Securing IoT in Industry 4.0 Applications with Blockchain

Securing IoT in Industry 4.0 Applications with Blockchain

Edited by
P. Kaliraj
T. Devi

CRC Press
Taylor & Francis Group
Boca Raton London New York

CRC Press is an imprint of the
Taylor & Francis Group, an **informa** business
AN AUERBACH BOOK

ISBN: 978-1-032-00810-3 (hbk)
ISBN: 978-1-032-10713-4 (pbk)
ISBN: 978-1-003-17587-2 (ebk)

DOI: 10.1201/9781003175872

Typeset in Garamond
by MPS Limited, Dehradun

Contents

Preface

The Industrial Revolutions Industry 4.0 and Industry 5.0 are changing the world around us. Artificial intelligence and machine learning, automation and robotics, big data, Internet of Things, augmented reality, virtual reality, and creativity are the tools of Industry 4.0. Improved collaboration is seen between smart systems and humans, which merges humans' critical and cognitive thinking abilities with the highly accurate and fast industrial automation. The fourth and fifth Industrial Revolutions affect the roles that Indian universities and colleges prepare students for, and educational institutions are committed to helping produce the workforce for this new world and the student experience to match it.

Bharathiar University has designed guidelines for Curriculum 4.0 and has prepared new syllabi for all subjects intertwining Industry 4.0 and 5.0 tools onto various disciplines such as science, social science, arts, and education. The university has identified the gap in knowledge resources such as books, course materials, interdisciplinary curriculum, and innovative programmes. To fill this gap and to prepare the future pillars of our globe to face the volatile, uncertain, complex and ambiguous (VUCA) world, and to help the academic community, Bharathiar University has prepared guidelines for revising the syllabus, designing innovative faculty development programs, establishing connectivity to the real world for students, incubating creativity and inculcating design thinking. Moreover, with the active participation of all stakeholders under the esteemed leadership of the Honourable Vice-Chancellor, Prof. P. Kaliraj, interdisciplinary books are being edited for Education 4.0 and 5.0.

Technology has always played a crucial role in the lives of people over the decades. Industry 4.0, the current trend of automation, comprises smart factories, cognitive computing, cloud computing, augmented reality, the Internet of Things, and cyber-physical systems. Most countries are adopting this to attain higher levels in automation, operational efficiency, and productivity. Though it was proposed only for the manufacturing industry, today with billions of people and machines interconnected by powerful networks, it is essential that higher education curricula should be redesigned to match this change. Students should be made familiar with

Industry 4.0 tools and should learn how to apply the tools in the specific domains they live or work in. This book discusses the key components of Industry 4.0, which are the Internet of Things (IoT), blockchain, and cybersecurity.

The world today is driven by Industry 4.0 and is connected in every sense. The Internet of Things, or IoT, refers to the billions of physical devices around the world that are now connected to the Internet, all collecting and sharing data. After the advent of IoT, it is possible to connect everyday things to Internet. IoT makes everyday objects "smart" by enabling them to transmit data and automate tasks without requiring any manual intervention. Every day trillions and trillion bytes of data are generated by billions of devices connected to the Internet, so much that 90% of the world's data has been generated in the past couple of years. IoT also bridges digital and physical realities and supports information-driven automation. Physical devices such as sensors and actuators play a crucial role in IoT systems. With sensors, it is possible to collect data in almost any situation and hence they are widely used in various fields. IoT systems help in collecting and processing data at the same time. The collected data can be processed in real-time, which helps in optimizing the performance. This also helps in rectifying the malfunctions as early as possible. IoT has various advantages, such as ease of information access, communication capability, and cost-effectiveness. These advantages facilitate IoT to be utilized in various applications, such as smart cities, agriculture, industries, and healthcare. In this context, this book will unleash the roles of IoT, blockchain, and cybersecurity during this time of the fourth Industrial Revolution and their applications aligning with Education 4.0.

According to Fortune Business Insights, the global IoT market was valued at US$190 billion in 2018 and is projected to reach US$1,102.6 billion by 2026. This, in turn, will create a lot of job opportunities in IoT. It shows that there is a great need for educated individuals who have expertise in this domain. And with the demand for talented professionals more than doubling in the last few years, there are limitless opportunities for professionals who want to work on the cutting edge of IoT research and development. It is essential for universities and higher education institutions to offer a prescribed set of courses for a major or specialization in IoT. At the same time, those with dedicated IoT programs may have unique approaches to the discipline. This will create graduates who are skilled in IoT and this book can aid in imparting the concepts and knowledge of IoT among the graduates. This book provides a blend of IoT's fundamentals and applications with a description of its fundamentals, architecture, technologies for IoT, cybersecurity, and blockchain. This book provides relevant theory and industrial applications of IoT in various domains such as healthcare, smart farming, smart city, education, industries, cybersecurity, and blockchain.

What's in the Book?

Chapter 1 entitled "*Internet of Things*" describes how IoT has been widely used to improve the performance of industrial systems in the Industry 4.0 era. It provides an overview of IoT architecture and the technologies that enable IoT applications. This chapter provides a systematic understanding of the programming languages and tools used for IoT development and discusses the role of IoT in Industry 4.0 and the security issues involved in developing IoT applications.

Chapter 2 entitled "*IoT Applications in Education*" introduces technology related to higher education. The chapter gives a brief idea about the different approaches in higher education and the incipient higher education system. Further, it explains IoT applications in the teaching–learning process.

Chapter 3 entitled "*Industrial Internet of Things (IIoT) and Smart Industries*" provides an understanding of the Industrial Internet of Things (IIoT) and its impacts across industries, specifically in the insurance industry. Addressing the challenges and opportunities, the chapter provides a roadmap of IIoT in line with Education 4.0. This chapter is written by academicians.

Chapter 4 entitled "*Internet of M-Health Things (mIoT)*" elaborates how the state-of-the-art IoT is made use of in the medical field and how it helps to provide quality treatment to patients, even in the time of the COVID-19 pandemic. This chapter introduces an mIoT system that captures medical data in real-time remotely and stores it in the edge fog cloud. The mobile app introduced in this chapter assists patients in taking medicine on time and alerts them when vital parameter values fall below critical levels.

Chapter 5 entitled "*Industrial Internet of Things (IIoT) Applications*" presents the evolution of IIoT, the proliferation and market share, and some examples across major industries. Moreover, the chapter provides a learning plan for students embarking on the IIOT journey. This chapter is written by an industrial expert.

Chapter 6 entitled "*Smart Farming: IoT-Based Plant Leaf Disease Detection and Prediction Using Image Processing Techniques*" explores how smart farming is helpful for farmers to prevent plant diseases. It provides insights on enhanced product quality, volumes, cost management, waste reduction, and process automation. This chapter shows how plant diseases can be predicted using image processing techniques and how a smart farming system is beneficial to those farmers who are unable to get expert knowledge and advice.

Chapter 7 entitled "*Artificial Intelligence and the Internet of Things: The Smart City Perspective*" gives a detailed view of AI and IoT technologies and their relationship with the smart city applications that helps in building smart cities.

It also describes the layered architecture involved in the development of a smart city.

Chapter 8 entitled *"Internet of Nano Things: An Amalgamation of Nanotechnology and IoT"* delivers the general and the key notion of the Internet of Nano Things (IoNT), highlighting its significance and usefulness. The chapter provides an overall outline of the technology, including the nanomachine and nanonetwork architecture and nano-communication paradigms. The chapter also discusses the various applications of the Internet of Nano Things, along with a case study of nano bio-sensors for a better understanding of the reader.

Chapter 9 entitled *"Blockchain and Cybersecurity"* discusses how blockchains can enhance cybersecurity. This chapter details how blockchains can be used in cryptocurrencies, smart contracts, transferring financial instruments, Distributed DNS, Public Key Infrastructure, Certifying Authorities, anonymizing data in the healthcare industry, as repositories of public registers, IoT, traceability and supply chain management, public register of antiquities, etc.

Chapter 10 entitled *"Blockchain"* provides an overview of the structure and working of a blockchain. It also covers the types, evolution, benefits, and applications of blockchain to the Industry.

Chapter 11 entitled *"Cybersecurity"* proposes a framework of technologies designed to shield networks, computers, and data from malware, vulnerabilities, and unauthorized activities. This chapter teaches the experts to spot illegal activities, fend off attacks, and instantaneously respond to risks.

Chapter 12 entitled *"PLC and SCADA as Smart Services in Industry 4.0 for Industrial Automation Techniques"* explains the automation system employed in the industries along with its classification, functionality, flexibility, limitation, and application. It also explains how the PLCs and SCADA have been implemented for industrial applications, parameters, and their working. The working of Boiler Automation based on SCADA, programming, and data handling techniques between PLC, SCADA, and IoT are detailed.

How to Use the Book?

The method and purpose of using this book depend on the role that you play in an educational institution or in an industry or depend on the focus of your interest. We propose five types of roles: student, software developer, teacher, member of board of studies, and researcher.

If you are a student: Students can use the book to get a basic understanding of IoT, its tools and applications, cybersecurity, and blockchain. Students belonging to any arts, science, and social science disciplines will find useful information from chapters on IoT, cybersecurity, and blockchain. This book will serve as a starting point for beginners. Students will benefit from the chapters on IoT applications in *education, healthcare, industries, agriculture and farming, and smart city.*

If you are a software developer: Software developers can use the book to get a basic understanding of Internet of Things, its tools and applications, cybersecurity, and blockchain. Readers with software development background will find useful information from chapters on IIoT, IoNT, AI, and IoT. They will benefit from the chapters on *smart farming, smart city, Industrial IoT, Nanotechnology and IoT, and m-Health Things (mIoT).*

If you are a teacher: This book is useful as a text for several different university-level college-level undergraduate and postgraduate courses. A graduate course on IoT can use this book as a primary textbook. It is important to equip the learners with a basic understanding on IoT, a tool of Industry 4.0. The chapter on *Internet of Things* provides the fundamentals of IoT. To teach the applications of IoT in various sectors, say healthcare, teachers will find useful information from the chapter on *Medical Internet of Health Things (mIoT).* A course on IoT and cybersecurity could use this book, too.

If you are a member of the board of studies: Innovating the education to align with Industry 4.0 requires that the curriculum be revisited. Universities are looking for methods of incorporating Industry 4.0 tools across various disciplines of arts, science, and social science education. This book helps in incorporating IoT across science and education. The book is useful while framing the syllabus for new course that cut across IoT and disciplines of arts or science or social science education. For example, syllabi for courses entitled Internet of Things and Cybersecurity, Internet of Things in Science, and the Industrial Internet of Things may be framed using the chapters in the book. Industry infusion into the curriculum is given much importance by involving more industry experts – R&D managers, product development managers, and technical managers as special invitees in the board of studies. Chapters provided by industrial experts in this book will help infuse the application part of the IoT into the curriculum.

If you are a researcher: A crucial area where innovation is required is the research work carried out by universities and institutions so that innovative, creative, and useful products and services are made available to society through translational research. This book can serve as a comprehensive reference guide for researchers in developing experimental IoT applications. The chapters on the Industrial *Internet of Things, Smart Forming, Artificial Intelligence and the Internet of Things, Internet of Nano Thingsand Blockchain* provide researchers, scholars, and students with a base for research in the area of IoT.

*****

Acknowledgments

From Prof. P. Kaliraj

First and foremost, I express my sincere gratitude to **Hon'ble Shri. Banwarilal Purohit,** Governor of Tamil Nadu, India, who was instrumental in organizing the conference on Innovating Education in the era of Industry 4.0 during 14–15 Dec 2019 in Ooty, which paved the way for further work in Industry 4.0 knowledge world.

My heartfelt thanks go to Hon'ble Chief Minister of Tamil Nadu, India, and Hon'ble Minister for Higher Education, Government of Tamil Nadu. I thank Principal Secretary to Government, Higher Education Department, Government of Tamil Nadu.

I would like to express my thanks to Secretary to Governor, and Deputy Secretary to Governor, Universities Governor's Secretariat, Raj Bhavan, Chennai.

I thank my wife, Dr. Vanaja Kaliraj, and family members for supporting and being patient.

From Prof. T. Devi

I record my sincere thanks to **Prof. P. Kaliraj**, Hon'ble Vice-Chancellor of Bharathiar University, who identified the knowledge world gap when the professor searched for a book on Industry 4.0 and triggered the process of writing and editing books in the Industry 4.0 series. His continuous motivation during the lockdown period due to COVID-19, sensitization, and encouragement are unmatchable.

I express my profound thanks to the vice-chancellor and registrar for the administrative support. Heartfelt thanks are due to the authors of the chapters for their contribution of chapters, continuous co-operation in improvizing the chapters as and when requested, and for timely communication. I thank all the expert members who served as reviewers for providing a quality and swift review.

We wish to thank **Mr. John Wyzalek, Senior Acquisitions Editor, Taylor & Francis/CRC Press**, who believed in this book's idea and helped us in realizing our dream.

Special thanks are due to Mr. Todd Perry, production editor, Taylor & Francis/ CRC Press, Florida, for his excellent co-ordination and Mr. Manmohan Negi, Project Manager, MPS Ltd., for his untiring and swift support.

Thanks are due to Dr. R. Rajeswari, Associate Professor, Department of Computer Applications for her continuous support; Sister Italia Joseph Maria, Ms. M. Lissa, and Mrs. S. Shalini, Project Assistants for providing earnest support.

Thanks to the faculty members Prof. M. Punithavalli, Dr. T. Amudha, Dr. J. Satheeshkumar, Dr. V. Bhuvaneswari, Mr. S. Palanisamy, Dr. S. Gavaskar, Dr. R. Balu, and Dr. J. Ramsingh.

Thanks to the assistant technical officers Mr. A. Elanchezian, Mr. A. Sivaraj, Mrs. B. Priyadarshini, and office staff Mr. A. Kalidas of Department of Computer Applications of Bharathiar University, India.

Thanks are due to Mrs. K. Kowsalya, Assistant Registrar, Mr. R. Karthick, Assistant Section Officer, and Mr. A. Prasanth of office of the Vice-Chancellor and staff of the office of the Registrar of Bharathiar University, India.

I thank my husband, Mr. D. Ravi; daughter, Mrs. R. Deepiga; son, Mr. R. Surya; son-in-law, Mr. D. Vishnu Prakhash; and grandson, V. Deera and family members for their encouragement and support.

*****

Editors

Prof. P. Kaliraj, Hon'ble vice-chancellor, Bharathiar University, a visionary and an eminent leader leading big academic teams has had more than three decades of teaching and research experience. He has held various renowned positions, such as officiating vice-chancellor of Anna University, head of the Centre for Biotechnology of Anna University, dean of faculty at A C College of Technology, and member of the syndicate for two decades at Anna University. Professor Kaliraj had research collaborations with the National Institute of Health in Maryland, USA; Glasgow University in Scotland, UK; and University of Illinois in Rockford, USA. University Grants Commission BSR Faculty Award and the Lifetime Achievement Award from the Biotechnology Research Society of India adorned the professor. **Forty-two scholars were gifted to receive the highest academic degree under his distinguished guidance. His remarkable patent in the area of filariasis is a boon in healthcare** and saving the lives of mankind. He is a great motivator and very good at sensitizing the faculty, scholars, and students towards achieving academic excellence and institutional global ranking. Professor Kaliraj is a recipient of the **Life Time Achievement Award and Sir J.C. Bose Memorial Award** for his outstanding contribution in higher education – research. (email: vc@buc.edu.in, pkaliraj@gmail.com)

**Prof. T. Devi, PhD (UK), Professor, Centre for Research and Evaluation, former dean of research, professor and head, Department of Computer Applications, Bharathiar University** focuses on state-of-the-art technology that industries adopt in order to make students ready for the future world. She is a **Gold Medalist** (1981–1984) from University of Madras and a **Commonwealth Scholar** (1994–1998) for her **PhD from the University of Warwick, UK**. She has three decades of teaching and research experience from Bharathiar University, Indian Institute of Foreign Trade, New Delhi, and University of Warwick, UK. Professor Devi is good in team building and setting goals and achieving them. Her research interests include integrated data modeling and framework, meta-modeling, computerassisted concurrent engineering, and speech processing. Professor Devi has visited the United Kingdom, Tanzania, and Singapore for academic collaborations. She has received various awards including **Commonwealth Scholarship and Best Alumni Award from PSGR Krishnammal College for Women (PSGRKCW), Proficiency award from PSG College of Technology and awards from Bharathiar University for serving for BU-NIRF, Curriculum 4.0, and Roadmap 2030 and guided 23 Ph.D. scholars.** Prof. T. Devi may be contacted at (email: tdevi@buc.edu.in, tdevi5@gmail.com)

Contributors

T. Amudha
Department of Computer Applications
Bharathiar University
Coimbatore, India

V. Bhuvaneswari
Department of Computer Applications
Bharathiar University
Coimbatore, India

R.S. Gopalan
UIDAI Regional Office
Bengaluru, India

K. Kalaiselvi
Department of Computer Science
Vels Institute of Science, Technology
    and Advanced Studies (VISTAS)
Chennai, India

R. Maheswaran
Department of Electronics and
    Instrumentation
Bharathiar University
Coimbatore, India

S. Muruganand
Department of Electronics and
    Instrumentation
Bharathiar University
Coimbatore, India

N. Ponpandian
Department of Nanoscience and
    Technology
Bharathiar University
Coimbatore, India

R. Rajeswari
Department of Computer Applications
Bharathiar University
Coimbatore, India

A. Sakila
Department of Computer Science
Bharathiar University
Coimbatore, India

A. Sangeetha
Department of Computer Applications
Bharathiar University
Coimbatore, India

G. Srividhya
Department of Nanoscience and
    Technology
Bharathiar University
Coimbatore, India

V. Srividya
PSG Institute of Management
PSG College of Technology
Coimbatore, India

P. Sudhandradevi
Department of Computer Applications
Bharathiar University
Coimbatore, India

Saravana Kumani Sundaram
Insurance Solutions
Virtusa Corporation
Bengaluru, India

J. Vijayakumar
Department of Electronics and
    Instrumentation
Bharathiar University
Coimbatore, India

S. R. Vijayalakshmi
Department of Electronics and
    Instrumentation
Bharathiar University
Coimbatore, India

S. Vijayarani
Department of Computer Science
Bharathiar University
Coimbatore, India

Chapter 1

Internet of Things

R. Rajeswari

Associate Professor, Department of Computer Applications,
Bharathiar University, Coimbatore, India

Contents

DOI: 10.1201/9781003175872-1

Objectives

After reading this lesson, the audience will gain knowledge of the following:

1. Fundamental concepts behind IoT
2. SComponents of IoT architecture
3. Technologies that enable IoT applications
4. Tools for IoT application development
5. Role of IoT in Industry 4.0
6. Security issues of IoT applications
7. Applications of IoT

1.1 Introduction

The advancements in technology have impacted every aspect of life over the decades (Nuvolari, 2019). The four Industrial Revolutions have a major role in the technological changes in society. The first Industrial Revolution started in the United Kingdom and slowly spread to various countries. The second Industrial Revolution started during the end of 19th century when

First Industrial Revolution 1760 – 1900	Steam Engine, Coal, Mechanization
Second Industrial Revolution 1900 – 1960	Metallurgy, Oil, Electricity, Automobiles
Third Industrial Revolution 1960 – 2000	Computers, Robots, Nuclear Energy
Fourth Industrial Revolution 2000 – present	Internet, IoT, Augmented Reality, Cyber Security, Genetic Engineering, Automation

Figure 1.1 Evolution of Four Industrial Revolutions.

industries started using lighter metals, alloys, and plastics. The ownership of the product of materials also got distributed. It was during this time that many countries moved to social realms. It was also during this revolution that oil and other energy resources were used widely. The third Industrial Revolution started in the 1960s when people started using nuclear energy as an energy resource. During the third Industrial Revolution only, electronics and computers started playing a vital role in almost all the processes of an industry. In early 2000, the fourth Industrial Revolution had begun which builds on the third Industrial Revolution. It was during this period that the Internet was widely used by almost all the people in the world. The revolution is currently changing the way people live and work. The technologies which contribute immensely to the fourth Industrial Revolution are augmented reality, big data and analytics, cloud computing, cybersecurity, Internet of Things (IoT), and robotics (Xu et al., 2018). The evolution of four Industrial Revolutions is shown in Figure 1.1.

One of the key technologies which is accelerating the current Industrial Revolution is the Internet of Things (Sathyan, 2020). Gartner has predicted that in 2020, 30% of communications with smart machines will be based on conversations with them. The main advantage of the usage of the technologies in the current industrial revolution is to produce things faster. Internet of Things helps in performing digital manufacturing quickly and perfectly. It intends to improve the performance of industrial systems. IoT will help in the collection of a large amount of data and help in the analysis of it, which would in turn help in revolutionizing the manufacturing industry. This chapter intends to provide the fundamentals of IoT that will help beginners intending to work with IoT. This chapter describes the architecture of IoT, technologies involved in developing IoT systems, applications of IoT, the role of IoT in Industry 4.0, and security in IoT.

1.1.1 Evolution of IoT

Research on making objects interact with each other has been happening since the 1970s. In 1982, programmers of Carnegie Mellon University had written software to connect to a Coke machine to check whether cold sodas were available so that they could go from their hostel rooms to purchase them. In 1990, John Romkey created a bread toaster that could be connected to the Internet to operate it. This device is considered the first IoT device. The device was presented at the October 1987 INTEROP Conference. In 1993, Quentin Stafford and Paul Jardetzky developed a coffee machine that could take pictures of the level of coffee three times per minute so that it could be monitored. In 1999, Kevin Ashton first used the term "Internet of Things" when he was working for Procter & Gamble Ltd. (Ashton, 2009). He used "Internet of Things" when he was making a presentation on radio-frequency identification (RFID). In 2000, LG Electronics Inc. developed its first Internet refrigerator. It had screens and trackers that could update the items that were available in the refrigerator. In 2002, a device called Ambient Orb was introduced by David Rose and his team from the Massachusetts Institute of Technology (MIT) Lab. The device could monitor the weather and other sources and could change its color. During 2003 and 2005 the term "Internet of Things" began to appear in a lot of publications including "The Guardian" and "Scientific American". RFID was mainly used in the United States (US) Department of Defense. In 2005, the United Nation's International Telecommunications Union (ITU) released a write-up on "Internet of Things". In 2005, a wireless fidelity (WiFi) enabled rabbit (Nabaztaz) was created by Rafi Haladijian and Olivier Manel. The device could talk about the stock market, news, and alarm clock. In 2008, the first International IoT Conference was conducted in Zurich, Switzerland. It was during this year only there were more IoT devices than people on earth. In 2008 only, the Internet Protocol for Smart Objects (IPSO) Alliance was established by a group of 50 companies including Google, Ericsson, Bosch, Intel, Cisco, and Fujitsu. The number of IoT devices including tablet PCs and smartphones were 12.5 billion, whereas the world population was only 6.8 billion. In 2008, IoT was declared as one of the "Disruptive Technologies" by the US National Intelligence Council. In 2011, IoT appeared on the ascending curve of the Gartner Hype cycle, and in 2014, it appeared on the peak of the Gartner Hype cycle. During 2014 and 2016, various products such as Google glass, Echo, and self-driving cars were developed. Various companies had started to develop many products. During 2017 and 2019, IoT product development was widely accepted. Various technologies such as artificial intelligence and blockchain were integrated with the IoT platforms. The various stages in the evolution of IoT are depicted in Figure 1.2.

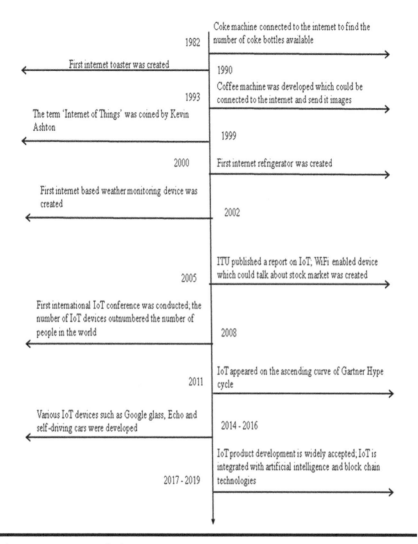

Figure 1.2 IoT Evolution.

1.1.2 *Definition and Characteristics*

IoT signifies a collection of devices that are composed of electronics, sensors, and software. They can communicate through the Internet. Security cameras, refrigerators, vehicles, and buildings are some examples of things that can communicate with each other using the Internet. Gartner defines "The Internet of Things (IoT) is the network of physical objects that contain embedded technology to communicate and sense or interact with their internal states or external environment" (Internet of Things, Gartner Glossary).

The Internet of Things has been defined in Recommendation ITU-TY 2060 as a "global infrastructure for the information society, enabling advanced services by interconnecting (physical or virtual) things based on existing and evolving interoperable information and communication technologies" (Recommendation of ITU-TY.2060, 2012).

Internet of Things exhibits certain characteristics (Martino et al., 2018), some of which are described below:

1. Connectivity: all the "things" or objects in IoT are connected to the cloud platform or server using the Internet. Sensors collect physical parameters which are sent through gateways to the cloud/server for further processing. Transfer of information happens for short distances or long distances using communication technologies such as WiFi.
2. Sensing: one of the important components of IoT systems is sensors that measure various physical parameters from other objects or the environment. The sensed data are then transmitted to the cloud or server.
3. Intelligence: IoT is a combination of hardware, software, and various algorithms that make the IoT objects respond to a particular situation in an intelligent manner. For instance, sensors in air conditioners sense the temperature and adjust the temperature accordingly.
4. Heterogeneity: IoT devices are used for various applications. They work in various hardware platforms, network connections, and software; hence, they are heterogeneous.
5. Voluminous data: Data plays an important role in IoT systems. Sensors collect data and send to cloud platform/servers, which are then processed and analyzed. There are several sensors connected to various IoT applications and all these sensors collect and transfer data at regular intervals. This causes a large volume of data from sensors to be sent to cloud platforms/servers where the data will be efficiently managed.

1.2 Architecture of IoT

IoT systems are built using sensors, actuators, and microcontrollers. It is a combination of various technologies (Ray, 2018). The typical three-layer architecture of IoT systems is depicted in Figure 1.3. The three layers of the architecture are as follows:

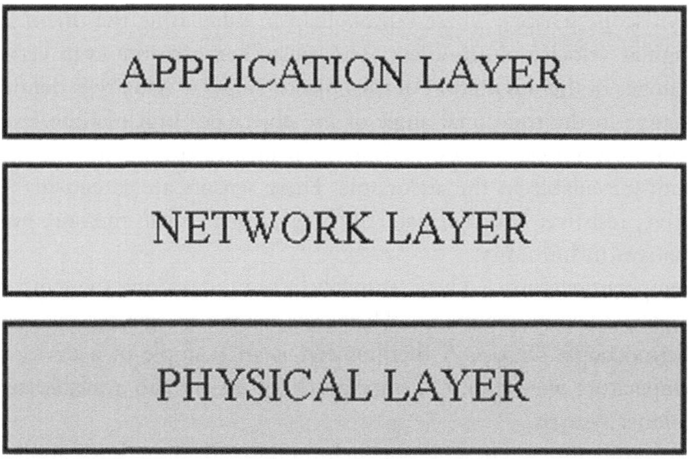

```
┌─────────────────────────────────────────────┐
│                                               │
│           APPLICATION LAYER                   │
│                                               │
└─────────────────────────────────────────────┘

┌─────────────────────────────────────────────┐
│                                               │
│             NETWORK LAYER                     │
│                                               │
└─────────────────────────────────────────────┘

┌─────────────────────────────────────────────┐
│                                               │
│             PHYSICAL LAYER                    │
│                                               │
└─────────────────────────────────────────────┘
```

Figure 1.3   Three Layer Architecture of IoT Systems.

1. Physical Layer: It has sensors and components that are responsible for obtaining data and converts them to digital format. This layer also identifies other smart objects in the environment.
2. Network Layer: It connects the objects in the physical layer with servers. It is used for transforming the data obtained from the sensors. In some IoT systems, this layer also processes the sensor data.
3. Application Layer: It is responsible for performing specific user services. This layer determines the application of IoT including smart homes, smart healthcare, smart metering, and smart transport.

1.2.1 Physical Devices

IoT systems consist of devices such as sensors, actuators, and other data transmission devices (Rayes and Salem, 2019). The main use of sensors is to take measurements of changes from their surroundings and send the data to actuators or applications that will further process the data. Depending on the types of signals generated by the sensors they are classified as digital and analog sensors. The output generated by analog sensors is continuous whereas the output generated by digital sensors is discrete. The various physical parameters measured by the sensors are sound, heat, motion, and biochemical parameters. Some of these sensors are described below:

1. Acoustic sensors: These sensors help in measuring the sound. An example of a device that uses an acoustic sensor is microphone. The ultrasonic vibration sensor has also an acoustic sensor embedded in it.

2. Gyroscope sensors: These sensors help in calculating the orientation and angular velocity of an object. The sensor can measure even very meager changes in the orientation of the objects. Angular velocity is defined as the change in the rotational angle of the object per unit of time.
3. Humidity sensors: These sensors help in measuring the amount of humidity available in the air or soil. These sensors are categorized as capacitive, resistive, and thermal. All three categories can measure even small changes in humidity.
4. Temperature sensors: These sensors help us in measuring the temperature of an object or environment. These sensors are categorized as resistive or thermocouple sensors. A thermometer is an example of a device that has temperature sensors in it. Temperature sensors are also available in air conditioner systems.
5. Pressure sensors: These sensors help in measuring the force applied to the sensors. These sensors are categorized as capacitive and piezo-resistive pressure sensors. They can be indirectly used to measure the flow of water, air, and altitude.
6. Proximity sensors: These sensors help in identifying objects that are near the sensors without any physical contact. They emit electromagnetic radiation such as infrared waves and wait for the waves to hit the object and return. There are various types of proximity sensors such as photoelectric, passive, radar, sonar, and ultrasonic sensors. They can be used in parking systems, conveyor systems, touch screens, and roller coasters.
7. Image sensors: These sensors covert the light into an electrical signal so that it can be converted to an image, viewed, and analyzed. For instance, vision cameras have image sensors inside them.
8. Light sensors: These sensors sense light energy and convert it to an electrical signal. Light sensors can detect various wavelengths of light ranging from infrared to ultraviolet rays. Some types of light sensors are phototransistors and photodiodes. Light sensors are used in smartphones, automobiles, and shipment cargos.

Actuators are devices that convert electrical energy into mechanical energy. Usually actuators make use of the data collected and analyzed by the sensors. Some of the actuators are described below:

1. Thermal actuators: These actuators convert thermal energy into mechanical energy. An increase in the temperature causes an object to expand and a decrease in the temperature causes it to contract. Examples of thermal actuators are bi-metallic strips that are used in micro thermostats.

2. Electrical actuators: These actuators are a type of gear motor that converts electrical energy into mechanical torque. Electrical line actuators cause linear motion. Rotary electrical actuators are digital current (DC) motors and alternating current (AC) motors.

3. Hydraulic actuators: These actuators utilize hydraulic power generated by compressing liquid. The hydraulic power is converted to mechanical energy by the actuators. The hydraulic actuators generate linear or rotary motion. Examples of hydraulic actuators are hydraulic jacks.

The physical layer also consists of hardware platforms which are mostly microcontrollers. Sensors are often connected to microcontrollers directly. Microcontrollers in IoT systems utilize their computational power to manipulate the data. Sometimes, if there is no need for processing the data, they just send it to the cloud/server through a gateway for processing. Some of the microcontrollers are given in Figure 1.4 and are described below:

1. Arduino Uno: This microcontroller depends on an ATMega328P processor for computation. The processing speed is 16 MHz and operates at 5 V. It has a flash memory of 16 KB and RAM of 1 KB. It supports a number of input/output (I/O) pins, out of which 14 are digital I/O and 6

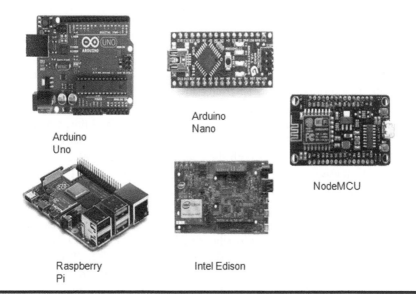

Arduino
Uno

Arduino
Nano

NodeMCU

Raspberry
Pi

Intel Edison

Figure 1.4   Sample Microcontrollers.

are analog I/O. It is able to communicate with a computer by sending and receiving data through an USB cable.

2. Arduino Nano: It is the smallest microcontroller which is based on an ATMega328 processor. It works at 5 V and the processing speed is 16 MHz. The size of its flash memory is 32 KB and that of SRAM is 2 KB.

3. Raspberry Pi: It is an open-source and miniaturized computer which runs on Linux. The usual model of Raspberry Pi has a processing speed of 700 MHz. It has 512 MB of RAM. The latest version of Raspberry Pi is Pi 4. The latest model has built-in WiFi and Bluetooth. It has 40 general-purpose input/output pins.

4. Intel Edison: It is developed by Intel. The initial version had a processing speed of 100 MHz with an operating voltage of 3.3V. It has a flash memory of 4 GB. The processor is Intel Quark SOCX 1000. The latest model supports Bluetooth and WiFi.

5. ESP8266 NodeMCU development board: It is an open-source IoT development kit that runs on ESP8266 WiFi SOC from Espressif Systems. It has a processing speed in the range of 80–160 MHz. It has 128 KB of internal RAM and 4 MB of external flash memory. It supports an 802.11b/g/n WiFi transceiver. It has 17 general-purpose input/output pins. These pins may be connected to peripheral interfaces including Analog to Digital Converter (ADC) channel, Universal Asynchronous Receiver Transmitter (UART), Serial Peripheral Interface (SPI), and Inter-integrated circuit (I2C) interface.

1.2.2 Gateways and Networks

Gateways are hardware or software that connect the microcontrollers and sensors with a cloud platform/server (Kang and Choo, 2018). Some sensors generate little data while others generate thousands of data per second that are collected and transferred by the gateways. They gather the information transmitted from various sources and interfaces and communicate that to the cloud. The gateway transfers data in both directions and takes care of the security of the data. Gateways are the glue for connecting all devices in IoT systems.

The data obtained using sensors have to be transmitted to the Internet through a smart gateway. Typically IoT devices connect using Internet protocol (IP) networks, which require power and memory (Montori et al., 2018). Sometimes IoT devices connect locally using Bluetooth and RFID. Some of the communication technologies viz., Wireless Fidelity (WiFi), IPv6 over Low Power Wireless Personal Area Network (6LoWPAN), Low Power Wide Area Network (LoraWAN), Bluetooth, and Zigbee are described below:

1. Zigbee: It is an IEEE 802.15.4 standard developed by Zigbee Alliance and mainly support wireless networking. It is useful for low data rates and short-range transmission. The data transmission range is 10–100 m.

2. Bluetooth: It is an IEEE 802.15.1 standard used for wireless transmission. It is also used for short-range data communication. The advantage of Bluetooth is that it requires low power for operation. One of the drawbacks of traditional Bluetooth is that it cannot directly connect to the Internet and an intermediate node is required. Hence, Bluetooth Low Energy (LE) was introduced, which provides quick communication using connectionless medium access control (MAC).

3. LoWPAN: It is a wireless personal area network that supports IPv6. It refers to IPV6 over Low Power Wireless Personal Area Network. It provides end to end data transfer using IPv6 and can provide a connection to various types of networks.

4. WiFi: It is the IEEE 802.11x standard and is most commonly used for connecting IoT devices to the Internet. It is useful for short-range data transmission and can connect to several networks. The power consumption is also less for WiFi. The communication range is 50–100 m.

5. LoRaWAN: It is mainly used for long-range data communication. The main advantage of LoRaWAN is to provide inter-operability across various networks. It has low power consumption and provides wide network coverage. The communication range is 5–10 km.

1.2.3 Edge Analytics

Traditionally all data collected from sensors were transferred to the cloud, where it will be processed and analyzed. For large applications, transmitting all the information obtained from the sensors to the cloud is cumbersome. In recent times, there is an increase in the use of edge analytics. In edge analytics, data is processed and analyzed in the gateways that are physically attached to the sensors. Hence, gateways store, process, and analyze the data instead of transferring it to the cloud. This makes the processing and analysis of data near the user. In some cases, the data is monitored and if it is in the normal range or if the data does not tell any significant information then, it is stored and processed in the edge devices. Otherwise, if the data is not in the normal range or if further processing is required to cull out information from the data then the data is pushed to the cloud. Cisco, Intel, and other companies have developed gateways to perform edge computing. IoT edge analytics is depicted in Figure 1.5.

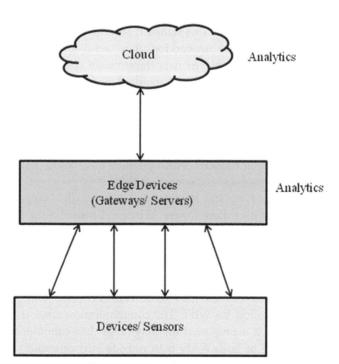

Figure 1.5 IoT Edge Analytics.

1.2.4 Fog Computing

Edge computing helps in saving time and bandwidth by making the computation in edge nodes present near sensors, rather than blindly pushing the information to the cloud. Similarly, fog computing helps in bringing the computational capability in the processors attached to local area networks (LANs) of sensors. So, the computational devices in fog computing are further away from the sensors or actuators compared to edge computing (Elazhary, 2019). Fog computing has features that resemble either edge computing or cloud computing. The advantages of fog computing are low latency, mobility of processors, and lesser transmission capacity. In fog computing, the processing is distributed, which is useful in applications such as environmental monitoring using large-scale sensor networks. Some of the challenges in adopting fog computing include management of Quality of Service (QoS) and security and regulatory requirements. The interface supported by fog should be able to provide interactivity with the cloud and sensors.

1.2.5 Cloud Platforms

Cloud platforms provide services for data storage, visualization, processing, data analysis, and decision making (Ray, 2016). These cloud platforms should be able to capture all the information created by billions of IoT systems in the world. Several vendors offer various cloud services that use advanced algorithms to perform predictive analysis. Cloud services for IoT are offered in three ways viz., Infrastructure as a Service (IaaS), Software as a Service (SaaS), and Platform as a Service (PaaS). The IoT cloud platform is different from the conventional cloud platform. The conventional cloud platform provides a pool of hardware and software resources to be available to all users. The IoT cloud platform offers services to process the real-time data coming from a variety of IoT systems. Some of the IoT cloud platforms are summarized in Table 1.1.

1.2.6 IoT Data Analytics

There are several sensors capturing data continuously which results in lots of data being transferred for storage in cloud platforms (Adi et al., 2020). The data collected are heterogeneous as they are collected by various types of sensors such as temperature, gyroscope, humidity, pressure, proximity, image, and light sensors. The data collected from sensors are raw. They have to be analyzed to interpret the information and take necessary actions. To analyze the information present in the sensor data various machine learning (Majumdar et al., 2021; Zhang et al., 2020) and artificial intelligence (Zhang, 2020; Greco et al., 2020) techniques have been used in several research works. Every day, more and more IoT devices are being used by people which leads to an increase in the data created and transmitted them. Cloud platforms enable the storage of large amounts of data. The usage of artificial intelligence based techniques helps in the extraction of correlation or features from data and prediction of future data. The usage of IoT data analytics helps in (a) identifying the platforms available in the pas data; (b) predicting the data in near future based on the collected data; (c) recognizing correlations among different types of data collected for an application; and (d) suggesting actions to be taken for a particular pattern in the data.

1.2.7 IoT Data Visualization

IoT systems generate a lot of data from sensors which have to gather and analyzed for various purposes. To interpret the information or to identify correlations present in the analyzed data correctly, it is necessary to display the data properly. In some situations, multiple visualizations of the same data help

Table 1.1 Sample Cloud Platforms

IoT Cloud Platform	Website	Services Offered	Cost
Xively	https://xively/com/	Data capture and visualization	Free
ThingSpeak	https://thingspeak.com	Data capture, visualization, and analytics	Free
ThingWorx	https://www.thingworx.com/	Data capture, visualization, and analytics	Pay per use
Amazon IoT	https://aws.amazon.com/iot/	Data management, analytics, visualization, and device management	Pay per use
Oracle IoT Cloud	https://www.oracle.com/Internet-of-things/	Data management, analytics, and visualization	Pay per use
IBM Watson IoT Cloud	https://Internetofthings.ibmcloud.com/	Data monitoring, visualization, analytics, and device management	Pay per use
Google IoT Cloud	https://cloud.google.com/iot-core	Device management, data management, visualization, and analytics	Pay per use
Microsoft IoT Cloud (Azure)	https://azure.microsoft.com/en-in/services/iot-hub/	Communication between IoT devices and device management	Pay per use
Cisco IoT Cloud Connect	https://www.iotone.com/software/iot-cloud-connect/	Data management and device management	Pay per use
General Electric Predix	https://www.ge.com/digital/iiot-platform	Data monitoring, analysis, and event management	Pay per use

to interpret the data from various dimensions. The data from sensors is presented in various forms such as bar/pie charts, histograms, graphs, and heat maps. Some of the challenges in the visualization of IoT data are (a) selection of right visualization and (b) appropriate display of heterogeneous and voluminous data coming from various sensors (Peddoju and Upadhyay, 2020). Hence it is essential to develop application-specific dashboard design that helps to visualize data to allow the users to gain insights from the data.

Several IoT data visualization tools are available globally. PowerBI (www.powerbi.microsoft.com) is based on Azure cloud-based services and provides several visuals based on the data. It supports both real-time streaming and offline data. Some versions of Microsoft PowerBI are free to use. Grafana (www.grafana.com) is a web application that supports the visualization of data, particularly time-series data. It is based on open-source software. Its dashboard is dynamic and supports several data sources. Kibana (www.elastic.co/kibana) is another popular open-source visualization tool for IoT data. It has a web-based user interface for viewing huge volumes of data in various forms such as bar/line charts, scatter plots, and maps. Tableau (www.tableau.com) is yet another interactive tool to visualize IoT data. It provides support for connection with servers such as Cloudera Hadoop and Amazon Aurora. It provides support for a wide range of charts apart from providing mapping functionality. The Tableau Public version is available for free to use. Thingsboard (www.thingsboard.io) is another open-source visualization tool. It provides various visualizations for both offline and real-time data. It supports IoT protocols such as Message Queuing Telemetry Transport (MQTT) and Constrained Application Protocol (CoAP) for device connectivity.

1.3 Technologies for IoT

1.3.1 Communication Protocols

Protocols that belong to the application layer of IoT architecture are essential for the transfer of data in IoT systems (Dizdarevic et al., 2019). These protocols ensure that there is no packet loss and low packet response time. They also should be able to support a wide variety of IoT devices and heterogeneous data. They should also support lightweight communication. Some of the IoT application layer protocols are described below:

1. Constrained Application Protocol (CoAP): This protocol is mainly used in low power and constrained networks. It is based on user datagram protocol (UDP). It is motivated by HyperText Transfer Protocol (HTTP)

Table 1.2   Summarization of IoT Protocols of Application Layer

Characteristics	CoAP	MQTT	XMPP
Transmission	UDP	TCP	TCP
Messaging	Request/ Response	Publisher/ Subscriber	Request/ Response
Security	DLTS	SSL	SSL
QoS	Supported	Supported	Not Supported
Open Source	Supported	Supported	Supported

and Representational State Transfer (REST) architecture is used. It supports asynchronous communication. The Datagram Transport Layer Security (DTLS) is used by CoAP to support integrity, security, and privacy.

2. Message Queuing Telemetry Transport (MQTT): This protocol is mainly used in constrained devices and unreliable networks. It is based on a publisher/subscriber client that uses Transmission Control Protocol/ Internet Protocol (TCP/IP). Hence, it supports reliability during message transmission. MQTT supports three Quality of Service (QoS) levels and the message is encoded using the Secure Socket Layer/Transport Layer Security (SSL/TLS) protocol. It supports asynchronous communication.

3. Extensible Messaging and Presence Protocol (XMPP): This protocol transfers data over the distributed network based on TCP. One of the biggest advantages of XMPP is that it is extendable. It depends on Extensible Markup Language (XML) technology and offers communication between client–client, client–server, and server–server. These protocols are summarized in Table 1.2.

1.3.2 Wireless Sensor Networks

Wireless sensor networks (WSNs) are part of IoT systems. Wireless sensor networks are wireless networks of a collection of sensors to monitor the physical parameters of the environment and pool the data to a single system/server to process and analyze the data (Kocakulak and Butun, 2017). The three main components of wireless sensor networks are nodes (sensors), gateways, and users. These components of WSN are shown in Figure 1.6. Nodes or sensors are connected and they transmit data through a gateway. The gateway and the users

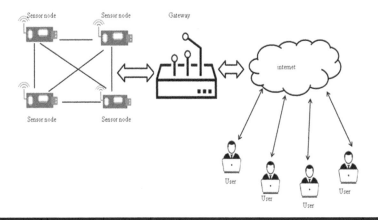

Figure 1.6 Typical Architecture of WSN.

are connected using a common network or Internet. All nodes in a WSN sense and collect information regarding a particular physical parameter from the environment such as temperature.

One of the main characteristics of the nodes in IoT systems is that they are connected to the Internet. The sensor nodes in WSNs have to be connected to the Internet so that they can be part of IoT systems. This can be achieved in various ways. Two of these methods are described here. In the first method, the entire WSN is connected to the Internet through a gateway. In the second method, individual sensor nodes in the WSN are connected to the Internet through separate gateways. In the first method, there is a single gateway and hence the entire network can fail if there is a problem in the gateway. This problem does not occur in the second method.

1.3.3 Cloud Computing

Cloud computing and IoT are increasingly being used in all aspects of life in recent years (Botta et al., 2016). Cloud computing is the usage of various computing services on a pay-per-use mode. The user cannot directly manage these resources. There are two categories of working models of cloud. The first category is called the deployment model which defines how the cloud is accessed. The deployment model is further classified as public, private, hybrid, and community cloud. In the public cloud, the services may be accessed easily by the general public such as email services. In the private cloud, the services may be accessed by a specific organization only and hence the security is also severe in this type. Hybrid cloud has the characteristics of both private and public cloud where important activities are carried out using private cloud and non-important activities are carried out using the public cloud. In the community cloud model, the services can be accessed by a group of organizations. Based on the reference models of the cloud, it is categorized as Infrastructure as a Service (IaaS), Platform as a Service (PaaS), and Software as a Service (SaaS). IaaS allows access to resources such as machines and virtual storage. PaaS allows access to runtime environments and tools. SaaS allows access to software applications. With the help of cloud computing, users can use any required hardware and software for a specific time without the need to install the hardware and software.

Cloud computing is the access to data and software from a centralized pool by consumers. IoT systems support communication between devices through the Internet. Both cloud computing and IoT support each other. A lot of data is generated by IoT systems which are transmitted to the cloud. When the user uses the resources in cloud computing, he has to pay only for the resources used. This characteristic is very useful for small IoT-based companies who want to reduce the overall costs. IoT developers also make use of the collaboration provided by cloud computing.

1.3.4 Embedded Systems

In today's world, embedded systems are found in almost all electronic equipments. These systems consume very little power and are used in almost all devices such as remote controls, digital cameras, microwave ovens, digital video disc (DVD) players, washing machines, and air conditioners. Applications of embedded systems include healthcare, automobiles, home automation, networking, and robotics. Embedded systems are part of a larger application that perform specific tasks. The major components of an embedded system are microprocessor or microcontroller, memory, networking components, and input/output units. With the advancements in very large-scale integration (VLSI), small chips come with enormous computation power and memory. The characteristics of embedded devices such as low power consumption and small size are very much suitable for IoT systems. Mostly, embedded systems can be programmed using languages such as C, C++, and Java.

IoT systems integrate microprocessors, memory, sensors, actuators, and communication (Serpanos and Wolf, 2018). Hence, embedded systems are part of IoT systems that enable a lot of IoT applications. Some of the computations of IoT systems can be performed by the microcontrollers themselves. The decision of whether the computation should be done at the embedded device or in other higher layers should be based on the type of computation, the energy status of the embedded device, and other parameters. With the powerful technological advancements in embedded systems, they will play a major role in computing, making it reside in the edge devices.

1.4 Developing IoT Applications

An IoT developer should be aware of a lot of domains such as networking, cloud programming, hardware device programming, and security. IoT development involves assembling the hardware devices; programming the devices which receive the data and send them to the server; programming the cloud/server to process the data and store it; and providing the data in an easily understandable manner by using appropriate visualization techniques. The languages and tools used should be specific to the domain of the IoT solution.

1.4.1 Programming Languages for IoT Devices

IoT systems are made up of three types of devices viz., sensors/actuators which generate data; gateways which organize them; and cloud/server which collect and process the data. Some of the popular languages used for programming IoT solutions are described below:

1. C: It is one of the popular languages used for programming the physical layer i.e., the hardware devices. It is widely used for programming constrained devices.
2. Java: It is another popular language used by developers for programming non-desktop systems. The application is developed on a desktop and then moved to a chip with Java Virtual Machine (JVM). Other editions of Java, such as Java Micro Edition or Java ME, are also used for programming embedded devices.
3. Javascript: It is one of the popular languages for IoT applications. The processing done in servers/gateways can be written using Javascript. The hubs and sensors that use Linux can also execute Node.js. Espruino and Tessel are some of the microcontrollers that can execute Javascript.
4. Python: It is a widely popular language used for coding IoT devices. Even microcomputers like Raspberry Pi, which runs on a Linux operating system, uses Python. It is used in several domains. Various versions of it, such as microPython, are also developed. Some of the Python packages used for IoT development are JSON, XML, HTTPLib, URLLib, and SMTPLib.
5. Swift: It is one of the popular languages used for developing Apple iOS and macOS applications. If the devices in IoT systems have to communicate with iPhone or iPad, then Swift is the choice.

1.4.2 Integrated Development Environments (IDEs) for IoT Development

Integrated Development Environment (IDE) is software with a coder editor, debugger, and automation tools that help developers to develop software applications. There are many IoT applications today, and this has led to the development of a lot of IDEs for working with these applications. Some of the IDEs used for IoT application development are described below:

1. Arduino IDE: Arduino is an Italy-based company that develops microcontroller boards and kits. It has developed the Arduino IDE to work with the microcontrollers. It has all preloaded libraries required to work with simple IoT applications. It supports C and C++ programming languages.
2. Raspbian: Raspbian is an operating system with the IDLE IDE to work with Python language. It is one of the environments suitable to program the Raspberry Pi device. Raspberry Pi is not just a microcontroller; it is a "microcomputer". It has lots of packages and precompiled libraries to work with Raspberry Pi devices.
3. PlatformIO IDE: PlatformIO is an open-source IDE that is cross-platform and supports a debugger. It supports various development boards, platforms, and frameworks. It provides an "intellisense" code editor for C and C++ programming languages. It has thousands of libraries to work with embedded devices.
4. Eclipse IoT IDE: It is an open-source IDE created by Eclipse Foundation for working with IoT applications. It has lots of tools and runtimes for IoT computing. In particular, an open-source development framework called Eclipse Kura is used for IoT application development. Eclipse Kura is based on the Java programming language.

1.4.3 Tools for IoT Development

The development and management of IoT applications are quite complex. Some tools are available to make these jobs easier. One of the advantages of these tools is that the IoT applications need not be built from scratch. Some of the tools used for developing IoT applications are described below:

1. NETCONF-YANG: Network Configuration Protocol (NETCONF) is based on a simple network management protocol (SNMP). NETCONF stores the details of its configuration and state using YANG, which is a data modeling language. The NETCONF-YANG tool helps in the

management of IoT systems by providing various features such as management Application Programming Interface (API), transaction and rollback managers, data model manager, and configuration API.

2. Puppet: Puppet is a popular tool that helps in managing the configuration of IoT systems. It helps in maintaining the servers, storage, and networks in IoT systems. All the operations in Puppet are carried out using resources such as services, processes, files, and users.

1.5 Applications of IoT

There are many IoT applications that are used in the day-to-day life of all people and industries. Apart from improving the lives of people, IoT systems have found applications in various domains such as transportation, healthcare, agricultural, industrial, and environmental domains. Some of the applications of IoT are represented in Figure 1.7.

1.5.1 Agriculture

With the rise in population, there is a huge demand for a multifold increase in food production in terms of quantity and quality in food (Tzounis et al., 2017). IoT systems are used to capture the images of plants to monitor plant diseases. Plants are cultivated in greenhouses where the climatic conditions have to be maintained at particular levels. Monitoring the climatic parameters in greenhouses is possible

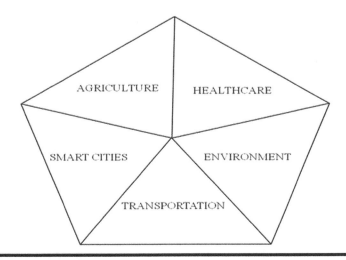

Figure 1.7 Applications of IoT.

through IoT systems. Sensors such as optical sensors and humidity sensors have been used to find the temperature and moisture content in the agriculture fields. The information is then utilized to control the amount of water used for irrigation. Wireless sensors have been used for tracking animals, monitoring them, and analyzing their behavior. RFID tags have been used for tracking agricultural products, thus enabling automation in the food supply chain.

1.5.2 Smart Cities

The number of cities is increasing globally every year. Smart cities are intended to make urban life easier by applying smart systems to the infrastructure and services of the city. IoT systems will help the buildings in the cities to efficiently utilize resources such as energy and water (Alavi et al., 2018). Sensors and smart grid technologies are utilized to make use of resources such as water and electricity appropriately to avoid wastage of these resources. Similar smart systems and innovative ideas are used to promote business employment which improves the economy of smart cities. These systems will help in monitoring the collection and disposal of garbage in the cities. IoT-based smart grids help in smart metering to optimize electricity consumption and billing. IoT also helps in controlling the traffic in roads of smart cities by learning the traffic patterns and controlling traffic appropriately.

1.5.3 Transportation

The number of private vehicles is increasing, which has led to an increase in traffic. IoT-based systems have been implemented to obtain information related to the location of vehicles, their routes, and traffic congestion, which in turn can help in the reduction of traffic and provide information related to travelers (Patel et al., 2019). IoT-based systems are implemented to schedule the vehicles in the routes to reduce the traffic congestion in the city. IoT-based traffic management systems also help in altering the traffic among various routes to facilitate the movement of emergency vehicles such as ambulance of vehicles of VIPs. IoT-based systems also help in monitoring accidents or various events happening on roads. The data obtained about these events can help in providing various services to people affected by accidents or to people participating in the events. Pressure sensors in IoT systems automatically find whether seats in a vehicle are occupied by a person or whether it is empty so that it can be allotted to another person.

1.5.4 Environment

Appropriate disposal of waste and its maintenance is essential to avoid polluting air, water, and oil. Pollution of air, water, and oil can be prevented with the help of IoT systems (Hart and Martinez, 2015). Sensors are used to monitor the quality of air all over the city throughout the year. pH in water is used to determine the quality of water and the health of aquatic animals in the water. Sensors are used to collect the data related to radiation levels near nuclear facilities to detect the leakage of nuclear energy. Sensors may also be fixed at places like electric poles and trees to monitor the levels of radiation in the city. Sensor-based IoT systems can be implemented to detect disasters such as floods, storms, volcanic eruptions, earthquakes, and other natural disasters. Once these disasters are detected, they can be communicated to people so that they can move to safe places. Sensors are used to monitor the glaciers so that any calamities can be predicted earlier. Sensors are used to monitor the temperature, which is important for the growth of roots and absorption of nutrients. Sensors are also used to monitor the moisture level of the soil to ensure the proper growth of plants.

1.5.5 Healthcare

With the rise in the human population and the average lifespan of people, there is a lot of demand from healthcare for providing better treatments. IoT has revolutionized the healthcare sector, making it move towards Healthcare 4.0 (Aceto et al., 2020). IoT helps in the remote monitoring of patients. Similarly, sensors and wearables help in monitoring the physiological signals of people at regular intervals so that their health status can be checked. These sensors and wearables can be used for patients who are in intensive care units or for any healthy people who want to have a regular check-up. Currently, various physiological signals such as temperature, electrocardiogram (ECG), glucose level, oxygen saturation, pulse rate, and pressure levels can be monitored. Recently, fog computing at gateways provides various healthcare services such as storage and analysis of healthcare data (Mutlag et al., 2019). IoT systems also help elderly people in taking appropriate medicines at the correct time. Examples of such systems include implantable insulin pumps.

1.6 Industrial IoT (IIoT)

IoT has invaded our everyday lives and has linked physical objects to the digital world, supporting communication between these objects (Lampropoulos et al., 2019). IoT has also found applications in industries particularly in intelligent manufacturing which is referred as the Industrial Internet of Things (IIoT). Industry 4.0 is associated with a highly automated, integrated, and efficient manufacturing environment. In every aspect of manufacturing, intelligence is incorporated which leads to the development of smart factories. With the integration of sensors, actuators, networking technologies, and storage systems, it is possible to monitor and control every process involved in industrial manufacturing. The IIoT services and applications can appropriately schedule and control the manufacturing operations. Moreover, the IIoT systems can communicate with the help of devices. It is possible to track the assets of the factory wherever it is transported. Hence, it is possible to monitor and manage all the processes such as procurement of raw materials, production, transport, and monitoring the finished products.

Although the incorporation of IoT in manufacturing has made the processes involved in manufacturing efficient, there are also some challenges (Khan et al., 2020). Some of the challenges are the enormous amount of data, the heterogeneous nature of IIoT systems, and the complex and decentralized processing of data. Efficient data management policies have to be considered for the transmission and storage of data. These policies should take into consideration the heterogeneous nature of IIoT systems. IIoT should also support wireless technologies.

1.7 Security in IoT

One of the challenges of IoT applications is the security issues associated with IoT systems. In IoT every object will be able to communicate with each other; hence, there is a need for security that is different from the traditional web applications (Kouicem et al., 2018). Moreover, the characteristics of IoT systems such as mobility of the objects, wireless communications, diversity of connected devices, and scalability of the IoT make security mandatory for IoT systems. Security challenges are present in every layer of IoT architecture, including application-based layer, network-based layer, and device-based layer.

Security solutions of the application-based layer include the usage of Datagram Transport Layer Security (DTLS), secure application proxy, password verification, secure coding, usage of file signatures, the establishment of a secure communication channel with authentication, and usage of lightweight encryption schemes. Similarly, security solutions of the network-based layer include the definition of timestamp and authentication parameter for packet verification, usage of encryption-based signatures, installation of threat hunting modules such as intrusion detection system (IDS), and usage of lightweight encryption systems. Security solutions of the device-based layer include measurement of signal strength, computation of the number of packets delivered, encoding packets, and usage of an appropriate intrusion detection technique.

1.8 Summary

In recent years, IoT has enabled people and/or things to be connected anytime and anywhere using the Internet. It offers various applications in various domains such as agriculture, environment, healthcare, smart cities, and transportation. In particular, IoT helps in automating the processes involved in industries. Industrial IoT will definitely impact the lives of people due to its role in factory automation to automotive connectivity. This chapter provided the fundamentals of IoT that will be useful to naïve users of IoT. This chapter described the architecture of IoT, technologies involved in developing IoT systems, and applications of IoT.

Acknowledgment

The author would like to thank Bharathiar University for all the support provided.

References

Aceto, G., Persico, V., Pescape, A., 2020. Industry 4.0 and health: Internet of things, big data and cloud computing for healthcare 4.0. *Journal of Industrial Information Integration* 18, Article ID 100129. doi: 10.1016/j.jii.2020.100129.

Adi, E., Anwar, H., Bay, Z., Zeadally, S., 2020. Machine learning and data analytics for the IoT. *Neural Computing and Applications* 32, 16205–16233.

Alavi, A.H., Jiao, P., Buttlar, W.G., Lajnef, N., 2018. Internet of Things-enabled smart cities: State-of-the-art and future trends. *Measurement* 129, 589–600. doi: 10.1016/j.measurement.2018.07.067.

Ashton, K., 2009. That 'Internet of Things' thing. *RFiD Journal* 22, 97–114.

Botta, A., Donato, W.D., Persico, V., Pescape, A., 2016. Integration of cloud computing and Internet of things: A survey. *Future Generation Computer Systems* 56, 684–700. doi: 10.1016/j.future.2015.09.021.

Dizdarevic, J., Carpio, F., Jukan, A., Bruin, X.M., 2019. A survey of communication protocols for Internet of things and related challenges of fog and cloud computing integration. *ACM Computing Surveys* 51(6), Article ID: 116. doi: 10.1145/3292674.

Elazhary, H., 2019. Internet of Things (IoT), mobile, cloud, cloudlet, mobile IoT, IoT cloud, fog, mobile edge, and edge emerging computing paradigms: Disambiguation and research direction. *Journal of Network and Computer Applications* 128, 105–140.

Greco, L., Percannela, G., Ritrovato., Tortorella, F., Vento, M. 2020. Trends in IoT based solutions for health care: Moving AI to the edge. *Pattern Recognition Letters* 135, 346–353.

Hart, J.K., Martinez, K., 2015. Toward an environmental Internet of Things. *Earth and Space Science* 2, 194–200. doi: 10.1002/2014EA000044.

Internet of Things, Gartner Glossary, www.gartner.com/en/information-technology/glossary/Internet-of-things retrieved on 10th April 2020.

Kang, B., Choo, H., 2018. An experimental study of a reliable IoT gateway. *ICT Express* 4, 130–133. doi: 10.1016/j.icte.2017.04.002.

Khan, W.Z., Rehman, M.H., Zangoti, H.M., Afzal, M.K., Armi, N., Salah, K., 2020. Industrial Internet of things: Recent advances, enabling technologies and open challenges. *Computers and Electrical Engineering* 81, Article ID: 106522. doi: 10.1016/j.compeleceng.2019.106522.

Kocakulak, M., Butun, I., 2017. An overview of Wireless Sensor Networks towards Internet of things. In: Proceedings of 2017 IEEE 7th Annual Computing and Communication Workshop and Conference (CCWC), Las Vegas, pp. 1–6.

Kouicem, D.E., Bouabdallah, A., Lakhlef, H., 2018. Internet of things security: A top-down survey. *Computer Networks* 141, 199–221. doi:10.1016/j.comnet.2018.03.012.

Lampropoulos, G., Siakas, K., Anastasiadis, T., 2019. Internet of things in the context of Industry 4.0: An overview. *International Journal of Entrepreneurial Knowledge* 7(1), 4–19. doi: 10.2478/ijek-2019-0001.

Majumdar, S., Subhani, M.M., Roullier, B., Anjum, A., Zhu, R., 2021. Congestion prediction for smart sustainable cities using IoT and machine learning approaches. *Sustainable Cities and Society* 64, Article ID: 102500.

Martino, B.D., Rak, M., Ficco, M., Esposito, A., Maisto, S.A., Nacchia, S., 2018. Internet of Things reference architectures, security and interoperability: A survey. *Internet of Things* 1, 99–112. doi: 10.1016/j.iot.2018.08.008

Montori, F., Bedogni, L., Felica, M.D., Bononi, L., 2018. Machine to machine wireless communication technologies for the Internet of things: Taxonomy comparison and open issues. *Pervasive and Mobile computing* 50, 56–81. doi: 10.1016/j.pmcj.2018.08.002

Mutlag, A.A., Ghani, M.K.A., Arunkumar, N., Mohammed, M.A., Mohd, O., 2019. Enabling technologies for fog computing in healthcare IoT systems. *Future Generation Computer Systems* 90, 62–78. doi: 10.1016/j.future.2018.07.049.

Nuvolari, A., 2019. Understanding successive industrial revolutions: A developmental block approach. *Environmental Innovation and Societal Transitions* 32, 33–44. doi: 10.1016/j.eist.2018.11.002.

Patel, P., Narmawala, Z., Thakkar, A., 2019. A survey on intelligent transportation system using Internet of things, In: Shetty N., Patnaik L., Nagaraj H., Hamsavath P., Nalini N. (Eds.) *Emerging Research in Computing, Information Communication and Applications*, Springer, Singapore, 231–240. doi: 10.1007/978-981-13-5953-8_20.

Peddoju, S.K., Upadhyay, H., 2020. Evaluation of IoT data visualization tools and techniques, In: Anouncia S., Gohel H. and Vairamuthu S. (Eds.) *Data Visualization*, Springer, Singapore, 115–140.

Ray, P.P., 2016. A survey of IoT cloud platforms. *Future Computing and Informatics Journal* 1, 35–46. doi: 10.1016/j.fcij.2017.02.001.

Ray, P.P., 2018. A survey on Internet of Things architectures. *Journal of King Saud University – Computer and Information Sciences* 30, 291–319. doi: 10.1016/j.jksuci.2016.10.003.

Rayes, A., Salem, S., 2019. *Internet of Things from Hype to Reality*, Springer, Switzerland.

Recommendation of ITU-TY.2060, June 2012, www.itu.int/en.ITU-T/gsi/iot/Pages/default.aspx retrieved on 10th April 2020.

Sathyan, M., 2020. Industry 4.0: Industrial Internet of Things (IIOT). *Advances in Computers* 117(1), 129–164. doi: 10.1016/bs.adcom.2019.10.010.

Serpanos, D., Wolf, M., 2018. *Internet-of-Things (IoT) Systems*, Springer, Switzerland.

Tzounis, A., Katsoulas, N., Bartzanas, T., Kitlas, C., 2017. Internet of things in agriculture: Recent advances and future challenges. *Biosystems Engineering* 164, 31–48. doi: 10.1016/j.biosystemseng.2017.09.007.

Xu, M., David, J.M., Kim, S.H., 2018. The fourth industrial revolution: Opportunities and challenges. *International Journal of Financial Research* 9(2), 90–95. doi: 10.5430/ijfr.v9n2p90.

Zhang, C., He, Y., Du, B., Yuan, L., Li, B., Jiang, S., 2020. Transformer fault diagnosis method using IoT based monitoring system and ensemble machine learning. *Future Generation Computer Systems* 108, 533–545.

Zhang, J., 2020. Real-time detection of energy consumption of IoT network nodes based on artificial intelligence. *Computer Communications* 153, 188–195.

Chapter 2

IoT Application in Education

K. Kalaiselvi

Department of Computer Science, Vels Institute of Science, Technology and Advanced Studies (VISTAS), Chennai, India

Contents

DOI: 10.1201/9781003175872-2

29

Objectives

By reading this chapter, the learner will gain knowledge on

1. Technologies for higher education
2. Influence of IoT on Education
3. Components of Internet of Things
4. Challenges in IoT
5. Smart Campus
6. IoT and virtual education

2.1 Introduction

In today's era, technology plays a vital role in higher education. In the education field, technologies help students to encourage involvement with the course material available online. It helps them to earn an easy learning experience. The technology involved with education is provided to students as ubiquitous learning. Technology will allow both instructors and learners to enjoy and have a meaningful teaching–learning process.

IoT produces a world that links all the artifacts (also known as smart objects) around us to the Internet and interacts with each other in limited human interaction (Ashton, 2009). Our mission is to create a safer atmosphere for people,

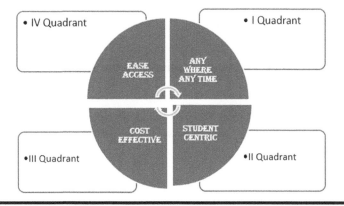

Figure 2.1   Incipient Higher Education System.

where things around us know what we expect, what we want and without any clear directives, what we need to do accordingly. Current Internet of Things (IoT) research focuses mainly on how generic artifacts can view, hear, and detect their physical world and connect them to express their opinions. Monitoring and decision making could also be moved from the human side to the robot side. Since IoT is understood to be the networking between actual objects or devices. One of the IoT principles of a scholar. A transparent and comprehensive network of intelligent objects that can co-ordinate themselves, share information, data, and energy, react, and operate in the face of situations and changes in the world. Knowledge exchange takes place through networking technologies such as Wireless Sensor Networks (WSNs) and Radio Frequency Identification (RFID).

2.1.1 Technology Related to Higher Education

The new educational system will be defined with these four attributes viz., anywhere anytime, student-centric, cost-effective, and easy access to learning content. In the near future, education will have a paradigm shift from traditional learning to online learning and in turn will have classrooms digitalized. Figure 2.1 shows the four phases of higher education systems clearly.

   Different approaches to higher education areas listed below:

1. Custom learning experiences
2. Cloud computing
3. Speech-to-text options
4. Virtual and augmented learning experiences

5. 3D printing
6. Learning analytics

Gartner identifies the few strategic technologies that will have the biggest impact on higher education are as follows:

- Next-generation security and risk management
- Artificial intelligence (AI) conversational interfaces
- Smart campus
- Predictive analytics
- Nudge tech
- Digital credentialing tech
- Hybrid integration platforms
- Career software
- Student cross-life cycle CRM
- Wireless presentation technologies

The biggest challenge in higher education is how technology can be incorporated into the education field. According to Wake Forest University Vice President David Brown, "the case for computers [in collegiate education] rests on scant amounts of hard evidence". Further, Brown says that technologies have been forced to use in higher education. He trusts that "available of more choices will lead to more learning". From a teacher's perspective, technology can be effectively used to reach all kinds of students.

According to Brown, all evidence says that education with computers will have proven results. In his further studies, says that collaborative learning, visualization, and animation will surely enhance the learning process. It proves that technologies incorporated in the educational strategies will move to a new paradigm shift. Brown concludes that in the near future more empirical evidence is required to say that technologies can be used in different kinds of learning centers.

2.2 Components of IoT

The Internet of Things consists of four major components:

1. Sensor
2. Internet (network)
3. Data processing and
4. Application layers

Further, IoT architecture includes protocols, actuators, cloud services, and layers that include four phases in the architecture.

a. What is IoT architecture?

It consists of four layers which include different kinds of sensors, protocols, actuators, cloud services, etc. shown in Figure 2.2. All items are linked to the Internet on first layer, which includes an ensemble of embedded sensors and actuators interconnected to an IoT gateway. In the second layer, unprocessed data are collected from IoT gateways and converted into digital streams, filtered, preprocessed and sent for the analysis phase. The third layer processes and enhances the analysis of data. This step can be carried out by using machine learning and visualization techniques. Finally, in the fourth layer data, are transferred and stored into the cloud server or local server.

b. Can IoT work without Internet?

Without an Internet connection, IoT cannot function but it can send an alert message for the lost connectivity to the system. In some applications like home appliances, vehicles already have a battery device to have connectivity, which helps to sustain the system to connect with sensors, actuators, and software.

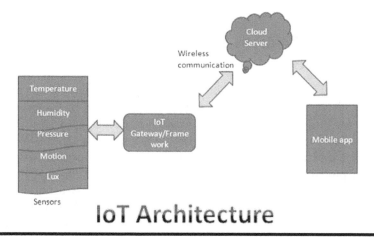

Figure 2.2   Architecture of IoT.

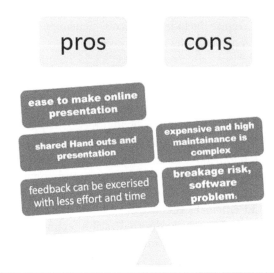

Figure 2.3   Pros and Cons of Smart Class.

c. What is the role of the Internet in IoT?

The Internet helps to connect people so they can communicate with each other and exchange their online data to access them. It also helps to do real-time analysis and to create desired outcomes for the specified application.

2.3 IoT Applications in the Teaching and Learning Processes

The use of IoT in the school is linked to the professional and healthcare topics. It adapts and improves tutoring by utilizing and permitting optimization of all content and procedures of distribution. It allows professors to stretch attention to individuals and their techniques. It similarly decreases charges and employment of edification over mechanization of mutual responsibilities external to the real teaching procedure. Use of IoT in modern colleges and tutorial rooms will transform the education and allow for progressive payments to the institutes. Figure 2.3 describes the pros and cons of IoT applications in the learning process.

Some of the methods to use Smart Boards in the Smart classroom are as follows:

1. Classroom management will be improved
2. Eyes strain minimized

3. Academics can experience digital learning
4. Kindergarten lessons can be animated with cartoons
5. The online test can be conducted with multichoice questions
6. Students will utilize the technology more smartly

The scope of using student ID cards is as follows:

1. Student tracking can be done efficiently
2. Library books can be easily accessible
3. Students can be provided with security
4. Attendance marking can be done

2.3.1 Interactive Whiteboards

Usually a traditional study hall has a slate or projector connected with a PC, in any structure. This kind of study hall does not record their movement. In any event, it can monitor teaching and learning movements that can be captured from any improved gadgets. The documented study hall behavior triggers all understudies, including people who do not have a confused understanding of the themes of those topics, from different perspectives. These gadgets were simply used to show and display data and images from associated PCs to understudies. Be that as it may, a selection of information from the study hall will be suggested, not just presenting information to understudies and collecting from their association. We should, therefore, store the data for some time later. Furthermore, by using a brilliant e-learning framework, this knowledge can also be transmitted in the appropriate arrangement without even a moment's pause. This program synchronizes certain words to get to the untouchables of the public space of study. So, in any case, everyone may become acquainted with those exercises, being outside the study hall. Some of the commonly used IoT applications are discussed.

i. Picture boarding into IoT-empowered panels

The association of the older era demonstration panels with current interactive picture boarding of the software has the same issue. This comfort has been altered by Internet devices such as Glogster and certifies us to produce ordinary prints short of difficulties uniting images, text, audio-visuals, transcripts, and hyperlinks. This allows for comparison with the other mechanisms and helps the academicians to proportion them immediately with others and eases the work of the academician. Such computer-generated photos can then be pre-valent over contact with generations and instructors, confidently retrieved via the URL contract of the image and dispatched on refinement blogs.

ii. Communicating acquisition of data

The mixture of manuscripts and photographs does not regulate the achievement of differentiating these existences. To provide comprehension, the limit of the workbooks is balanced with net-primarily created websites consisting of additional content, images, examinations, animations, and different materials. This expands the scholars' perspective to analyze new possessions with increased concern and engagement with teachers and their classes.

iii. Knowledge at any period and anyplace

In creating a net over the use of separate Internet-based organizations, IoT plays a significant role. Progressive knowledge enables researchers to demonstrate the researchers' progress. Edmodo is an infinite form of a vocal conversation between teacher and student. Edmodo styles are conceivable for strangers to profit somewhat from data from everywhere. At a similar time from the tutorial room or uniform reacting to uprights, IoT allows scholars and educators to communicate through strange techniques, examination mails, and forthcoming proceedings. It is by far a real app that offers a harmless mechanism and robust privacy. It also helps an operator by promising occupied privacy.

iv. Greater security structures

The IoT application in teaching is important, as the institute locations and training areas could be very useful by applying greater knowledge to confidential responses. It includes alternative pointers, auditory enhancement, Wi-Fi chronometers, and hearing-impaired announcements that give a security numbness to the academics and labor. IoT application helps in disaster management of public services by linking the locations and the relevant staff and students through pre-recorded instructional communications.

v. Good-bye to chalkboards

The use of a real, powerful stage containing smart boards is here. It helps presenters to explain the added addresses that are deprived of difficulties with the contribution of relevant exhibits and films. Pupils are promoters of gaming as a real place to talk. The ingenious age group helps coaches and students to browse the web or handle audio-visual and section tasks universally.

vi. Being present monitoring system

An efficient gadget for faculty attendance guarantees the security of an academic initiative and can provide different approaches to colleges and tutoring facilities. This helps the researchers to directly integrate the records into the system. This might enable the operation to reduce the time it takes to circulate proof of involvement and encourage institute generals to direct a portion of correspondence to the parents. Also, apart from the number of examples a student has told the specialist, it will help to follow an evaluation of the experimental requirements of academics and the remedial medication that they would be attractive. It also provides the student with the best quality to validate their mealtime for the day.

vii. Mobile applications and tablets

The criterion is a constraint of the ambitious pupils' system method. The survivors of these contemporary students, however, seem to rotate around smartphones, tablets, and other screen-oriented computer electronics inappropriately. This extra focus on computers for gaming and communal engagement with instructive themes has been delightfully eliminated by the IoT authorities. Now it is unproblematic to connect the planet diagonally to individuals with parallel regions and healthcare. In teaching, the computers of the Internet of Things collect knowledge and suggest theoretical themes of attention robotically to the scholars involved on the other side of the computer. Smartphones and tablet activities have been completed that are virtually helpful for the student's assessment.

viii. Fine-tuning infirmity

A few years ago, it was very difficult for autistic children to learn and replicate new items. Any additional able pupil has grown probable with the latest technological techniques, information new items, and results in impartial comparable. A portion of individuals have experiences with the intellect of the audible spectrum. They may seek aid from an organization of similar gloves and a pill, interpreted from a linguistic sign, to produce voiced speech. Its brilliance in transitioning into the printed language in a wide variety is noteworthy. All the creatures of incapacitated children of God are brighter just as IoT devices indulge in imagination to provide the deactivated children with instructive support in a meaningful way. This channels unimportant achievements into their intelligence and desire.

ix. Smart campus inventiveness progress pupil experiences and save money

Gathering data from IoT devices can also allow campuses to develop "smarter," which in turn can help students make healthy and varied additional money-making choices by styling them. Lecturers from Circumstance Western Reserve University established an allowance from the U.S. Energy Subdivision to test roughly ground-breaking concepts, as well as a computer that can generate energy from the emotions of touching individuals and transitory carriages. Two IoT apps were previously developed by researchers at Carnegie Mellon University: Snap2It, which associates operators with a copier or projector after they have occupied an image of it on their smartphone; and Impromptu, an organization that calls up communal apps when they are needed, such as when a student enters a supply or is near a car stopover.

x. Task-based education

The transition from a perfect information transfer to a cooperative, information sharing organization is a person of the organizational movements taking place in education. Since associated organizations free-up educators from footage and intensive care students, IoT will have a thoughtful impact on the method we interact, enabling them to ease information somewhat rather than just bring up results. Students learn-by-doing in task-based education and educators aid when appropriate. IoT systems mechanically provide reaction, assistance, and classroom-level control. No pupil falls too far late or becomes too far in advance by promoting teachers for assistance and by increasing trouble when needed, a problem that has continuously continued in the tutorial room.

2.3.2 Students ID Cards

ECUS in conjunction with an up-to-date ECUS stamp marks you as a student. This can be used as an identification card at college, but it is not a substitute for the official identity documents. The ECUS can be used in the canteen and cafeteria as a digital payment tool, as well as for scanning, copying, and printing on Konica-Minolta machines. White scanners are fitted in the canteen and cafeterias at all checkouts. To pay, simply place the ECUS on the scanner until the completion of the payment. The Konica-Minolta company photocopiers are also fitted with scanners that read the ECUS.

2.3.3 Tracking Attendance

RFID engineering has been commonly used in various segments for a long period, such as in education, transportation, horticulture, creature agriculture, store deals, and other divisions. Using RFID in training is an understudy participation testing system, using Internet of Things (IoT) and cloud technologies, it will create a genuine observing framework for time participation that can be accessed by various parties, such as speakers, campus organization, and guardians. With this observing system, it is possible that understudies that are not seen can be quickly identified and fast activity can be taken and the learning planning can run easily (Buhalis and Amaranggana, 2013).

2.3.3.1 Sensors and Actuators

Physical quantities such as temperature, sound, humidity, vibrations, etc are degree sensors and transform into an electrical quantity over this physical quantity. These transformed signals move to the system and function in the same way after the framework.

2.3.3.2 Connectivity

Using various communication media, such as Wi-Fi, Bluetooth or BLE, LoRaWAN, LTE, and many more, the received signals must be submitted to the network.

2.3.3.3 People and Process

A critical part of IoT is people and planning. At that point, in Figure 2.4, the ordered inputs are combined into a bidirectional structure that coordinates data, individuals, and forms for making superior choices. On his mobile/web application, the user will get to his outcome.

2.4 Challenges in IoT

IoT brings impossible challenges and openings to instruction. The select improvement of ubiquitous computing, growing IoT propels like cloud computing, and colossal information related analytics are confirmative not because it was in civilizing the middle values of teaching and quality of investigation be that because it may grow an IoT culture and propelling a substitution computerized culture (Chen et al., 2014). With extending on-line degree openings and steady get to educator substance in each organized and unstructured organize, the IoT leads computerized vitality into instruction establishments. IoT can be an outstanding move interior the old educator worldview although

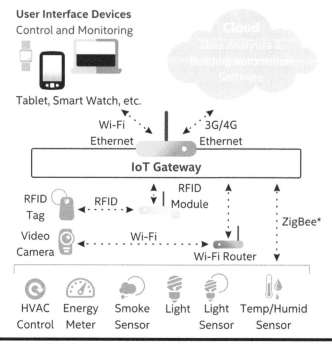

Figure 2.4   General feature of IoT Gateway.

integration broader disciplines, close to science, to complement the worth of immense information accessible from social media. several the IoT challenges in the instruction division get a handle on.

2.4.1 Cloud Computing

Various colleges are abuse half breed cloud as they try to arrange for encouraging IoT applications. the mix of millennial's, the preeminent tech-savvy understudies interior the colleges, empower since the rise of the pill and versatile advancement, has opened present-day methods to extend the reason-ability of undertaking arrange, educator developments, examination, and learning circumstances. With show computing, the cloud gives steady affiliations and organizations to data advancement organizations. Straightforwardly, undertaking arranges in many instruction establishments depend upon hybrid cloud systems with computing stages on person clouds, although undertaking and teacher applications step by step move to open clouds. Endeavor arrange in these establishments require a cutback inertia time due to the ask for substance in educator propels, the tremendous increase in sound and recordings for heading, furthermore, the require for energetic undertaking frameworks.

2.4.2 Instructional Technologies

The developing utilize of getting to know administration frameworks LMS like Moodle and chalkboard is making an expansive amount of prepared and unstructured statistics like sound and video substance. Delicate digital schoolrooms prepared with deal with seize frameworks and net gushing provide a danger for college understudies to get to instructive substance on request at any time.

2.4.3 Mobility Applications

IoT programs are being increasingly utilized to facilitated transportable learning applications and for evaluation and checking on systems (Rivera and van der Meulen, 2013). The culminate computer program will help understudies to memorize from getting to know possessions, manage assignments, and work on errands. Teaches conjointly utilize besides those programs to appear incredibly particular intellect, ventured forward real, consistent diversions, and social subject things.

2.4.4 Security and Privacy

The executions of IoT improvements display present-day and unmistakable protection and safety demanding situations and issues (Rivera and van der Meulen, 2013). Tending to these demanding situations and to verify to create beyond any doubt safety in IoT devices and administrations must be an essential want. One most of the fundamental criteria for IoT is that they should grasp robust and reliable protection and security instruments. Instruction is vulnerable to the safekeeping and shield of the IoT framework. Although there was extra electricity to supervise the guarantee of the IoT framework, there's still no technique to identify commerce risks associated with records breaches. The education segment needs to create hints to secure IoT applications. As coaching makes variation destiny staff, it's to understand IoT degrees and frameworks certainly with the challenges of IoT subsidizing, advancing superior instructions educational method, preparing, and facts area investigation. Also, IoT applications should join the long-run labor ethically and morally to deal with cyber protection problems as society relies upon the part of IoT applications. Subsequently, an agreeable approach to security and security is progressing to be required to create preparations in success and suitable a whole lot obliged to confront IoT security demanding situations. Additionally, the overall capability of the IoT relies upon methods that take into consideration people's safety. Subsequently, to fulfill those openings, there's must create better approaches that take into consideration an individual's safety selections and desires, whereas nevertheless advance development in cutting-edge improvements and administrations.

2.4.5 Research Computing

Higher coaching proceeds to gain from IoT integration. seeing that the fee of equipment decreases, information space investigation has picked up energy inside the final a long time. Furthermore, with the delivery of gigantic information, indeed small faculties will increment their records area investigation impact and put in tall execution computing (HPC), enormous records ranges, and analytics. STEM instruction has seen the prerequisite of spotting broader collaboration with IoT biological structures by misuse of machine innovations, remote-managed Ethereal Vehicles (UAVs), and microcontrollers. Designing research centers make use of sound video innovations, UAV, Raspberry Pi, and open supply frameworks (OSS) that unit of size driving developments and upgrading studying bureaucracy in the building comes. Logical teach analysts captivated with the aid of the excessiveness of colossal statistics created by using social media and omnipresent computing unit never-endingly misuse conveyed computing levels like HPC, GPU clusters, Hadoop clusters, and huge data analytics to improve IoT study.

2.4.6 Quality and Ethics

The quality of learning each on-line and on-field and hence the rising fetched of higher instruction has been heightening wrangled around in later a long time. The IoT offers specific openings to communicate computerized courses. In any case, it conjointly presents challenges to keeping up the standard of instruction and examination of students' work. IoT insightful applications would like disobedient and advance for instructs, instructors and so the consistent community to boost the standard of examination and address ethics issues among instruction.

2.4.7 Financing

These application stacks still create each on a level plane and work out progress, examination computing, and wander progress. onboard the data advancement and inquire about office costs, most colleges do not have a methodology for sharing costs related to recognizing an IoT establishment. educator activity must return up with unused considerations to finance relate data development establishment and administrations.

2.4.8 Network Devices and Connections

Teachers are also utilizing immersive technologies and devices to enable their students to learn more. There are a variety of views about the negative impact on young students. There are a few reasons why teaching and learning love technology (Patel and Patel, 2016).

1. One of the main reasons students appreciate innovations and are pleased with these services. They became more active and committed to the usage of learning technology.
2. The other theory is that it involves four learning components: positive interaction, group involvement, daily communication and feedback, and connections to real-world experts.
3. It also provides job learning services to students. When these children go to work and work, their programming skills would help them to do their work more efficiently. In contrast, a small incident or viral social networking video can make someone famous.
4. Technology has made it easier for students to understand. They can get preparation tools, apply auto-correction tests online, and have an online meeting with their parents to save time.
5. Research reveals that the application of technologies has improved the test score. Students are carrying the material they have gained at their own pace and are performing well in the exams.
6. Code helps low-level learners. Technology is a well-known means of educating children with special needs and teaching languages.
7. It's an opportunity to pass past class. Learners may learn from experts in the classroom, even if they have accessible learning resources.
8. Improved answers to homework. Technology helps children to do their homework on a computer utilizing online platforms. They're going to review the lessons of the videos and watch some related resources.
9. It helps to save money and electricity. More efficient teachers will be encouraged to utilize technologies in classes. The goal of technology is to eliminate obstacles. i.e., audio-visual assistance via multimedia and amplification. If audio-visual assistance is effective, class management is much easier and more powerful.

Knowledge learned in the past has changed in modern times and is continuously changing via immersive and intelligent technologies. "Books are going to be outdated soon" Thomas Edison. In the age of no more lectures, no more journals, no more teachers, no more timetables. E-books, digital machines, and intelligent systems make a huge improvement in learning feasible. Learning can now be achieved from a distance without time and space restrictions.

Education is evolving into a virtual world of artificial intelligence and technical sophistication (Rose et al., 2015). The introduction of robots will bring about a larger shift in the economy and minimize human interaction. The new education system platform changed job learning and centered on the partnership of appraisal, development, progression, experience, exploration, creativity, ethics, and risk.

A variety of leading researchers cautioned about IoT equipment and teaching technology: microcontroller improvement forums, advanced built-in computers, mobile phones, iPods, laptop and tablet automated electricity lighting, smart HVAC systems, RFID-enabled student ID cards, wireless door locks, security cameras, and video conferencing, biometric involvement, and visionary participation.

Developing school rooms via digital virtual white forums helps students to learn additionally and continually along the way, or makes it easier to share, incorporate, and edit knowledge with students by utilizing on-the-fly web material to facilitate discussions in school rooms. You've got to market devices like laptops, tablets, smartphones, etc. In the classrooms that allow them to test their devices. This would inspire students to do the work they have completed in the elegance room, since returning to their homes, to reconsider and reinforce the values of their time of entertainment. Students may use small IoT platforms with microcontroller updates, including Arduino, Raspberry Pi, and STM32 Nucleoid. It is a rather distinctive example of British schools where children will learn how to use a BBC microphone: bit, a Bluetooth and USB single-board laptop, an LED display, and two programmable buttons. All these forums have accessories to extend their functionality to fulfill the different requirements for updating the IoT program.

2.4.9 Sensors

Things Network (IoT) apps – for urban frames, factory installations, or wearable equivalents – use giant sensor clusters to gather news for site transmitting to a centralized, cloud-based computer asset (Sintef and Norway, 2014). Analytics program utilizing the cloud computer frameworks decreases the colossal quantities of data produced in extraordinary truths for customers and commands for actuators in the region. Sensors are straightforward gadgets, which transform into electric markers or shifts in electrical homes shown in Figure 2.5 by actual causes.

Whereas this utility is a considerable starting point, the taking of properties as IoT components by sensors must be considered:

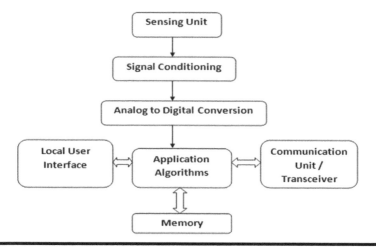

Figure 2.5 Smart Sensor Building Blocks.

- Low-cost meaning they can be shipped financially in big numbers
- Subtly "vanish" mentally under every condition
- Online, as wired membership is typically impractical
- Self-identification and auto proofing
- Quite a low capacity, such that it may be due without a battery shift for such a long time or making up with energy selection
- Robust assistance to limit or erase
- Self-analytical and self-recovery
- Self-adjusting or understanding remote link alignment instructions
- Preprocessing data for gateway, PLC, and server load constraint

Data from various sensors may be integrated and connected to generate choices on inert queries. To differentiate between mechanical disappointment, for example, temperature sensors and vibration sensing details may be used. The sensor functions are found in a single device; in other gadgets, the programming capabilities of a sensor are consolidated.

Savvy sensors are designed as IoT pieces that are transformed into a computerized data stream for passage to an entrance through the show reality vector. A certain chip unit is used to measure the application (MPU). This may be sifted, stipend, and all other flag conditioning errors listed for the method.

The MPU's insight can be extended to a few other capabilities to reduce the heap on the IoT's modern imperative resources, for example, data alteration can be sent to the MPU so that the sensor can be set up for any development change. The MPU will apprehend any occurrence of parameters that start drifting past ok standards and generate signals appropriately; the administrators will then be able to take measures and move earlier before a catastrophic failure occurs.

On the off chance, the sensor should view the "file by using exception" mode in which the data is likely to be transmitted when the expected variables are significantly changed from past sample variables. This decreases both the load on the vital processing aid and the possible requirements of the smart sensor, usually with a simple benefit, since the sensor can rely on battery or power harvesting without the associated power.

If the smart sensor recalls two additives for processing, self-diagnosis of the sensor may be implicit. Any flow in one of the sensor outputs can be distinguished immediately. Also, if the sensor fails; for example, because of a quick circuit, the process can proceed with the second estimation. On the other side, a look at can be made up of two sensors that collaborate for advanced gazing input.

2.4.9.1 Image Sensors

Image sensors are rebellious and are employed to modify optical pictures into electronic signs for appearing or putting away the documents electronically (Stankovic, 2014). In specialized camera and modules, clinical photography, and night-vision gadget, warm imaging gadgets, radar, sonar, media home, biometric, and IRIS gadgets, the vital application of the image sensor is identified.

- CCD (charge-coupled device)
- CMOS (complementary metal-oxide-semiconductor) imagers

While each type of sensor uses exclusive innovation to capture images, each CCD and CMOS imager uses metal-oxide semiconductors with a similar degree of light impact and no innately friendly contrast. A typical user might feel that this is an ordinary camera, but even though it's not a long way from reality, image sensors are connected to a wide range of different gadgets, making them far more useful. One of the most popular uses is the automotive industry, where imagery carries out a significant activity. With these sensors, the framework can detect signs and symptoms, hazards, and a variety of different items that the driver might often notice. They expect a great challenge in the IoT enterprise, as they have a direct effect on the production of driverless cars. Also, they are carried out in specialized safety frameworks, where images help to capture insights about the attacker. In the retail industry, these sensors are used to gather consumer data, helping companies display signs of development expertise to whom their store's move, race, gender, age are just a portion of the valued parameters that retail owners get through using these IoT sensors.

2.4.10 Physical Objects

It is the Internet functioning of the strong physical elements that are empowered to gather and trade information through IPv6 addressing modes. It also refers to the use of cleverly related objects, specialists, and gadgets to track the information generated by installed sensors in machines and other physical-virtual devices. IoT has been described as the global framework for a data society that can promote the interconnecting of a wide range of artifacts, such as physical and virtual items, which rely on existing media transmission conventions and innovations. IoT-GSI also underscored the growth of other Learning with high urban areas and networks. IoT, because of the Internet Society (ISOC), refers to the situations where organize availability and processing capacity spreads to gadgets, articles, and sensors to produce, send/get, trade information without human intervention.

IoT offers the propelled availability of tools, gadgets, and structures that run past machine-to-machine (M2M) communications that center around sensor systems and computers. It's all about cloud creativity, choosing, and exchanging info. By IoT, objects can be sensed around the environment and can be detected and remotely managed through the existing device base, such as the Internet, in which each article is interestingly recognizable via its installed equipment structure and can be connected within the current Internetworking engineering. These products, such as PCs, advanced cell phones, PCs, laptops, phablets, and gadgets that can get an IP address, contain a heap of the Internet of Things (IoT). Also, other gadgets with/without human involvement that can collect and transfer information and make a control decision can be attached to them. Communication Technology has been modified to a simple section of the current instruction models. It makes it possible to shift from a knowledge transfer model to a collaborative, interactive, self-coordinated, and engaging model that helps to broaden the information and skills of students (digital students) just as to develop their skills in the "learning computerized Society".

2.5 Digital Transformation among the Knowledge Seekers

2.5.1 Content Preparation

Hyper Immobility of the IoT within the instruction proposes that the interfacing of the various institutes, the coordinating, and scholarly centers should take place during the instruction (Sundmaeker et al., 2010). A vast array of sensors, actuators, and IP-based virtual or physical objects are progressing to be connected, producing gigantic knowledge. The most important Virtual Mechanical Measures will interface all the IP-based focal points around the outline, uniformly. Universal video-conference execution, worldwide foundations, and scholastic centers are regularly implemented and the inner instruction cluster on the outside is integrated. It's a sensible vision: the worldwide use and administration of examinations, and it comes in real and fiscal terms. This universal imaginable vision is expected for the long run that could reconstruct the individual's instruction frame, all because of IoT's hyper-property choices. Measurability is one of the intrinsic characteristics of the well-designed Internet of Things.

As a property of IoT, it is regularly thought of as a built trait within the system and can involve a variety of impacts on IoT-based instruction frameworks. There is no obstacle to the inclusion or absence of any protests from the structure and it is flexible to changes in the topology. IoT brings with it is its vast details, which may be due to the large space of objects that the unit has been empowered to transfer and generate a vast collection of data. The measurability of IoT is anticipated in terms of estimation of virtual school rooms, an assortment of physical and virtual IPv6-based objects, sensors, and actuators, and specifically in the variety of Hubs. Understudy and teacher execution square measure a very common marker that has been defined by a few analysts and there is no common parameter for that. In any case, a few critics have tried to verify the influence of the student's achievement and the power of the teacher.

The key qualification between dual thoughts is that the scope and space of the IoT are mechanical. IoT will cover the gigantic components of ICT topics. Instruction work by IoT would conceivably enable researchers and trainees to share their knowledge and information within a genuinely time-consuming system. The speed of exchanging and accessing data generated by various institutes around the world along with the number of artifacts concerned within the learning strategy is impressively growing. Misuse of IoT within the instruction environment has the same outcome as ICT-based instruction frameworks. It's going to make teaching and learning strategy a spurt and a success. As defined, IoT will have coordinate and roundabout impacts, as far as those parameters are concerned, within the instruction that does not appear to be the concentration in the middle of this chapter, be that, as they may be thought, within the related math shape as a back for this reason.

2.5.2 Assignments/Seminars/Projects

The cutting-edge under-studies offer the impression that they spin around smartphones, medicine, and distinctive screen-oriented physical science. IoT experts have superbly pushed this overabundance specializing in tasks, seminars, and scholarly topics (Vermesan and Friess, 2013). Nowadays, interfaces with individuals around the world with comparative goals and interfaces are as simple as ever. Sensors, commands and mechanically direct instructional exercise subjects are fascinated by researchers sitting on the inverse view of the computer. Sensitive use of phones is assisted by the student's analysis of the night. IoT innovation kills physical proximity constraints and improves the freedom to adapt to any kind of education, such as teachers, any apparatus, and anywhere e-learning is promoted, easily. IoT ensures an immense impact on the education policy by offering access to common assets and opportunities for college children and speakers.

Subsequently, one of each of the main impacts of IoT-based learning circumstances is that the traditional understudy and teacher assignments are changed regularly. Understudies and teachers can keep illuminating materials and/or testing facilities at any moment, wherever they interface. It is anticipated to advertise the gigantic assortment of examination openings for students, understudies, and analyst's circular the country. The researcher chosen would motivate them to be part of the learning plan by linking $64,000 items to their homework, homework, and logical tests. At the end of the day, the hypothetical and brief territorial arithmetic linked seems to think that the adequacy and effect of IoT within the teaching and learning strategy is certain and should not be ignored. Adaptation, hyper-connectivity between $64,000 and virtual objects, transparency, capability, and measurability are IoT properties.

2.6 Conclusion

The chapter concludes by explaining how the Internet of things influences the advanced education domain. A study has been carried out on how IoT impact on higher education scenario. Many survey results reveal that how IoT have higher interaction while using in education. Since IoT is scalable and an intelligent network can be done it is used in schools, colleges/universities, and education centers. An effective and interactive ensemble can be done between IoT and virtual education with intelligence features in it. Despite existing challenges, IoT plays a vital role in the new mitigation of higher education. Hence the chapter has been written by exploring the IoT applications in higher education.

References

Al-Fuqaha, A., Guizani, M., Mohammadi, M., Aledhari, M., Ayyash, M., 2015. Internet of things: A survey on enabling technologies, protocols, and applications. *IEEE Community Survey Tutor* 17(4), 2347–2376.

Ashton, K., 2009. That 'Internet of things' thing. *RFID Journal* 22, 97–114.

Buhalis, D., Amaranggana, A., 2013. Smart tourism destinations. Paper presented at: Proceedings of the 2014 International Conference on Information and Communication Technologies in Tourism; Dublin, Ireland.

Chen, S., Xu, H., Liu, D., Hu, B., Wang, H., 2014. A vision of IoT: Applications, challenges, and opportunities with China perspective. *IEEE Internet Things Journal* 1(4), 349–359.

Patel, K.K., Patel, S.M., 2016. Internet of things-IOT: definition, characteristics, architecture, enabling technologies, application, and future challenges. *International Journal of Engineering Science and Computing* 6(5), 6122–6131.

Rivera, J., van der Meulen, R., 2013. Gartner says the Internet of Things Installed base will grow to 26 billion units by 2020. *Gartner.* http://www.gartner.com/newsroom/id/2636073, [accessed 5 April, 2016].

Rose, K., Eldridge, S., Chapin, L., 2015. *The Internet of Things: An Overview,* The Internet Society (ISOC), Reston, VA, 1–50.

Sintef, O.V., Norway, P. F., (Eds.), 2014. *Internet of Things–From Research and Innovation to Market Deployment,* River Publishers, Aalborg, Denmark.

Stankovic, J. A., 2014. Research directions for the Internet of things. *IEEE Internet Things Journal* 1(1), 3–9.

Sundmaeker, H., Guillemin, P., Friess, P., Woelfflé, S., 2010, Vision and challenges for realizing the Internet of things. Cluster of European Research Projects on the Internet Things, *European Commission* 3(3), 34–36.

Vermesan, O., Friess, P., 2013. *Internet of Things: Converging Technologies for Smart Environments and Integrated Ecosystems,* River Publishers, Aalborg, Denmark.

www.gsma.com, [accessed 2 January, 2018].

Chapter 3

Industrial Internet of Things (IIoT) and Smart Industries

S.R. Vijayalakshmi[1] and S. Muruganand[2]

[1]*Post Doctoral Research Fellow, Department of Electronics and Instrumentation, Bharathiar University, Coimbatore, India*
[2]*Associate Professor, Department of Electronics and Instrumentation, Bharathiar University, Coimbatore, India*

Contents

DOI: 10.1201/9781003175872-3

Objectives

By reading this chapter, reader gains knowledge on

1. Definition of Industrial Internet of Things
2. Industrial Internet of Things and digital transformation
3. IoT in making smart city
4. IIoT in different industries

3.1 Industrial Internet of Things (IIoT)

Machine learning, machine vision, machine to machine communication, embedded systems, big data analytics, and microprocessor/microcontroller developments reduce human input required and develop the new concept of IIoT. For example, the washing machine is connected to the user's cell phone. The cell phone receives the message from the device for any service required from the user. In the oil industry, oil spills cause damage. If there are any loose or rusty connected pipes, they could not be effectively and accurately checked by humans. On the other hand, if the industrial PC is installed with big data analytic software, it could predict the oil spill occurrence with high accuracy and efficiency. This software alerts users to make necessary arrangements. IIoT expands the manufacturing sector and connects every industry, as shown in Figure 3.1.

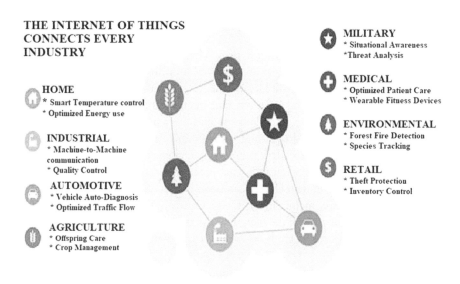

THE INTERNET OF THINGS
CONNECTS EVERY
INDUSTRY

HOME
* Smart Temperature control
* Optimized Energy use

INDUSTRIAL
* Machine-to-Machine
communication
* Quality Control

AUTOMOTIVE
* Vehicle Auto-Diagnosis
* Optimized Traffic Flow

AGRICULTURE
* Offspring Care
* Crop Management

MILITARY
* Situational Awareness
*Threat Analysis

MEDICAL
* Optimized Patient Care
* Wearable Fitness Devices

ENVIRONMENTAL
* Forest Fire Detection
* Species Tracking

RETAIL
* Theft Protection
* Inventory Control

Figure 3.1   Industrial Internet of Things.

Industrial IoT benefits are predictive maintenance efficiencies, increased operation speed, asset/resource optimization, and increased revenues. It increases industrial output considerably. If IIoT is implemented in oil drilling, it will increase oil production by 5 lakh barrels per day. IIoT is not only boosting industrial production, but it also increases profits by decreasing production costs. Electronic business industries have a demand for sensors, system boards, and network devices. IoT is significantly growing in all the industry sectors. The number of IoT devices connected across the world increases day by day and year and year. An average of a 12% increase per year happens in IoT devices, leading to 125 billion IoT devices by 2025.

IIoT is a network of industrial products and physical objects such as machinery, automobile vehicles, household products, etc. These physical objects comprise embedded technology such as electronics, hardware devices, embedded software, miniaturized sensors, and network connectivity techniques. These devices could sense their internal hardware device state. It also could be enabled to communicate with external environments such as persons and other physical things. The field of invention in these categories is continuously growing and the speed of innovation is difficult to predict.

3.1.1 Digital Transformation

Interaction with the world around us is changed by the IIoT with digital technologies. Digital technologies are involved in industries such as agriculture, farming, the internal infrastructure of the city, healthcare products, medical industry, textile industry, oil industry, and many more industries.

IIoT technologies give tremendous modifications in sensors, equipment, city infrastructure with flying drones and autonomous cars, new shopping experiences, and real-time analysis. IIoT is gradually changing the way of the industry into the digital path and digital industrial process. It moves efficiency forward.

Digitalization eases human life as a consumer of industrial products. Humans are using it in e-commerce, mobile Internet, social media, digital cash transformations, from start to end of all parts of the economy, and many more. Digital transformation takes effect via four levels as given below and it is shown in Figure 3.2.

1. Digital data – Capturing, processing, and evaluating enormous amounts of information is possible. It permits enhanced calculations, guesses, calculations, and conclusions to be prepared from big data.

Figure 3.2   Digitalization.

2. Automation and computerization – Combining technologies such as artificial intelligence with IoT are enabling intelligence in systems to work and think like a human.
3. Connectivity – Connecting the complete value chain and goods via networks to coordinate supply chains. It enhances supply chain management by reducing both construction time, fabrication of product period, and innovation in product cycles.
4. Digitally accessible customers – The mobile app or Internet behave as new mediators to customers. Customers directly access offers such as choice, transparency, and new services of producers.

Sensors in all main items or embedded devices form a network of an interface between the analog physical world and digital computer system. Facial recognition with biometrics plays an important part in linking humans with their computer-generated world. It recognizes daily entities with approved operators on roads, public places, or in workshops. Headsets, tablets, or screens are known as brain waves or EEG waves, or mind-controlled devices. These devices permit new kinds of communication between human beings and embedded products in all different spaces. Innovative hardware and sensor devices integrated into dresses, glasses, and vehicles made IIoT a reality. The latest technology trend is shown in Figure 3.3. These technologies are involved with IoT in one or

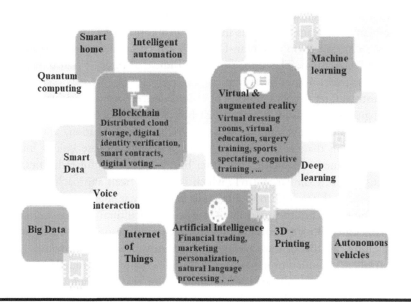

Figure 3.3   Technology Trends.

another way to bring the real world into the virtual digital world. The world objects will become intelligent like humans.

E-therapy in healthcare is possible with IoT. Virtual counseling by doctors could be effectively done by IoT. Electronic health records (EHR) are accessible by authorized medical staff, administrators, and patients only. Accessing these records helps to offer innovative insurance products and forecasts pandemics or infection hotspots.

3.1.2 Industry 4.0

The domain of sensor devices, actuators, and network-connected devices deals with countless openings for automation in industrial goods, facilities to customers, and a lot more services to humans. But these connected devices have to process an unlimited data stream, which is the main task in IIoT. Cloud computing, graphical processing units (GPUs), quantum computers, microcontroller units (MCU), and high-speed microprocessors are high-tech computing processors developed for providing solutions to these huge data processing and big data analytics. The progress in the vast volume of data brings analysis of marketing techniques, competitors, product data, and customer behavior.

Intelligent machines, advanced data analytics, and a man-machine interface bring focus to the manufacturing industry. These techniques focus on optimization in the production process. The new word "Industry 4.0" was created in Germany ten years before this industry revolution and revolves in the production technique (Kim and Tran-Dang, 2019). Figure 3.4 shows the industry version 4.0 ecosystem. This Industry 4.0 or Industrial Internet is also identified as the Industrial Internet of Things (IIoT).

Industry 4.0 represents a network of various devices linked by communication technologies such as WiFi, Bluetooth, Zigbee, WiMax, etc. It develops a system that could collect data, monitor systems, exchange information, and analyze them. Based on that, it delivers a valuable new vision. These visions increase product outcomes, and smarter and faster business decisions for industries.

Industry 4.0 is similar to IIoT, which is an American approach for similar phenomena. Both are applied to numerous areas such as engineering, industrial, energy, transport, healthcare, utilities, services, agricultural science, cities, and also many more. Both are concentrating on the optimization of resources as well as limitations in the manufacturing practice. Advanced developments in microcontrollers and microprocessors, sensors and actuators embedded in systems, and development of embedded boards enable best rearrangements of processes such as monitoring machine performance, increasing machine work effectively, inventory track and management, production completion tracking, increasing

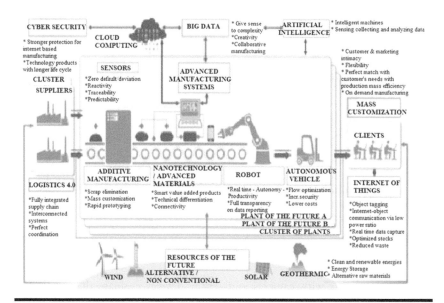

Figure 3.4   Industry 4.0 Ecosystem.

efficiency in product outcome, and anticipating problems in production, logistics, customer services, and rising resource efficiency.

3.2 IoT Is Making a Smart City

Sensors all around the vehicle could be able to trace all obstacles and it could respond automatically and immediately to avoid accidents and any malfunctions. If a vehicle needs a service, predictive repairs will sense it and check the car routinely. Vehicles communicate with one another on the road. If there is a traffic jam congesting a particular road, it will be communicated to approaching vehicles to take a different route using a GPS (Global Positioning System) navigation device. IIoT in air leak detection is shown in Figure 3.5. The sensor placed in an air tube detects leakage immediately and sends the message to the dashboard of the vehicle and an automatic alert message is sent to all connected devices before any malfunction occurs in the vehicle. In the picture, when a sensor connected with a tire detects an air leak, it sends an automated alert to several connected devices such as mechanic, owner phone message, and smart devices of an automobile service center to avoid a malfunction before it happens to the vehicle.

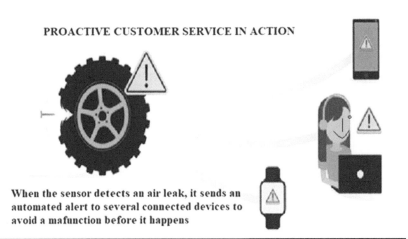

PROACTIVE CUSTOMER SERVICE IN ACTION

When the sensor detects an air leak, it sends an automated alert to several connected devices to avoid a mafunction before it happens

Figure 3.5 IoT Air Leak Detecting System.

Highway lights with cameras and sensor devices evaluate the number of highway operators in the location. It will operate traffic signals based on the current number of users in that location and independently switch from red to green. The car will find the adjacent existing car parks through navigation if car parks are linked. Speed control of the car will be done automatically in the pedestrian crossings and in front of schools.

Cameras on highway lights post surveillance and instantly recognize the thief or purse snatcher so that streets become much safer than earlier days. Suppose the bag has an embedded SIM card. It will alert or send a message of its location and situation by itself. Smart highway lights turn on/off lights automatically as soon as somebody or a car approaches the smart LED highway light. This technique saves power consumption of the street light by avoiding unnecessarily turning on the light bulbs.

Smart waste container trucks will send an alert message to the people to deposit dustbins from their housing apartments if a corporation develops a clean city app and asks people to install it on people's mobile devices. All people in that locality could download the clean city app from the municipal corporation website or the Google play store. They configure the location of housing apartments in the app. People get information about current pollution levels such as PM1.5 in that location. Figure 3.6 shows a highly connected smart city through the Internet of Things.

A city becomes a smart city with the interconnection of utilities like energy, transport, waste and water supply management, hospitals with blood banks, homeland security, and schools. The smart city is well defined as "A city that interconnects physical, corporal, social, public sharing and business infrastructure

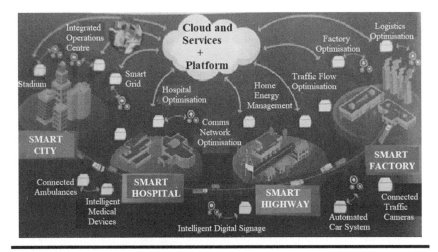

Figure 3.6   Connected Utilities in a Smart City.

to control the city through its collective intelligence through ICT (information communication technologies)" (Zanella et al., 2014).

The smart city is designed with three layers in the IoT. First is the application layer. This layer collects data, processes it, and displays data and information in various required formats by the user. The second layer is the network layer. It forwards IoT packets over reliable communication networks and connects and synchronizes various networks. The third layer is the perception layer. This senses and gathers the information or data using sensors. This layer captures, identifies, and differentiates information of the different objects in this physical world. It contains sensors to gather various data from the real world. This layer also has a camera, RFID (radio frequency identification) tags, GPS, laser scanners, and many more input devices.

The IoT captures data and sends the information to a server or cloud. It helps in monitoring remote devices and making an intelligent decision on data capture and remotely controls devices through activating actuators. IoT products improve traffic management in cities. Road signals becomes intelligent devices and recognize the number of vehicles on the road and control the signal automatically and intelligently based on vehicle strength.

The IoT platforms connect multiple heterogeneous systems in a city. Pediatric hospitals in a city can be connected to the school to get health data of children. The distribution of grants could be based on this statistical information. Wireless sensors are deployed in the multiple concrete structures available in the city. These sensors are monitored periodically. Radio signals are emitted from building structures that can be accumulated by the city municipal councils.

Water levels of dams, lakes, sewage, and all other water-related items could be watched using the IoT technique. Water leakage will be sensed automatically and immediately for proper use of water. Garbage container capacity exhaust information sensed by the IoT devices is sent to the garbage collector track to pick up garbage containers. Figure 3.7 gives smart city components.

Wireless patient monitoring systems are implemented in hospitals. All different medical sensors can be placed on patients to monitor their physiological and vital medical parameters. But highly secure IoT systems must be created to maintain privacy laws. Sensors can be placed in the home patients to monitor their health remotely in real-time.

A smart grid is needed and intelligent power controllers are designed. Smart e-meters are used to read consumption of electricity remotely and deduction of cash in their account automatically. IoT plays a good role in cost-effective efficient power generation, power distribution, and power transmission within the city.

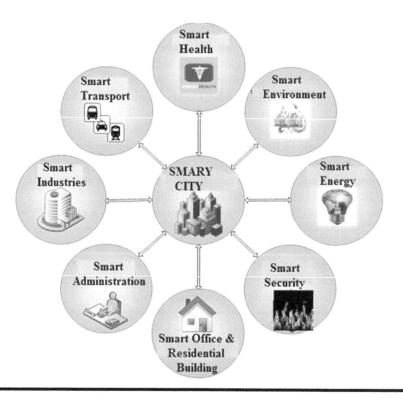

Figure 3.7   Smart City Components.

Automatic driverless cars and air taxis are other components of connected ultra-smart cities. Smart monitors and controls across the city transform automatic traffic-free accident-free city life. Transport, infrastructure, environment, utilities, buildings, fire monitoring, and police control are the components of the smart city.

Some of the smart cities with the Internet of Things implemented in areas are listed below:

- Green apartments or houses or buildings – Rooftop gardens and plants or vegetation on the side and front of the buildings help insulate from the sun's heat, absorb carbon dioxide (CO_2), and produce oxygen to help healthy life.
- Apartment or office management – Automatic services for heating, energy usage, lighting, parking, and ventilation and optimization of services to reduce the cost and demand.
- Security management – City is fully covered with closed-circuit television (CCTV) to make the city free from theft, security, and control of the crowd. They are controlling access and monitoring the city for intruder detection and alarm with CCTV, if necessary.
- Wind turbines on buildings – Rooftop wind turbines to generate power are installed on top of high-rise buildings for renewable energy production. High-rise buildings are now integrated with solar or wind power generators in the building design itself. Helically twisted wind turbine towers across the city for efficient use of space help in power generation.
- City pollution control – Sensor nodes are installed in many places to monitor the air pollution of the city, control the emission of CO_2 by the factories, and monitor pollution by automobile vehicles.
- Photovoltaic cells in building – Conventional materials are replaced by renewable sources of energy such as solar panels. These are integrated into the building fabric.
- Smart grid – Power flow in both directions is efficiently done by the smart grid. Energy consumption monitoring and management for the entire city.
- Gas/chemical leakage detector – Sensors are implemented to detect gas leakage at home and every building in the city. The factories are using sensors for detecting chemical leakage and monitoring of waste that are left in the river by factories.
- Traffic management – Real-time management and updating of traffic are possible using IoT. Instant traffic updates are sent to smartphones to help plan routes. If there are traffic jams in one route, it will show alternate route plans to avoid congestion and fast movement within the city.

Adapting fast and slow lanes for walking and cycling, and monitoring vehicles and pedestrian levels using IoT will help to optimize traffic according to conditions.

■ Waste and e-waste management – Waste monitoring in the dustbin containers and automatic collection from the dustbin. With optimization of the collection route within the city and updating collection time to the people, electronic product waste (e-waste) management could be done properly.

■ Smart parking – Parking system is combined with the traffic monitoring system. It monitors the availability of parking spaces across the city and informs the user instantly.

■ Disaster detection – Sensors are deployed to monitor and detect the disaster in specific places susceptible to vibrations such as an earthquake. Landslide, mudslide, and storm prevention systems could also be implemented. This system monitors soil moisture, humidity, vibrations, and soil thickness.

■ Water quality monitoring – The quality of drinking water monitoring and leakage in water tap detection across the city could be done by a sensor-based Internet system. Water leakage detection in the city in real time is possible. The system detects the presence of water outside the tanks or overflow and variations in pressure along pipes and activates an alert message.

■ Internet access – Free citywide or metro WiFi or Internet access for public use.

■ Street lighting – Intelligent and weather-adaptive street lights to monitor the city and to reduce power consumption.

■ Electric transport – Electric vehicles and public transport with electric vehicles are implemented throughout the city. Charging stations across the city are available for electric vehicle charging.

■ Building structural health – Vibrations or material conditions in buildings and infrastructures are monitored to avoid any undesired events.

■ Fire safety – An entire city is monitored for fire safety. Fire detection and intelligent extinguishing are kept in every important location.

3.3 IIoT in Different Industries

3.3.1 Smart Grid Technology

Increasing demand for power and industrialization and population growth put a strain on power grids. Consumers want to know their energy consumption and usage and want to take measures of their power consumption. Consumers want to know the shut-off reasons and improve infrastructure. The smart grid gives the balance between demand and production. In a smart grid system, supply is automatically adjusted constantly with the demand. To do this, huge collections of different sensors and computerized monitoring devices are embedded throughout the smart grid. Smart meters are implemented in individual homes and offices in entire nationwide power grids.

Power plants could maintain a constant relationship with all residents and businesses and communicate among all. If the power grid capacity is strained, electrical appliances self-adjust to consume less power in time. They turn off themselves automatically when the system or appliances are not in use and idle. By this method, demand and production is well balanced. Automatic consumption of power control is achieved greatly in real time within the grid itself. This system greatly reduces the need for supplemental sources or alternate peak plants. During high-demand requirements, algorithms calculate the amount of power needed and turn on extra power generators immediately and automatically.

Energy demand peaks and troughs are calculated by the computers. The computers help in adjusting the level between high peak and trough. Sensors could detect the time power consumption is high in the grid and when and where the high power consumption occurs. Based on the time of high power requirement and place of requirement, the production can be automatically shifted to that place. Over time, based on the predicted rise and fall in demand, production is automatically adjusted. Smart meters can then adjust for any differences. It allows varying prices on power based on demand and requirement. Electricity providers raise electricity prices on demand and high power consumption periods so that it helps to even out the peak. Overall, this makes the power grid more reliable and reduces the variable count needed for accounting.

Smart grid has the capacity for bidirectional current flow. Today, the creation of local power generation from bio-waste, photovoltaic panels, solar panels, wind power, and fuel cells is possible, and this energy production is much more decentralized. In earlier days, power generation could be done in one direction only. The smart grid now takes into account power generated by the consumers. Homes, offices, and businesses generate power that can add their surplus electricity to the grid power system. It allows power transmission in both directions through the power lines. Energy is generated at home and surplus generation is given to the power grid. This value is taken into account by the smart meter for accounting purposes. Figure 3.8 shows power generation and implementation of the smart grid system and smart meter at a smart home.

This trend of redistribution and localization makes large-scale renewable energy generation more practical and possible. The grid could now be adaptable to all different power outputs such as solar and wind etc. Smart grids are designed

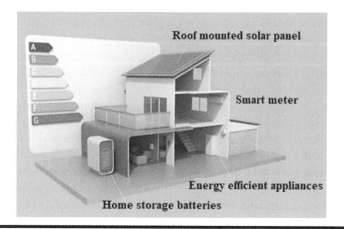

Figure 3.8   The Smart Grid at Smart Home.

with multiple routes for full load power transmission. Suppose if someone broke a transmission line and caused a shutoff in an area. It will be instantly detected by the sensors. The sensors locate the damaged area in real time and find the best reroute to give electricity to the affected area. Manpower is not needed to investigate multiple transformers to isolate the problems. The smart system reduces shutoffs. This prevents any adverse effects from shutting off.

This smart grid or Internet energy system is far more sustainable, reduces energy costs, is more efficient, and highly reliable. This system helps in using reusable, renewable energy systems and reduces carbon emissions and thus smart grids are better. Greenhouse gas emissions and CO_2 emissions are reduced by the smart grid system.

3.3.2 Smart E-Waste Management

Artificial intelligence (AI) and various sensors with radio frequency identification (RFID) tags are used in smart waste management. Dustbins are equipped with AI programs and Internet of Things sensors to make them behave intelligently in the waste management sector. RFID tags and various sensors are used to collect garbage. A pneumatic garbage disposal system reads RFID tags and can sort tons of garbage daily. The main computer system stores all data and it determines the appropriate method to dispose of the waste.

A mobile app that uses embedded vision technique to generate a quick assessment of waste. The embedded vision technique uses a camera and sensors to monitor dustbins. This device mounted on garbage trucks visually analyzes roadside dustbins. The combination of sensors, image recognition, and AI could differentiate objects and could recognize them. The glass, plastic, paper, metal, and all different materials are separated using this system. The system automatically compresses these objects before placing them in containers.

Smart trash robot uses an AI program to sort recyclables from landfill waste. This recycling equipment ensures the highest recovery rates from any material type. Material type includes commercial, industrial, electronic waste, food waste, and green waste recovery. A high-resolution color camera is used with all kinds of sensors in this system. This system is installed with a sorting method to provide accurate color and size separation of small particles. This method is suitable for electronic scrap, chemical waste, plastic flakes, animal-plant waste, metal scrap, glass, paper, and any other small particle segregation.

Robots are involved in a waste sorting system. Robots are installed with an AI program for smart recycling and sorting of waste materials. The e-waste system uses the concept of embedded vision, computer vision, embedded system, machine learning, AI, and robotics to sort and pick recycled materials from moving conveyor belts.

3.3.3 Smart Home

The Internet of Things enables control and monitoring of the products used in the home. Internet service technology helps make people's lives easier and more comfortable. It enables people to control things or devices from any corner of the room or anywhere through the Internet. A smart switch can be used to turn on or off the light or microwave oven or smart speaker or any home appliances from anywhere. This switch can be used through a virtual assistant to enable any device. The smart home utilizes many technologies. Wireless, Bluetooth, broad, and many other wireless technologies are used to offer home networks. Using one wireless network, the electronic devices could communicate with each other as well as any other through the Internet. It offers many services to make the home smart. It helps to reduce electricity and water usage is reduced. Through the mobile app, any electronic appliances or devices or switches are turned off or on.

Smart switches are turned off when we asleep or occupied with other work in another room. Smart ovens with digital thermometers and cameras are operated to monitor the food. These are also useful to new users who are not sure about the required temperature to cook the dish. The skill-based program is loaded in the oven and knows the temperature required for the dish, which it can get from the connected app.

The refrigerator is loaded with AI and sensors. These smart refrigerators monitor the condition of vegetables, fruits, and all edible items through sensors and cameras. It also provides the food recipe for available items in the refrigerator. The refrigerator is installed with many apps. These apps can be synchronized with the smartphone. The fridge has a huge screen to display them all. There are 3D food printers that can create a pizza and various other items.

Smart speaker devices allow speaking to apps easily as humans ask apps to do the jobs. The device can ask apps to turn on or off the light as we do. It could now close the garage, lock the door, adjust the light, and temperature of the air conditioner. They allow every activity to be easily accessible and controllable to make a smart home.

Smart mattresses help to monitor our sleep. It acts as a supervisor of our resting time every day. Apps give information about sleep cycle, time, and health conditions accurately. They give all details required to monitor our health. A smart clock with an alarm provides time, weather, and news. It also can sense the sleep pattern of the user and send a notification to the caretaker or health adviser accordingly.

Smart lighting can adjust brightness depending on the mood of the user and the availability of the person. Ceiling fans' speed can be adjusted through a connected app that adjusts the room temperature smartly. The doorbell has a camera vision sensor for security purposes. This security system sends alerts to the phone or system when someone is near the door. Smart lock security equipment has the potential to communicate with a smartphone via wireless technology. This enables the lock or unlocks the house anywhere from the world. This security camera can be viewed on the smartphone through the Internet.

3.3.4 Smart Apartments/Offices/Buildings

All different kinds of buildings are enabled with a heating, ventilation, and air conditioning (HVAC) system. This HVAC system will work smartly with the use of sensors. The sensor can detect the presence of the person in the office space and switch on/off the light based on the detection of the person automatically. This smart building system is shown in Figure 3.9. The energy meter is connected with an HVAC system to get the data about the energy-consuming equipment in the buildings. The data is analyzed to decide how energy is used by every device at the office. The energy usage information is sorted as either optimally utilized or over-utilized. These modules detect the fault in the device through abnormal usage identification. Everything is possible through sensors and machine learning techniques.

3.3.5 Hospital Industry

IoT in the hospital industry has been modernized service delivery. It has a better-quality consumer experience for in-hospital visits. It reduced the cost to

Figure 3.9   Smart Building.

an individual in their health care. IoT sensor devices have taken precautionary care one stage advanced. It has taken predictive care into reality. These sensors identify harmful movements and send a piece of alert information for proper preventive care in advance before an issue can worsen. IoT is a web of a smart physical device that can be linked to the Internet and connected with one other. These devices can comprise anything like coffee makers, headphones, TVs, security systems, light bulbs, wearables, and a lot of devices in the hospital industry. All of these devices can collect data and automated actions to make a connected hospital.

IoT-enabled robotic devices could perform surgical operations. The operation will be performed more precisely and in a controlled manner. This robotic surgery helper is shown in Figure 3.10. During wartime, it can operate from a distant place to save the lives of patients. The use of robotic devices solves the problem of performing surgery over a long time. IoT body scanning performs smart body scanning and tracks body changes using 3D cameras and mobile applications. For body fat, the circumference is analyzed and displays in a graphical form to show the status of the body.

Biomedical chip implant technology will emerge with the web to relieve many illnesses of the human body. This technology allows human and machine communication. It allows the chip implanted inside the human body to communicate with the human brain and to bring back the function of the brain that was lost due to illness. Using this, the disabled patient gets the ability to control a cursor on a computer screen. By thinking about the movement of one's hand, it simulates typing on the keyboard.

AI could detect a change in inpatient mental health. It is applied to listen to hundreds of voicemails to detect the change in the patient's clinical state. Tracking changes is important for the need of changing the treatment. Machine

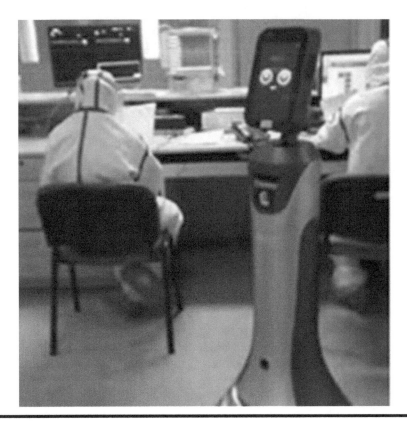

Figure 3.10   Robotic Surgery Helper.

mechanism tools, asset tracing, and inter-connected programmable logic controllers (PLCs) experience the most growth in terms of inter-connected service. Machine mechanism tools such as 3D printers/copiers, computer numerical control (CNC) machines, lathes, mills, engineering products, and industrial drills will develop in the usage of IoT.

3.3.6 Water Industry

The IoT in water confirms accurate control over the water resources through the available data. This IoT allows efficient and optimized management of water by the water companies. Smart water management improves unnecessary usage and avoids water scarcity. This system efficiently uses available water resources. This enables smart water meters, detectors, and irrigation systems. The new method of irrigation will be used in agriculture, industries, and households to avoid waste.

3.3.7 Oil and Gas Industry

Embedded sensors and IoT help to capture the production of oil in real time. This permits the collection of relevant information from resources, allowing decisions at the right time. Greater accuracy is achieved in detecting leakage and any relevant information with computerization, automation, and data communication system. Digital IoT in the oil and gas industry builds their profits considerably.

3.3.8 Transport Engineering Industry

Internet of Things in the transport engineering industry enables real-time access to data to make self-driving automatic cars in the world. IoT transportation reduces pollution by monitoring it through sensors. It optimizes the movement of people and goods. Hence, it saves the lives of people. The auto industry is equipped with IoT and sensors. IoT helps in asset tracing, road traffic management, route optimization, car driver behavior monitoring, and many other activities. Smart transportation system monitors the dangers and conditions of the road and warns the driver about real-time information. This IoT system helps in supervising the real-time parking of vehicles. It monitors the traffic and informs the driver. Free parking lots are relayed to the driver instantly. Multilevel parking systems help to reduce maintenance and operating expenses.

3.3.9 Mining Industry

Industrial IoT is cheap in the industrial mining zone. The sensor technology is used for real-time monitoring of mining resources. IoT removed waste in each stage of the mining process. This IoT displays the processes at the granular level to make saving results based on real-time data. Mine avalanches and apparatus failures are supervised and organized by the adaption of IoT in the mining industry. Various challenges in the industry are monitored and controlled in the industry and it increases the accuracy of the detection. IoT improves productivity and reduces the cost of production. IoT improves industry production and safety through real-time data analysis. It decreases the asset interruption and cost of operations.

3.3.10 Smart Drones

Efficient motors, more accurate sensors, better onboard processors and software, advanced autopilot system, and built-in compliance technology for safe, effective flight control are installed in the smart drones for new opportunities in transport and logistics. The flight is monitored and controlled by smart sensors. These drones are guided by an embedded vision system along with an object detection and collision avoidance facility. Autonomous drones are constructed with high-impact plastic which makes them lighter and more robust. They do not need input or control from the pilot. These drones deliver data or products in real time once the destination or task is set. These can monitor the fuel level of the engine. The damage to their propellers is watched by the sensor and cameras in real time. Identification of drones is done by the visible color blink sequence light-emitting diode light. The app installed in the smartphone identifies the code of the drone. Drones are used for the automatic delivery of goods or emergency services. This drone helps in delivering the packages to their intended destination through a global position system (GPS). Drones are applied to industrial inspection, delivery of goods, surveillance, and agricultural applications.

3.3.11 IoT in Business/Retail Shopping

RFID is mainly used in all kinds of industries, including retail shopping. It will be interfaced with web and 3D browsers via virtual reality. Virtual reality allows the customer to travel through the web or Internet and go into showrooms and stores to browse for products they like virtually. If the consumer likes to purchase an item, they would receive a chat message on their smartphone app and be given information about price comparisons from all other shops.

IoT allows several different kinds of companies to share information. IoT combines all companies' services for every user to decide the service they want to proceed with. IoT offers a budget home security system using the web and video camera surveillance. It allows homeowners to continuously check their homes wherever they are. IoT help with bus transportation. Driverless cars depend on signals to navigate cars on their routes automatically. Intelligent building construction is possible by integrating sensors with IoT. Sensors placed in the building and appliances will able to detect instantly if there are any changes.

Inventory management is efficiently done using IoT and machine learning. It manages efficiently and tracking constantly existing stock in the warehouse, its expiration date, and future demand forecasting. Robots and RFID tag sensors now scan the shelves to check stock availability and replace the stock without any human involvement. It reduces warehouse maintenance costs. These technologies reduce delivery or shopping items. Machine learning helps in watching which items sell more and needed by the customers. Predictive analysis and remote sensors notify the distributers when restocking or to top off the item in the vending machine.

Robots help to check inventory, prices, and misplaced items. These increase efficiency and accuracy of the inventory management process. Consumers can simply order through their phones and be notified when their order is complete. They need to visit the store and scan QR codes to get their package of goods from the conveyor belt. This technology reduces the consumers' in-store time to a few minutes from hours.

3.3.12 IoT in Ocean Exploration

AI and IoT sensors help to identify the link between the world oceans. An autonomous robot or Autonomous Underwater Vehicle (AUV) with high-altitude 3D visual mapping cameras with sensors are deployed on seafloors. Seafloor images could be drawn and explored. Biological hotspots could be discovered. The environmental ocean parameters such as temperature, depth, and pressure monitoring are easily done and marine life could be watched. A tsunami is detected by the pressure sensor deployment. Earthquakes could be detected. These are possible by sensors, underwater drones, and AI. AUV for ocean deep-sea exploration is shown in Figure 3.11.

3.3.13 Agriculture Industry

IoT sensors on equipment simplify and streamline the collection, inspection, and overall distribution of agricultural resources. Robots help in improving

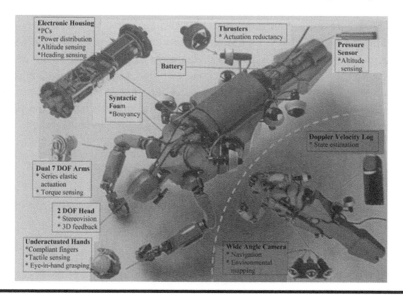

Figure 3.11 AUV for Deep-Sea Exploration.

productivity and result in higher and faster yields. Smart drones are used for spraying and weeding. It reduces chemical use. Machine learning predicts crop production based on their location and climate. Remote sensing, geographic information system, crop fitness monitoring, and soil health checking, and livestock and farm administration will make a change to smart farming.

In the agriculture industry technologies like robots, sensors, drones, satellite imagery, big data analytics, embedded systems, and IoT are involved. These technologies are engaged in agriculture such as environmental monitoring, irrigation, landscape plotting, and soil study to crop analysis (Lele and Goswami, 2017). They help in timely crop damage assessment, reliable quality data analysis, and contingency planning.

AI can help farmers in resource utilization, crop determination, and best hybrid seed selection. It could be able to support increased effectiveness and optimize scheduling to upsurge harvest. Its aim to provide effective decision making for farmers along with big data and cloud computing. Seed drill machines help in seed planting and flowerpot apparatus. This equipment usage improves the location of farming ideas and decreases product application overlay. This ensures all seeds are placed and planted where planned. It finds most of the unwanted plants/weeds and destroys them. It does not spray pesticides all over the crops. It helps in making the food cleaner. Machine learning algorithms to process data are captured to monitor crop and soil health. Figure 3.12 shows IoT in the agriculture industry.

Drones are applied in farming. These drones help in increasing the production of the crop. They monitor crop production and plant growth. Digital imaging of the field gives a picture of the farm to the farmer. These drones, along with cameras, capture multiple images of the farm. These images could be processed to create vegetation index maps. It gives accurate predictions for the market and predicts crop conditions, thereby increasing the harvest and profits of the farmers. It predicts the environmental impact on agriculture, too.

Figure 3.12 IoT in the Agriculture Industry.

Robots are used for a lot of work in agriculture. Some of them are harvesting and picking, weed control, autonomous mowing, spraying and thinning, sorting, utility, and many more activities. Weather analysis and environmental monitoring and accurate predictions are possible with these techniques. Robots are involved in harvesting crops. Automatic robotic operations permit milking thousands of cows at a single time. An AI-based dairy farm collects data virtually. It integrates the farm's data and streams it in real time. It then uses AI to evaluate that data, which helps farmers to make better management assessments. The motion-sensing sensor is attached to a cow's neck. It transmits its movements to the farmer. Farmers monitor cow behavior such as walking, drinking, lying down, or eating through the sensed data. This helps to detect health issues in a cow before they become critical.

A few more examples of IoT in the agriculture industry are listed below:

- Weather forecasting and monitoring are applied to provide more accuracy in the short, medium, and long term.
- Solar-powered equipment is used for irrigation and cold storage. It eliminates electricity and helps small farm holders.
- Eco-friendly crop production methods are implemented to minimize the significant loss caused by pests. It reduces diseases without overdosing crops and plants with chemicals. It prevents water and soil pollution.
- Sensors can provide statistics and figures about the harvest, rainfall information, pest control data, and soil nutrition. This information is valuable in production. It offers precise data to improve farming techniques over time.
- Wet or dry soil, cattle feed levels, and growth of crops can be detected by IoT sensors.
- IoT sensors could manage and control smart connected cutters, machines, reapers, and irrigation equipment.
- AI-based analytics with weather information to provide new awareness about the environment. This helps in decision making for crop selection, crop outputs, etc.
- Field scanning, seeding, and analyzing plant health, and much more work could be done by drones to help farmers.
- Cameras in drones capture high-quality field images to solve irrigation and variation of soil for the pest.
- Drones are used to spray micronutrients on crops without penetrating groundwater.

3.3.14 Food Industry

Many sensors are used for the automation of processes in the food industry. Some of the sensors used in the food industry are pressure, temperature, flow, and level. Smart senors help to reduce cost and increase production. The temperature sensor has two different sensor elements to measure chamber temperature. The two sensor elements are PT1000 and an NTC thermistor. Both operate independently of each other. A microprocessor integrated into the temperature sensor evaluates the signal of both elements and checks the measured value. With this sensor, the prescribed regular calibration is not necessary. In the food industry, some processes need exact temperature. Sensors are used for finding chemicals and identifying pollutants in food quality. Food safety is monitored. Safety applications are used all over the food manufacturing method which includes process monitoring, freshness evaluation, and quality study.

Electronic nose sensors are used in the detection method of food quality. IoT is used in logistics, food safety, wastage reduction, and food quality. Sensors can help to track products, worker activities, and real-time analysis for production. It can inspect the color of the food and specks in flour production, It helps to rectify any inaccuracy. Sensors monitor moisture content along with protein. It allows real-time optimization of the production procedure. IoT assures high quality in food products at any time and anywhere.

3.3.15 IoT in the Fire Industry

The Internet of Things could be implemented in any industry. The fire industry is used here, for example. The first step of the project is requirements gathering. Sensors to collect the fire information are selected. Smoke sensor, light sensor, temperature sensor, humidity sensor, infrared sensor, light-dependent resistor sensor, image sensor, CO gas sensor, and many more sensors to collect information are selected to detect fire or smoke from the environment. The micro-processing unit gathers all sensor information and the actuator or motor or water sprinkler are activated if it senses fire or smoke. It gives a feedback signal to control the event. All collected information is stored in a database. This information is exchanged between many customers.

The historic data reference from the building's database server offers absolute suitable response mechanisms. This is shown in Figure 3.13.

This system treats control mechanisms, prevention, stoppage, and removal of fire from the buildings. After getting the requirements, methods to implement are designed. Figure 3.14 gives a brief methodology to implement a sensor network. These methods are 1) data collection, 2) data storage, 3) data retrieval. Data collection will be implemented by the sensors connected with the system

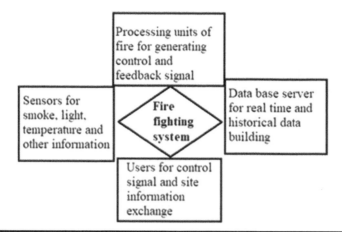

Figure 3.13   IoT Fire Monitoring System Requirements.

Figure 3.14   Fire Application Diagram.

board. Collecting, processing, and sending data are done by the data collection section.

The sensor board that collects information is shown in Figure 3.15. It shows sensor nodes with all different kinds of sensors, fire extinguishers with RFID tags, and video image sensor nodes for collecting environmental data. Packet handling, data buffering, data encryption, and data authentication are adapted by the network connection.

Data storage takes place in a PC station. Software is designed to store all the data received by the different nodes from different locations of the city. Displays

Figure 3.15 A Sensor Node, Fire Extinguisher with RFID, Video Image Sensor Node.

of information in the form of numerical values and graphical plots are done in this section. The database is created by any free database server language. The database structure is designed in such a way that all collected information about the event by the sensors in a sensor network. The data retrieval section is used to get the data that are stored in the database. The query feature allows the user to select data from the database.

Fire IoT can be divided into three layers for the fire industry. The perception layer, network layer, and application layer are three layers for monitoring fire (Ying-Cong and Jing, 2013). This layer consists of sensors, system boards, gateways, and interfaces for the network to observe the environment and to identify the event through the collective information about the environment. RFID tags are used to give unique identification physical addresses to the fire-related objects.

The network layer contains all different specialized kinds of networks for communicating and processing information provided by the perception layer. It is used for data saving, data processing, and decision making about the event. The application layer is the interface between the system and users for providing intelligent information from the observed environment data. It provides services for users by analyzing collected data done by the perception layer. Figure 3.16 shows the screen output for the user to detect the fire accident events.

Every fire-fighting product (shown in Figure 3.15 with RFID tags) has a unique identification code by classification and standardization. Production, design, logistics, construction, commissioning, and any units related to the fire industry's physical location and services related to them can be coded. The direction of the flow of products in the supply chain can be managed by this

Figure 3.16 Application Layer Sample Output for the User in System and Mobile.

identification to the device. After quality certification from the authorities, the products are marketed. Any quality problem can be traced easily and intelligently monitored through the Internet.

The fire monitoring system is constructed around the city to make it a smart city to transmit fire information to the data center. When the mistake is detected, IoT finds it in time and informs relevant authorities to make repairs and control the event. The physical location of the product or the fire accident event can be traced in real time so that maintenance of the product or the accident control can be properly handled. IoT makes a centralized management system for fire fighting. Digital video information along with geographic information allows the smart city to monitor fires in real time.

Fire system management software for fire IoT is divided into different modules, as shown in Figure 3.17. A system management module performs validation of users and managing systems of fire event detection. The system configuration module provides an interface for any new equipment installed with the fire control unit. Device management maintains all the

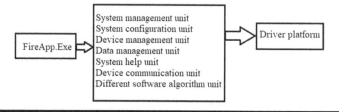

Figure 3.17 System Software Design for Fire IoT.

work related to the system. Import-export of data and database managing is done by the data management module. System help unit, alarm management module, software algorithms to detect the fire, data manager, database manager modules are included in the system software design of fire detecting event.

In fire IoT, all buildings have installed automatic fire sprinklers. Heat sensors can be added to control the temperature efficiently with the sprinklers, easily calculate insurance requirements, help with an insurance claim, and minimize risks and protect people and property by using IoT.

3.4 Conclusion

Privacy and security are the two main problems of data with IoT in industries. Once devices are connected to the web, they become helpless insecurity. Hacking, phishing of data, and frequent data leakage are possible. This disadvantage has to be overcome in IIoT. Information security standards should be maintained in IIoT to avoid this. IIoT is prone to very few industrial accidents. IIoT enables a smart factory.

The automobile industry, manufacturing plants, finance industry, and energy utility industry are the IoT-implemented industries. IoT-embedded devices with sensors make a variety of applications in different industries to increase automation. Factories, human beings, and machinery are interconnected through the computer system and embedded system to provide an intelligent industrial operation to increase product outcome.

The global standard will be formed worldwide for the successful IIoT. Computers are free from errors. Workplace accidents are can be recognized mostly by human errors. With IIoT, one can expect fewer explosions, oil spills, and any other industrial accidents. In the medical field, users can get more accurate patient support systems.

References

https://www.businessinsider.com/

i-scoop, 2021. https://www.i-scoop.eu/internet-of-things-guide/industrial-internet-things-iiot-saving-costs-innovation/industrial-internet-things-iiot/, IIoT- the Industrial Internet of Things (IIoT) explained, 5 August.

Kim, D.-S., Tran-Dang, H., 2019. *Industrial Sensors and Controls in Communication Networks*, Springer Science and Business Media LLC, Switzerland.

Lele, U., Goswami, S., 2017. The fourth industrial revolution, agricultural and rural innovation, and implications for public policy and investments: A case of India. *Agricultural Economics* 58(1), 87–100.

Ying-Cong, Z., Jing, Y., 2013. A study on the fire IOT development strategy. *Procedia Engineering* 52, 314–319, doi: 10.1016/j.proeng.2013.02.146.

Zanella, A., Bui, N., Castellani, A., Vangelista, L., Zorzi, M., 2014. Internet of Things for smart cities. *IEEE Internet of Things* 1(1), 22–32.

Chapter 4

Medical Internet of Health Things (mIoT)

S.R. Vijayalakshmi[1] and S. Muruganand[2]

[1]*Post Doctoral Research Fellow, Department of Electronics & Instrumentation, Bharathiar University, Coimbatore, India*
[2]*Associate Professor, Department of Electronics & Instrumentation, Bharathiar University, Coimbatore, India*

Contents

DOI: 10.1201/9781003175872-4

Objectives

After reading this chapter, the reader gains knowledge on

1. Medical IoT definition
2. Advantages of medical IoT
3. Architecture of mIoT
4. Internet of mobile health things

4.1 Medical IoT

IoT can be utilized for providing an intermediate interface in a patient's monitoring system wherever the patient will be and provides monitoring through a healthcare management system. The IoT devices will collect vital parameters through built-in sensors. The collected information is transferred to the network automatically. The embedded software and hardware in the object help to interface between the environment and object. They provide the interface between internal electronic components and the external atmosphere in such a way that helps caretakers in making decisions. This IoT hospital management provides diagnosis by accessing previous history treatments of the patient by physicians and taking immediate conclusions about the next step for on-time decisions for saving a precious life by real-time data. This makes us provide in-depth imminent patient care and employ fog devices and gateways through mIoT.

The objectives of medical IoT include the following:

■ Highly developed and accurate medical decision making
■ Reducing replication of analysis and diagnosis of patient's reports, imaging scans, and comparative patient-related analytic data
■ Enhanced medication and drug prescription management
■ Sophisticated enhancement of screening programs and preventive life-saving healthcare measures

4.1.1 Advantage of Medical IoT

Rural and urban peoples can get treatment through Internet-connected devices. Though they are away from hospitals, they can get specialist advice for treatment. Before they arrive at the hospital, hospital staff know which rooms and beds are occupied and the time of their release from the hospital. This room occupancy information can be seen by the patients at arrival for treatment. Doctors could easily watch the patient's physical health condition and everything from the prescription schedule. The system is easy and efficient. Patient monitoring remotely is possible. Patients feel safe and healthy because of constant monitoring by the physicians. It reduces the length of stays in the hospital and prevents unnecessary admissions. Cost is reduced and treatment outcomes are improved. mIoT helps patients, medical doctors, hospitals, clinics, and insurance companies.

> **IoT used for patients:** There are two forms of devices connected with patients. One may be a wearable device and other wirelessly connected devices. Wearable devices such as smartwatches monitor body temperature, sugar level, and many more will help access patient's information. Device sensors are used for monitoring vital parameters of the patient. Body temperature, pulse rate, blood pressure, blood volume, heart rate, and many more vital parameters of the patient are monitored. Wireless devices check the vital parameters of the patients such as oxygen saturation, pulse rate, and all required data. It transmits the information to the caretaker wirelessly to a short distance. Using these devices, they can track the health condition and decide on patient health. The mechanism detects undesired signals from the patient and alerts the concerned healthcare providers.
>
> **IoT for physicians:** Wearable devices or wireless health monitoring equipment help physicians track the health conditions of people efficiently and effectively. Based on the wirelessly received information, they make plans for medical treatment and decide whether they require urgent medication. The more powerful and best treatment for patients can be provided. Even doctors ensure the safety of themselves from infected disease during virus patient treatments.

IoT for hospitals: Hospitals have all kinds of equipment. They are wheelchairs, defibrillators, nebulizers, ECG machines, X-ray machines, oxygen pumps, and much more monitoring equipment. These equipment and devices are tagged with RFID tag for its location tracking, asset management, and real-time maintenance. Inventory control and stock maintenance in pharmacies and checking the environment conditions are effectively done by the IoT. Even hospital staff performance can be monitored. The COVID-19 disease causes the easy spread of infections for people in hospitals. Easy isolation of equipment and patient is possible by the IoT system and device. Hygiene monitoring is done to avoid the spread of disease. The environmental monitoring system monitors the temperature of the refrigerator automatically. Pharmaceutical supply chain management improves medication management.

IoT for Health Insurance Companies: Insurance companies easily check the truthfulness of the patient record to check the eligibility of claim with intelligently IoT-connected device. The risk assessment process is easy and no fraud claim is possible. Insurer data for all operation processes will give customers the ease of visibility of data. Wearable and wireless devices of the patient will send data to the insurers for data validity and be used for decision making about the claim.

4.2 General Architecture of IoT

IoT has a four-step architecture, as shown in Figure 4.1. The first step is wearable devices, wireless devices, medical sensors, cameras, and healthcare equipment to collect health-related data. The output by the sensors or wearable transducers is sent to the next stage. The sensed data is preprocessed and aggregated in the next stage to retrieve only useful information from the medical data. The output data of this stage is stored by the data storage and moved into the data center or cloud. The last stage is data analysis. All the medical data are analyzed for further processing of medication and used for medical decision making.

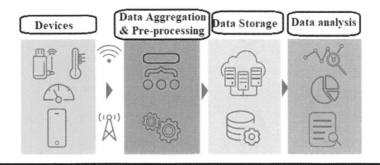

Figure 4.1   The Four Stages of IoT General Architecture.

4.2.1 Devices

Medical wearable sensors/devices are the first stage in IoT architecture. Wearable devices are used to monitor the health of the patient. It observes readings and sends alerts if needed. The collected data from the wearable device is used for diagnosis of disease, improved treatment, and enhanced customer service. In IoT architecture, the medical sensor is the device used to collect vital medical data from the patient. A medical device is used for many purposes, such as diagnosing the disease, monitoring the patient, or treating diseases, or as supportive assistance for physically challenged persons. Numerous kinds of sensors are implemented in medical uses. A few of them include force sensors, airflow sensors, temperature sensors, and pressure sensors. Temperature probes are used for body temperature measurement. Force sensors are used in kidney dialysis machines. Airflow sensors are implemented in anesthesia delivery systems. The pressure sensors are placed in infusion pumps and also in the sleep apnea machines. Some of them are discussed in this. Pacemakers, shown in Figure 4.2, are an embedded sensor system for giving synchronized stimulus to the heart to maintain cardiac function effectively. Sensors in pacemakers detect heart/muscle activity. The detected data send wirelessly to the system. So, these are life-saving sensors. These sensors are used for safety-critical medical applications.

The high-volume pressure sensor is shown in Figure 4.3. It is calibrated based on piezo-resistive technology. It is integrated with thin-film temperature compensation. It is designed for use in patient monitoring. Digital airflow sensors have many features. Accurate measurement, very fast response time, high precision, high accuracy, high stability, and high sensitivity are a few features of airflow sensors. They are designed for suitable critical medical uses. The airflow sensors are used in medical applications such as anesthesia delivery machines, laparoscopy, and heart pumps. These sensors allow easy integration

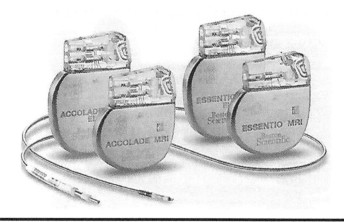

Figure 4.2   Typical Pacemaker.

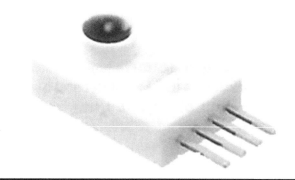

Figure 4.3   MPX2300DT1 Pressure Sensor.

to microprocessors or microcontrollers (MCU) because of their I2C digital output feature. The data processing is carried out by microcontrollers.

Sensors provide a digital electrical output that can be easily processed. These have to be wearable, non-invasive, and capable of offering painless and comfortable measurement and prevent infections and contamination. Peripheral sensors are used to monitor information from the outer environment. Thermistor sensors are used for monitoring skin temperature. The sensed temperature output from the thermistor sensor of the environment is displayed in real time and skin temperature of the patient is sent to the system of the Doctor for analysis (Figure 4.4).

Pulse oximetry sensors are used for sensing oxygen saturation in the blood. Heart rate was also measured by an oximetry device. An infrared emitter/

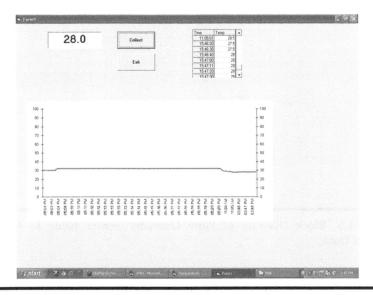

Figure 4.4 Temperature Output Display.

receiver device worn on the finger or ear lobe transmits light through the skin. Continuously, the blood oxygen concentration is measured by the receiver, and heart rate is determined from the measured value of the receiver. It is shown in Figure 4.5. The pulse probe output such as (72) pulse rate and SpO_2 97 (oxygen saturation) are displayed in the liquid crystal display and also wirelessly transmitted to the doctor.

Figure 4.5 Pulse Oximetry Sensor Node in Detecting the SpO_2.

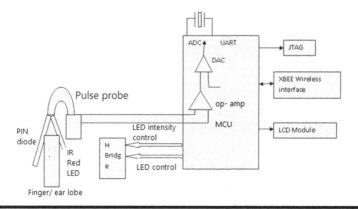

Figure 4.6 Block Diagram of Pulse Oximetry Sensor Node to Measure Medical Data.

The block diagram of the pulse oximetry medical sensor node is shown in Figure 4.6. The medical sensor to sense data, interfacing components to connect peripheral with the microcontroller, Wireless interface to transmit/receive information to distant are interfaced with the micro controlling unit (MCU). The data is sensed by the sensor. The sensed data is preprocessed by the MCU and transmitted to distant locations wirelessly through Xbee and also displayed in the LCD module of the medical device.

Photoplethysmography (PPG) sensors are used for detecting blood volume changes. Infrared light emitted using IRLED is fed into the skin. Light is immersed proportional to the volume of blood and backscattered proportional to the variation in the volume of blood. The scattered light is measured to compute blood volume variation. The same concept is used in pulse oximetry to measure oxygen saturation. Galvanic skin sensors are used for detecting skin conductance.

Micro-electromechanical sensors (MEMS) are piezo-resistive silicon pressure sensors based on the wheat stone bridge and are used to measure blood pressure. Microelectronic biosensors (MEBS) are of two types such as calorimetric or electrochemical biosensors. Both sensors are used to measure medical data. Calorimetric biosensors are used for monitoring enzymatic reactions by detecting the heat of the biological reactions. Electrochemical biosensors are used to monitor enzymes.

Amperometric biosensors are used to measure current at an electrode. Wearable sensors include medical sensors, GPS, etc. Wearable sensors are also connected with various accessories like clothes, wrist bands, eyeglasses, headphones, and smartphones. Then they are called wearable devices.

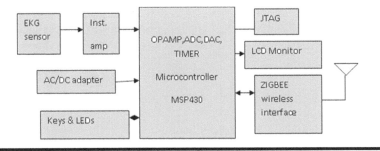

Figure 4.7   EKG Medical Sensor Node to Measure Heart Rate.

Non-invasive sensors like electrodes are used in ECG and electromyography (EMG) and many more. The EKG medical device block diagram is shown in Figure 4.7. The EKG sensor to measure heartbeat and pulse is connected to the microcontroller through the amplifier. This instrumentation amplifier amplifies the measured medical signal to the level required for processing. All peripheral devices such as LCD module, Zigbee wireless interface, LEDs, and switches are interfaced with the microcontroller. After preprocessing of received medical data by the microcontroller, it is transmitted to the persons needed in real time or to the cloud.

Figure 4.8 shows multiple sensors connected to the patient for monitoring health through which vital parameters are extracted for analysis. Various sensors

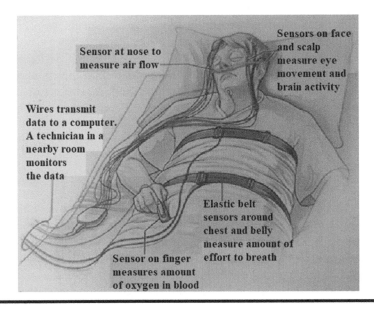

Figure 4.8   Medical Sensors.

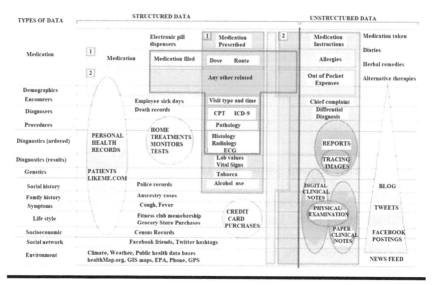

Figure 4.9   Type of Data.

are incorporated into smart devices to measure different parameters of the person who wore them. Wearable technology facilitates the capability to collect patient healthiness conditions or user surroundings. All collected real-time data are uploaded on a cloud database or fog layer. There are many sensors available to collect medical data from the patient.

Different varieties of data that are to be collected from IoT devices is shown in Figure 4.9. The data model can be developed based on their application in healthcare to get quality care for the user. The collected data stored in the database depends on the requirement. All required data are extracted from the sensor and environment to give excellent medical care to the patient. Table 4.1 gives types of sensors used for diseases.

4.2.2 Data Aggregation and Preprocessing

Medical sensor networks use Zigbee communication protocol to transfer information. Using Zigbee protocol, information of few kilobits per second is transmitted to a short distance. Zigbee protocol is intended to deliver low data transmission wireless communication applications. It's a simple, easy protocol with less cost. Any one of the architectures such as a star, mesh, tree, and cluster combined network is selected based on resource requirements in medical sensors.

Table 4.1   Type of Disease and Their Sensors

Disease/Condition	Sensors
Diabetes	Glucose sensor, IR LED (infrared light-emitting diode), contextual sensor
Asthma	Pulse probe, body temperature sensor
Heart disease	Blood pressure sensor, ECG sensor, pulse rate sensor
Hyperthermia and hypothermia	Thermopile infrared (IR) sensor, wearable thermometry
Tele-surgery	Micro electro-mechanical sensors, robot
Ebola	Lightweight body sensors, radio frequency identification (RFID) reader
Wheelchair management	Camera sensor, accelerometer sensor, a force sensor
Rehabilitation, medication non-compliance	Force sensor, distance sensor, RFID
Neuromuscular diseases	EMG sensors
Respiratory disease	SpO$_2$ pulse oximetry sensor

The data signals picked up by the medical processing unit should allow correct visualization of signals by the software application. The software app must consider many factors to identify the signals feature to implement. The software platform is selected in such a way that it can accommodate the high volume of medical data. It should allow easy integration of hardware and software. Software platforms should have a virtual instrumentation tool for aggregating, measuring, displaying, and storing.

The design stage of the medical app display visual information of medical data for proper medical diagnosis by the physician. Different sections are designed to receive the acquired biomedical signals for visualization and preprocessing. The input section receives the biomedical signals. In the preprocessing section, the different signals are recovered. In the processing section, every signal is translated into visual form in its units; for example, the temperature in degrees Celsius or Fahrenheit, relative humidity in percentage, and pulse rate per second. The signal is presented visually to the user by the display section. GUI section eases the information analysis process for the end user.

Medical sensor devices are designed in such a way to reduce cost and power consumption. The slight change in information transmitted will cause an erroneous diagnosis of information by the doctor. Hence, it must ensure the reliability of information transmitted to the physician. An optimum signal is transmitted to the caretaker to make proper decisions on the patient's condition.

4.2.3 Data Storage

Edge, cloud, and fog are different techniques for data storage, retrieval, and access. Either they are combined and or used separately based on requirements. The cloud provides the necessary computational structure to access, process, store, or archive capability for data. It has the necessary network configuration for centralized storage and effective processing. The minimum amount will be spent on configuration. It also avoids latency and performance issues. These resources are available both for centralized private cloud, public cloud, or localized data sources.

In this architecture, equipment contains all data. These are transferred to the cloud for storage and effective analysis. The connected health in a collaboration edge example is shown in Figure 4.10. In the cloud, the data is used for cognitive prediction, extrapolative protection, forensic problematic investigation, and a minimum of optimal process optimization. Cloud computing deals with a range of services such as the following:

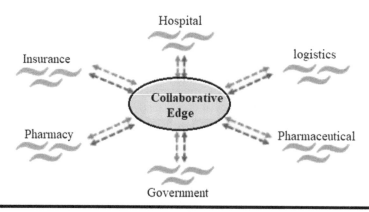

Figure 4.10 Collaborative Edge Example: Connected Health.

■ IaaS (Infrastructure as a Service) is a service of the cloud through which it provides an isolated data center with resources that possess the capacity for data storage, processing, and networking infrastructure related to hospital records management.

■ PaaS (Platform as a Service) is a platform for enlargement where tools and components are provided to the users for creating, investigating, and instigating the related particular patient to the respective doctors but none other.

■ SaaS (Software as a Service) is well organized for software for the needs of medico-legal ethics. This can be utilized as it is; otherwise, it can be re-modeled according to their hospital values, needs, and ethics.

The healthcare sector is connected with the cloud, for getting access to its services from any location via different devices. Hence, the availability of the hospital records and patient history can be stored forever with security in any unavoidable situations. Moreover, there is no requirement to employ local servers. It responses quickly for saving a patient's life by providing the necessary care and medical treatment. It provides real-time analysis and solutions. The cloud provides various services and deployment models for multiple metho-dological solutions and even through virtualization concepts. Figure 4.11 shows the architecture of cloud computing.

Cloud computing provides various networking services. It enables to gain less amount of capital but immense services to control entire premises. It is a

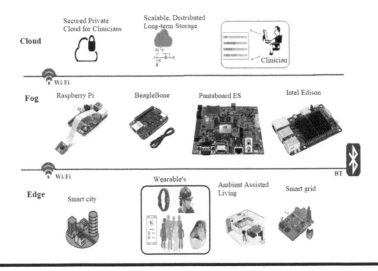

Figure 4.11   The Architecture of Cloud Computing.

representation of pay per usage of services by giving access to various computing resources as adapted by the user.

a. It can be released with nominal organization effort.
b. It provides a high-level abstraction of computation and storage models.
c. MIoT responsibilities involve real-time risky applications in human life. Cloud computing delivers data with a high delay, which is undesirable in mIoT.
d. It is unable to compete with a medical smart device control system that is highly crucial and needs a milli- or microseconds of low delay response time.

Fog computing is close to the end user, as shown in Figure 4.11. Fog computing is applicable when the data are collected from the smart devices through edges like sensors, smart devices, a pacemaker, or any chips. In Figure 4.12, fog computing collects data from the system board. Multiple devices are connected to the fog network. All data are sent to the network. The collected data from the devices, which have to be practiced in microseconds for providing any kind of solution for decision making. Hence it is latency sensitive. It has been implemented with many embedded nodes, device networks, virtualized data centers, and smart IoT devices. These are arranged to work in real time, have high storage, and have high-tech computations. Figure 4.12 shows fog computing for mIoT.

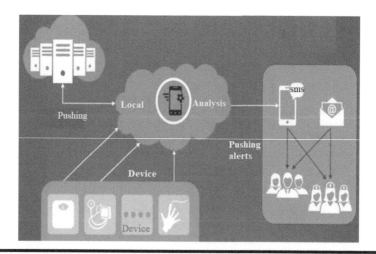

Figure 4.12 Fog Computing for mIoT.

The difference between cloud and fog is mainly on the delay time. The work is distributed as per the time-delay requirements. Fog offers millisecond to sub-second delay so that it works more rapidly than a real-time communication job. Fog deals with multi-nodal smart devices. It performs for no delay or latency responses such as healthcare i.e., mIoT systems. Similarly, emergency and health monitoring services may be practiced well while transmitting data to the cloud through smart devices. mIoT cloud system processes and sends the diagnostic reports to the respective physicians for clarification.

The selection of fog is based on response time. For example, neurological diseases offer fog computing because it requires high response time and no delay time. The fog computing nodes has to be significant, competent, dynamic, and scalable by avoiding redundancy, and elasticity for expanding fog structure. Benefits of fog mIoT in the application areas are low delay, awareness of location, and wireless sensor networks on a large scale, mobility support, device heterogeneity, smart utility services, and smart traffic management.

Fog computing offers massive support in monitoring and maintaining the delay-sensitive fog-based application. It is implemented through a wireless sensor network (WSN). It can transmit data and reports in real time in low-power, low-cost embedded products. The fog layer will surely improve and assures the mIoT implementation. That in term ensures security. Fog maintains the confidentiality of data. Data access to other physicians could be avoided. Wearable devices are an example of edge computing that stores small data collected by the wearable device. For example, a wristwatch that is used to collect skin temperature stores that information in its local memory. The fog, edge, and cloud-based mIoT are shown in Figure 4.13.

4.2.4 Data Analysis

Limited power usage, small compact size, and affordable cost are the factors that determine data analysis of the medical device. The data analysis section of medical devices answer queries for locally processed data. It is achieved with limited processing and caching for storing data. Medical software network architecture will have provisions to add new additional devices with dynamism. New devices register their abilities during initialization with the network. This feature of the network allows flexibility. This allows network adaptability to change over time as sensors are developed and additional monitoring of newly added devices.

Table 4.2 shows medical network software architecture for sensor device software stack, gateway software stack, and back-end analysis and storage servers. Network software architecture is divided into three sections, namely sensor device software stack, gateway software stack, and back-end analysis and storage.

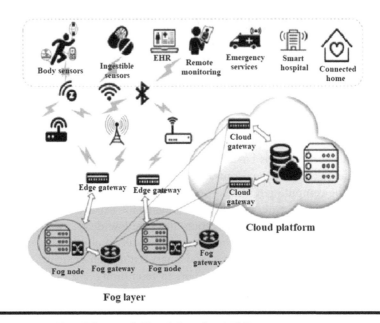

Figure 4.13   Fog, Edge, and Cloud-Based mIoT System.

Table 4.2   Medical Network Software Architecture for Sensor Device Software Stack, Gateway Software Stack, and Back-End Analysis and Storage Servers

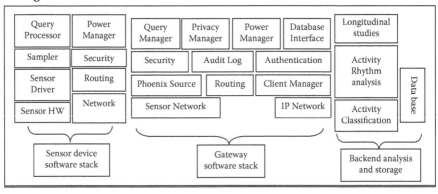

Query Processor	Power Manager	Query Manager	Privacy Manager	Power Manager	Database Interface	Longitudinal studies	
Sampler	Security	Security	Audit Log		Authentication	Activity Rhythm analysis	Data base
Sensor Driver	Routing	Phoenix Source	Routing		Client Manager		
Sensor HW	Network	Sensor Network			IP Network	Activity Classification	
	Sensor device software stack		Gateway software stack			Backend analysis and storage	

The internal parts of each section are shown in Table 4.2. Query processor, power manager, sampler, security, sensor driver, routing, sensor hardware, and network are the internal parts of the sensor device software stack. Query manager, privacy manager, power manager, database interface, security, audit log, authentication, phoenix source, routing, client manager, sensor network, and IP network are internal parts of the gateway software stack. Database, activity classification, activity rhythm analysis (ARA), and longitudinal studies are the back-end analysis and store internal parts.

Gateway software stack serves message communication gateway. It's an application-level gateway. This interfaces between the medical sensor network and any other IP networks. Energy consumption, power supervision, query administration, confidentiality, safety, privacy, and security are the system operations performed by the gateway software stack. Gateway stack performs these major operations due to its greater resource. The back-end analysis program performs sensor data analysis. It performs online. Context-aware power supervision and confidentiality are done through a feedback behavior profile. System structure, user data, privacy policy, audit details, and medical vital information are stored in a database for the long term.

Sensor data stored in the database is the input to the activity rhythm analysis (ARA) unit. It processes this data and studies the behavior configurations of occupants and detects any deviations from normal values. This unit decides any change in the signal causes a short- or long-term decay in the occupant's health. The back-end is extended to add new additional devices. They are designed to perform the tasks as discussed below. The sensor input data is received by the program, filtered to get the usable part, processes them, and produces output data for other units to use for further processing. It collects a low-level sensor data stream and processes it to decide high-level inference of indications of disease hierarchically. It facilitates the user interface. Medical physicians, staff nurses, occupants, caretakers, and others query sensor data subject to privacy policy using the user interface unit. Staff nurses have patient tracking GUI and it produces a graphical representation of sensor data in real time. This facility of accessing sensor data is connected through the gateway. The user could not be provided with direct access to the database. This enables new interface development and easier and customized interface as per user requirements.

Query manager fulfills the user requirement in the application field. It enables high-level ideas for expressing queries dynamically. Any device issue queries the manager. All queries are uniquely acknowledged with a source ID and query ID. Back-end, user, and devices issues query through a network protocol. They also request the current value of medical data or periodic data of medical sensor devices. To avoid repetitive queries, all queries may be cached. Query managers efficiently restart or reissue queries later.

Zigbee or any other communication protocol used in a medical network is expensive. If data is processed at its source before transmission, it may reduce the amount of data that are reported to the user. But medical sensor devices have limited memory and processing ability. Hence, only lightweight processing is possible in the device. Query managers retain device state, sensor type, hardware ID, query ID, and dynamic network ID. It also questions background queries to newly added additional devices. For example, a medical sensor device battery voltage falls below the set value, sample sensed medical data in periodic time duration such as oxygen saturation, heart rate, ECG samples, etc. A query manager is a key point for the user. All users receive the active device information. Power managers concentrate on reducing energy consumption. Sensors collect data of occupants based on changes in their behavior. It gives freedom to the system administrator for setting policies based on application type. Radio components and sensing unit components are controllable by the power manager. For example, it may set a high value for temperature, a low value for light, turn off some devices, and a radio device duty cycle. Based on location and context awareness, it controls sensor characteristics for power management.

NN-based medical image processing, image segmentation to find thin vessels in medical images, an expert system for medical image processing, OOPS concept in medical image processing environments, embedded vision in image shaping, threshold technique in finding sensing value, compressing medical data, and image restoration are a few advanced technologies in medical networks to analyze data. Medical imaging requires a specialist to deal with the details of the image. An artificial vision system is designed to analyze medical data set using numerical simulation tools.

Picture archiving and communication system (PACS) stores all the image information of the patients. It permits the supply and transmission of images to the medical experts to help find the condition of patients. Medical experts use the image search tool to search and retrieve images. A content-based image retrieval tool has increased in the retrieval of images.

Computer neural networks (CNNs) for the medical task are designed for classification, recognition, segmentation, and identification in medical imaging. Machine learning is also involved in these imaging tasks. Classification draws a boundary box around different objects in the image. Recognition identifies the objects in the images and gives a name to them. Segmentation outlines the edges of the objects and marks them. Identification finds normal anatomy such as the kidney in the ultrasound image. Segmentation finds abnormal images such as tumors in the CT scan of the lung. Hence, it helps the medical expert to determine a lung tumor location from the main anatomical structure. Based on the image segmented information, experts decide on whether the operation is to be carried out on the patient or not. Using classification in imaging, the expert identifies the growth of abnormal tissue on chest X-rays.

Computer-aided diagnosis (CADx) helps in classifying the images to identify the presence of the abnormal tumor or tissue in the scan images. Computer-aided detection (CADe) is a fully automatic application. This radiological image is automatically analyzed to study any missing lesion on CT and MRI scan images without human interference. It helps in determining the exact edges of the tumor in surgical operations to direct the surgeon for resection of the tumor without any neurological deficits.

Big data perform an important part in mIoT. Medical sensor devices and image modalities are increasing, resulting in a fast increase in the medical data quantities. It requires the new excellent method to process these data in short time scales. PACS uses map-reduce programming concepts to store, process, and retrieve images. These systems store petabytes of medical data images and error-free processing of these images. Precision medicine is based on big medical image data analysis. It includes IoT, genetics, medical data imaging, patient information, and monitoring data during mobility as in Figure 4.14. Deep learning and embedded vision techniques are used to discover required data from medical big data images that are received from mIoT, genetics, image modalities, and medical sensor networks.

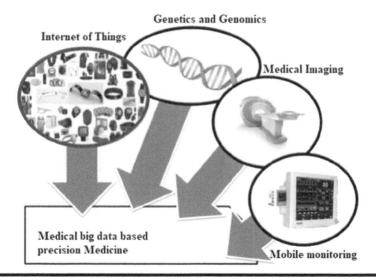

Figure 4.14   Precision Medicine.

4.3 Internet of Mobile Health Things (mIoT)

Mobile health is also called m-Health; monitoring of one's health via mobile devices. In m-Health, "m" refers to mobile or medical. Nowadays, everyone has many smartphones for their use. Providing a mobile app for health monitoring of patients will be a true lifesaver technique. M-health handles situations like critical care and regular treatment. Medical information is accessed by the physician through the app to analyze patient behavior trends to avoid unnecessary patient visits to hospitals. The government and health ministry monitor the people's health and can accumulate and generate health statistics.

Some mobile apps are medication management apps, fitness app, elder monitoring apps, and patient health recording apps. Medical cost, easy management of medical drugs, error reduction, and wastage control in healthcare are a few advantages of mIoT.

MIoT is defined as using embedded vision, medical data computing, mobile communication, and cloud computing to observe patients' vital information instantaneously. It utilizes all wireless technologies to onward medical information to cloud computing. Medical data can be accessed by all required from the cloud. Real-time treatment is done for the patient after observing and diagnosing data.

Figure 4.15 shows the implementation of IoT in the healthcare system. RFID tags are assigned to patients and devices. All collected medical data are stored in the form of Electronic Health Records (EHR). The efficiency is high in the case of an EHR system. All clinical requirements are taken care of by the EHR system.

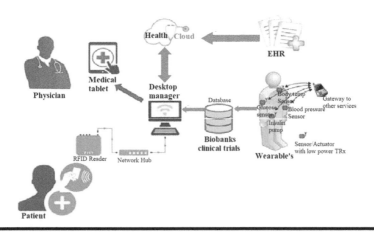

Figure 4.15   Implementation of IoT in Healthcare.

EHR record is stored on a database management system or in the health cloud, edge, or fog. IoT and cloud computing in healthcare integration allows the patient to interact with physicians through the mobile app and communicate online. EHR records available on the net can be accessed by a doctor at any time. There is a problem with the safety, security, and privacy of patients when the data is available on the net. It could be solved by blockchain technology. It gives a secure mechanism for sharing medical records. Storing medical data on the blockchain has greater control over the flow of data between medical professionals. The private data are protected from medical data hackers.

Desktop managers receive this information whenever required and this will be used for multiple purposes. The purpose may include various kinds of treatment approaches and research. The fog layer is implemented at the mIoT gateway as the scheme needs exact replying with the least time delay. This increases the communication link security. Fog computing provides reliable user authentication. Fog IoT also has a privacy management mechanism. Edge IoT is used in wearable devices.

The medical Internet of Things (mIoT) aims to access the history and analyze patient's data from resources through the deployment of smart devices that are located nearest to the hospital, patients, and their doctors as fast as possible to take life-saving actions. This data is generated by physical smart sensors or actuators closest to the fog layer. These are installed near the necessary area whereever it is necessary to grab data. Data are sent as well as received to prevent or to take immediate action by carrying out crucial functions through mIoT. The medical IoT is shown in Figure 4.16.

In the present technological domain, the medical Internet of Things is about employing any kind of smart device for the welfare of health-related issues through various layers such as cloud, edge, and fog. These layers enable active in

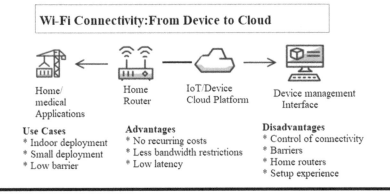

Figure 4.16 Medical Internet of Things.

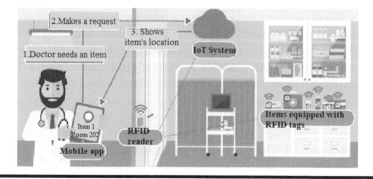

Figure 4.17 Hospital Operations Management.

obtaining live-saving or any kind of critical data. In mIoT, data processing, analyzing, and providing a real-time response for further investigation, diagnosis, and management of patients through medication or even surgical intervention or just a first aid could be done. The main benefits of IoT in healthcare contain less cost and error, improved treatment, faster syndrome analysis, positive cure, medications, and apparatus management.

Hospitals are busy places and equipped with huge costly medical equipment. Doctors observe multiple patients simultaneously. Figure 4.17 shows the hospital operations management system. This system manages all the equipment available in the hospital. The equipment is easily maintained and secured from unauthorized access. Doctors identify the present position and exact location of the essential tools or equipment.

4.3.1 mIoT Layer for Patient Monitoring

The security and privacy issues of a medical data network have to be resolved by allowing the three-layer concept as given below for mIoT:

   1. **Device Layer**

Medical devices, medical sensors, fog nodes, and mobile devices are a few examples of device layer devices. This layer of devices collects data from the user. Data is analyzed and transmitted to the database for storage. Identification authentication, management of authorization, secured booting, and password protection are the prevention attacks in the device layer for security measure. Security algorithms are written based on memory, power processing, and embedded operating systems used in devices.

2. **Network Layer**

WiFi, Bluetooth, Zigbee, Light Fidelity (LiFi), and Near Field Communications (NFC) are all wireless technology with the latest developed versions that could be implemented in IoT network protocols. This layer is responsible for establishing communication between embedded system boards, smart medical devices, fog sensor nodes, and cloud computing that use communication network protocols. This layer is protected from all attacks by applying secured routing.

3. **Edge, Cloud, and Fog Layers**

Information received by the device layer is sent to these (edge, cloud, and fog) layers for storage. These layers provide computing energy and storing areas. This layer is also protected from all attacks by applying a secure, adequate, and efficient approach.

4.3.2 Wearable Medical Devices

An autonomous, non-invasive medical device for monitoring a user over a prolonged period is called a wearable medical device and is placed either in clothing or in the human body. Usually, the term refers to a sophisticated device with the capability for integrating electronic, mechanical, computing, and some degree of artificial intelligence (AI). Such a device can collect, store, process, and analyze data to provide necessary feedback, and instantly send alerts or medical decisions to patients and medical supervisors. The wearable device layout is shown in Figure 4.18.

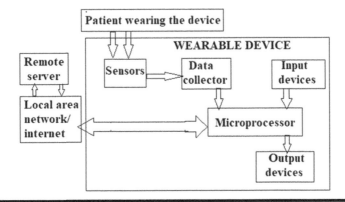

Figure 4.18 Wearable Medical Device Layout.

Wearable devices are designed for a specific purpose, such as monitoring vital medical parameters. It provides long-term support, medical aid, and re-habilitation assistance to users. This non-invasive device is used for sensing, communicating with patients, and also for receiving feedback from them. A wearable medical device receives inputs from sensors and the data collector. The microprocessor, which is the heart of the wearable medical device, provides data processing, data storage, and wireless communication with the remote server. Sensors positioned on the body of the patient monitor him/her and the sur-rounding environment parameters, and feed this data to the data collector. The patient enters the information into the microprocessor using input devices, such as a keypad, touchscreen, etc. The wearable device to monitor heart rhythm is shown in Figure 4.19.

Figure 4.20 shows a watch app for depression monitoring. The collected data about the patient's level of depression is stored by the cloud for further analysis of psychologists to understand the patient's problem from a distant place instantaneously. The information collected by the wearable device is fed to the microprocessor. These devices communicate with each other through LANs, WANs, Internet, or telemedicine services. Output devices provide display/ feedback/alert or implement required actions, such as functional simulation and drug delivery. The components used in this wearable are miniature, light, durable, low cost, and provide require functional reliability and safety.

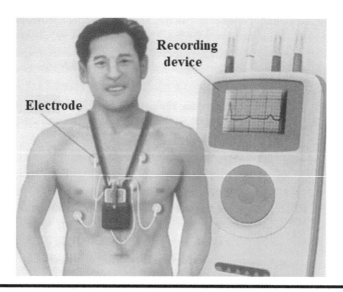

Figure 4.19 Wearable Device to Track Heart Rhythm.

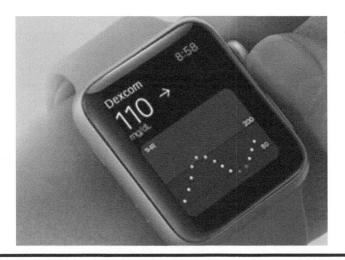

Figure 4.20 Watch App for Depression Level.

E-clothing uses a combination of textile and electronics technologies. In e-clothing, electronic sensors, circuits, or piezoelectric materials are attached or included or integrated into conventional clothing or accessories. These are used to store, process, retrieve, and send information. It is shown in Figure 4.21. Examples are conductive fabrics woven with silk fibers that have fine gold, silver, or copper wrapping. Smart garments with integrated processors and transmitters are other examples.

Fabrics have also been developed using a micro-super capacitor with conductive threads to store charge in self-powered smart garments. Special sewing technology creates a flexible mesh of aligned electrodes on a textile backing for a solid-state wearable device with the ability to store a charge that can monitor health in real time. An example of an accessory is smart shoes that monitor the impact on the ground to detect the runner's speed and send information through the Internet to the coach.

Smart fabrics can perform electronic operations. It could collect data from heating fabrics. It sends an alert message if anything is abnormal. Electronic components are knitted in fabrics through 3D-printing technology. These electronic components could be biomedical sensors, microprocessors, integrated chips, coin cells, wearable communication antennae, and so on. These fabrics have sensing capabilities, are very flexible, and are lightweight. Medical health devices are placed into any wearable shirts. Information received from these medical devices track the physiological condition of the wearer efficiently. Hence, remote monitoring of the ill-health person and health status of the patient is possible with quantity reduction in healthcare center visits.

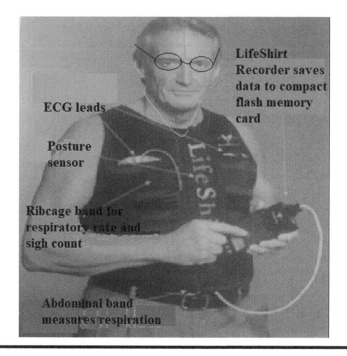

Figure 4.21   Life Shirt Monitors the Wearer's Vital Signs.

4.3.3 Wearable Medical Rehabilitation Devices

These devices provide long-term support, medical aid, and rehabilitation assistance to users. Some examples are:

Rehabilitation device for nerve stimulation: Iit is used for therapeutic purposes to block pain by providing functional stimulation through electrical impulses to the patient.

Wearable motion analysis device: The device is used as a biofeedback device during rehabilitation to monitor patients with balance disorders.

A wearable device for healing fractures: The device is used for accelerating the healing process of long bones for patients with open fractures.

Parkinson patient monitoring: Movement disorder of Parkinson's patients needs to be monitored at every moment by the doctor to analyze and detect abnormality or instability. The doctor checks data from the cloud and gives suggestions to the caretaker of the patient on what is to be done. This is a continuous automatic procedure. Figure 4.22 shows a Parkinson's patient monitoring system to help early detection of disease by analyzing symptoms of the patient.

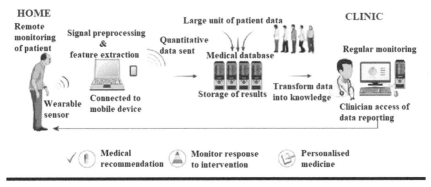

Figure 4.22   Parkinson Patient Monitoring.

Connected inhaler: Asthma disease is not treatable, but manageable using an inhaler. A sensor connected with an inhaler device monitors air pollution and temperature of the surrounding location of the patient. When the value exceeds, it triggers the event which can alert the patient from an asthma attack. The sensed data from the sensor recommend patients take the essential steps. The connected inhaler is shown in Figure 4.23. The monitoring of a breathing disorder for an elongated period through the mobile app is possible. Doctors track the situation of a disease from a distance and advise the patient for medication help. Early, accurate detection helps to avoid hospital visits and saves the hospital charges spent by the patient.

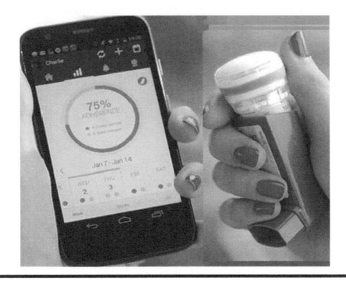

Figure 4.23   Connected Inhaler.

Ingestible sensors: These sensors are coated with magnesium and copper. They activate a pulse if the medicine is not taken at the precise time for the ill mental health patients. This is a cost-effective system to ensure the consumption of medication to avoid side effects. This is shown in Figure 4.24.

GPS smart sole: Elderly people, infants, and Alzheimer's patients forget daily tasks and are often found lost. This GPS smart sole device is embedded with a global positioning system to monitor its location. It easily fits with shoes and conforms to the user. GPS tracking is possible even if the user falls into a lake or river because it is waterproof, shown in Figure 4.25. It will send a notification to the caretaker about the user location.

Waste management system: Every dustbin is embedded along with sensors. The dustbins are placed in many locations of the hospital and report the quantity of garbage in the bin. The threshold value is set in each bin. If the value exceeds the set value of the threshold point, a computerized robot collects

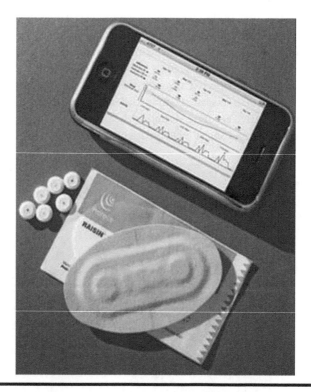

Figure 4.24   Ingestible Sensors.

Figure 4.25   GPS Smart Sole.

the trash and dumps it outside of the hospital. A sensor-fitted dustbin is shown in Figure 4.26.

Electronic glove: An electronic glove has sensors to sense pressure, temperature, and hydration which are thin flexible, and miniaturized silicon-based chips. It can be worn over a prosthetic hand to provide human-like softness and sensory perception. It is connected with a wristwatch for real-time display of sensory data as shown in Figure 4.27.

Robot assistant: COVID-19 disease brings a huge amount of patients to the hospital for monitoring. The COVID-19 disease virus spread through humans. To monitor this kind of patient, robots help in giving medication and food. It also gives an alert to the nurse about the task. All over the world robots are involved in helping and monitoring patients. The robot involved in disinfection work is shown in Figure 4.28. They help nurses while treating patients with a disease like coronavirus in social spread. All hospitals are deployed with a robot to serve the coronavirus patients to reduce infections for doctors, nurses, and health workers.

Figure 4.26   Medical Waste Management.

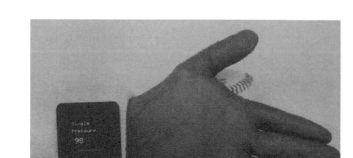

Figure 4.27   Electronic Glove.

Figure 4.28   Robot Assistant.

Robots are trained in dispensing food, medicine, collecting the trash used by the patients, performing UV-based disinfection, targeted detergent spray enables video calls between the doctor and patients, etc. It is incorporated with temperature sensors, cameras, and light detection and ranging (LIDAR). LIDAR is distant detecting technology. LIDAR uses a laser light for distance measurement. Using a temperature sensor, a robot is enabled to check the contactless temperature of patients. The camera visualizes the location and stores a 3D view in its memory of where it travels in the hospital.

Telemedicine: COVID-19 forced the healthcare world to do telemedicine. It is impossible to predict the range of the spread of COVID-19's consequence on humanity. The whole world and many nations are under lockdown to control the extent of the COVID-19 virus. Digital health is the solution in these critical circumstances. All adopt work-from-home solutions. Distant discussion about medication has become a more and more smart choice in healthcare to avoid hospital visits.

The COVID-19 pandemic carried out telemedicine and mIoT into an innovative bright. For instance, it is essential that medical specialists stay well and uninfected from viruses, the World Health Organization (WHO) advises telemedicine to observe patients and decrease the risk of increasing the COVID-19 virus spread. It is linking the gap between people, patients, surgeons, and health monitoring schemes. It enables everybody, particularly pandemic disease patients, to stay well at home. It enables communication with doctors through communication channels like a web/mobile app so that the method is facilitating the decrease of the range of the COVID-19 virus to people, staff nurses, and frontline workers, and medical supervisors. Video conference calls allow doctors to take care of high-risk ill people without coronavirus risk assessment. Frontline workers or experts expand their service to patients even though they are quarantined. It facilitates the distant monitoring of more pandemic disease persons in a short period and minimizes the amount of patients' hospital visits.

Cognitive IoT: Cognitive IoT is a smart device. It mimics the brain of human-beings in giving solutions. Body wearable sensors and environment sensors are placed to monitor medical data. The appropriate decision is taken on collected data to deliver necessary services.

3D-printed liver transplantation: 3D printers create artificial human organs like the patient's rib cage and other bone implants. Bio print with bioengineering helps in bone replacement, liver transplants, and organ implants.

Biomedical chip implant technology: This allows ill patients give the ability to control the cursor on the screen by thinking about the movement of the hand. It allows the machine to communicate with the brain. Scientist, physicist, Professor Stephen Hawking had a motor neuron disease. The sensor is placed on his cheek. He uses this sensor to type characters and numbers on the keyboard. He wears a motorized wheelchair system that enables him to write and speak with greater ease and no typo error.

Brain-computer interface: A brain-computer interface system consists of several sensors to collect brain signals. The decoder can detect and interpret neural signals related to brain activity. Computers translate these electronic neuro signals into corresponding actions.

Technological advancements have made available wider data memory capability augmented reality (AR)-based head-mounted displays, and artificial intelligence-based decision-making capability, and improved communication in the future. Superior components and sensors are helping in improving functionality, wearability, reliability, and security of devices. Devices are being integrated with implantable devices to provide real-time patient management. Futuristic wearable devices will include automatic infusion of insulin when blood sugar levels are high, serve as implanted micro-pump–assisted medicine supply systems, DNA diagnostics transplants, and imitation retinas.

4.4 Conclusion

An IoT-based healthcare system should find a solution to some kind of obstacles such as:

- Medical information storage on gateway servers as the investigation of the medical big data has been increasingly very difficult.
- Security and privacy issues.
- Communication is costly but also energy-hungry.
- Designing smart sensors that provide vital data to the edge devices.
- It generates huge amounts of data and has inadequate memory to store it all.
- Regulations are to be developed worldwide.

All of these obstacles will be overcome in the near future. Medical big data analysis, security, and privacy analysis are solved by strong algorithms. NEMS, MEMS, nanotechnology, miniaturization, material science, and sensor technology developments create smart sensors for measuring medical data reliably, effectively, and efficiently. More health data tracking is easily possible with mIoT.

During the COVID-19 pandemic, a community-spread disease, patients could be efficiently and 100% securely monitored by the doctors using mIoT and telemedicine. The whole world is under a great depression in this case to handle patients. The patient population increases and is very tough to provide treatment to them. Mobile app or telemedicine or mIoT or robots are the best solutions to this pandemic disease. Artificial intelligence embedded robots predict the disease and help them with further treatment advice. AI robots could do surgery precisely like real doctors. Mobile device usage increases the use of mIoT in the medical industry. Many mobile apps are developed to monitor people's health.

Wearable sensors, artificial intelligence, machine learning, wearable device advancements, blockchain, smart devices, big data, robotics technology, embedded products, miniaturized sensors, mobile computing, mobile technology, and iPhone app developments will boost the power of mIoT even further in the coming years.

References

https://econsultancy.com/Internet-of-things-healthcare/, Date accessed 14 Apr 2021
https://www.finoit.com/blog/the-role-of-iot-in-healthcare/, Date accessed 20 Apr 2021
https://www.i-scoop.eu/Internet-of-things/, Date accessed 25 Apr 2021
https://www.ubuntupit.com/iot-in-healthcare-20-examples/, Date accessed 15 Apr 2021

Chapter 5

Industrial Internet of Things (IIoT) Applications

Saravana Kumari Sundaram

Vice President, Insurance, Virtusa Corporation, Bangalore, India

Contents

DOI: 10.1201/9781003175872-5

Objectives

After studying this lesson, the audience should be able to understand.

"THE INTERNET OF THINGS IS NOT A CONCEPT; IT
IS A NETWORK, THE TRUE TECHNOLOGY-ENABLED
NETWORK OF ALL NETWORKS" EDEWEDE ORIWOH.
(Marr, 2018a)

1. Evolution of IoT for industrial applications
2. Market share and growth projection of IIoT
3. IIoT and impacts by industry
4. Insurance and healthcare
5. Anatomy of a user journey in Insurance
6. IIoT in healthcare during COVID-19
7. The fusion of IR 4.0 technologies
8. IIoT implementation examples in insurance
9. Challenges and opportunities
10. Crystal gazing into the future
11. Learning road map

5.1 Evolution of IoT for Industrial Applications

Internet of Things (IoT) means that everything around us connects to the Internet with an intelligent behavior adhering to the autonomy and privacy requirements (Hassan et al., 2015). This chapter explores how IoT applies in industries and its impacts in the various facets of our day-to-day life. When writing this chapter, the world is unprecedentedly battling with COVID-19

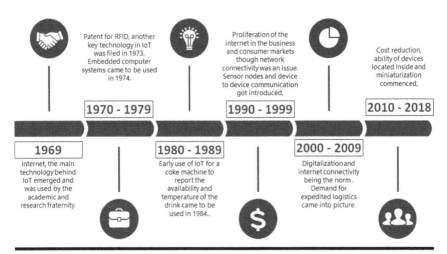

Figure 5.1 Evolution of IoT.

with phenomenal applications of technology. The uses of IoT are witnessed across the globe, from mobiles loaded with apps to ensure quarantine compliance, drones monitoring the roads during the lockdown, and more advanced uses to manage patient care and optimize and track medical equipment usage. Most of the IoT evolution occurred between the third and the fourth Industrial Revolutions (i.e., between 1969 and 2018) (Figure 5.1).

The Internet of Things's industrial applications has evolved to a subfield known as "Industrial IoT (IIoT)". The Industrial Internet of Things (IIoT) comprises interconnected devices across industries networked together or connected with computers' industrial applications. I-IoT solutions involve using cloud as the data and processing platform to connect, relay, store, process, and analyze sensor data (Cano et al., 2018). The industrial applications could range from Commercially Off-The-Shelf (COTS) products or custom-built industry applications. This connectivity allows for user interaction, data collection, exchange, and analysis, potentially facilitating business parameter improvements, otherwise known as Key Performance Indicators (KPIs). The KPIs could be in terms of productivity gains or cost reduction in terms of efficiency, market share increases, customer increase in terms of growth, customer loyalty, and a positive brand image through customer experience. The Industrial Internet of Things (IIoT) is an evolution with a higher degree of automation using cloud and edge computing, big data analytics, AI/ML and Cyber-physical systems (Wikipedia, 2020).

5.2 Market Share and Growth Projection of IIoT

There are also many misconceptions about IR 4.0, IIoT, and Industry 4.0. To put it in perspective, IoT applies for consumer use or industry use. The industrial uses of IoT are IIoT (Marr, 2018b). IIoT applied for manufacturing is called "Industry 4.0". In 1999, K. Ashton first used the term "The Internet of Things (IoT)" to indicate the use of the Internet by machines and not just humans. General Electric first used the term IIoT to indicate the industrial application of IoT. Industry 4.0 is the current automation and data exchange trend in manufacturing technologies. It is also known as the "Smart Factory".

Worldwide spending on the IoT is forecast to pass the $1.0 trillion mark in 2022, reaching $1.1 trillion in 2023 (IDC, 2019a). The Industrial Internet of Things (IIoT) market worldwide is projected to grow by US $38.1 billion in 2020, driven by a compounded growth of 7.1% (Markets and Markets Research, 2020). Factors such as technological advancements in semiconductor and electronic devices, increased use of cloud computing platforms, standardization of IPv6, and support from governments of different countries for R&D activities related to IIoT determine the IIOT sector's growth. IDC expects 70% of automobiles to connect to the Internet by 2023 (IDC, 2019b). Accenture estimates that the IIoT will lift real gross domestic product (that is, adjusted for inflation) by 1.0% in 2030 over trend projections for 20 major economies studied (Accenture, 2015; Worldometer, 2017) (Table 5.1).

Table 5.1   IoT Contribution to GDP (Top 4 Countries)

Country	GDP (in US $ Billions)	IIOT Contribution to GDP* (in US$ Billions)	% Contribution to GDP
United States	19485	7100	36%
China	12238	1800	15%
Germany	3693	700	19%
United Kingdom	2638	531	20%

5.3 IIoT and Impacts by Industry

IoT has its implication upon almost every industry. In the era of the Internet, human beings connect through the Internet. With the advances in IoT, machines communicate over the Internet. Furthermore, with Industry 4.0, production transforms. The nine key technology trends form the building blocks for the transformation leading to greater efficiencies and changes in traditional production relationships among suppliers, producers, and customers and between humans and machines (Boston Consulting Group, 2020) (Figure 5.2).

The Fourth Industrial Revolution is therefore not a prediction of the future but a call to action. It is a vision for developing, diffusing, and governing technologies in ways that foster a more empowering, collaborative, and sustainable foundation for social and economic development, built around shared values of the common good, human dignity, and intergenerational stewardship. Realizing this vision will be the core challenge and great responsibility of the next 50 years" (Schwab, 2015).

With advances in artificial intelligence, machine learning, deep learning, blockchain, cloud computing, edge computing, automation and the like, the analytics and decision making (Next Best Action: NBA), and the actions needed are automatically taken care of by the interconnected devices.

Figure 5.2   IoT Devices.

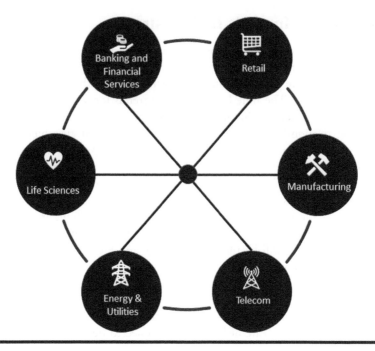

Figure 5.3   IoT Impact across Industries.

Example: the water pipe at home understands a leakage and informs the family member while calling the Home insurer to protect the home from inadvertent flooding or damage to the property. It can also take preventive actions to switch off the water source and inform the owner and other liable parties. The water pipe also sends all the data about this to the device provider. The device provider analyzes this data and understands the conditions that lead to a leakage in the pipe. With this information, the device provider alerts the customers on the maintenance required or offers value-based services such as being responsible for the pipe's wear and tear. It is also an excellent example of the onus for usage moving from the consumer to the manufacturer. IoT is disrupting businesses and leading to newer business models and evolving ecosystems (Figure 5.3).

5.3.1 Retail

The retail industry is one of the first industries to pave the way for IoT by using Radio Frequency Identification (RFID) to identify goods by transmitting a radio signal. More than 50% of the significant retailers worldwide have implemented IoT across multiple value chains such as supply chain management, smart inventory management, enhanced customer experience, automated checkout, and the like (Gaikwad, 2018). Retailers use sensors to monitor and take appropriate actions on the supply chain management, such as knowing the volume, status, and location of the materials in transit from the distributors to the retailer. In more advanced cases, the temperature, humidity, and status sensors transmit the materials' condition in transit, enabling the retailers to take corrective and preventive actions to ensure material safety. For example, it could offload a part of the inventory with a discount rather than traveling to the destined location. Alternatively, it could be to alter travel conditions, such as increasing moisture or adjusting the temperature so that the materials would last longer.

It is well-known that data mining leads to astonishing insights. For example, the men who buy diapers on a Friday evening also buy beer (McHaney, 2002). This shows how advanced the retail industry is and how it has used data insights for customer experience. The cameras in the retail stores and the sensors show the retail on the customer's journey into the store and future stocking of products and the duration. The location is all determined by using IoT to enhance the customer experience.

In recent days, the industry uses automated machines for Straight Through Processing (STP) by offering self-servicing kiosks and allowing RFID to auto recognize the items in the customer's shopping cart. The invoice is automatically generated by adding up the items' prices and offering scheduled discounts. On the automated acceptance of the customer's digital payment, the kiosk allows the customer to step out of the retail store. This process makes it very easy and quick for the customers to avoid lengthy queues and prevent fraud in a very non-intrusive manner. Needless to say, while the customer experience is made better, the cost of operations for the retailer also comes down due to this implementation. Depending on the seasons and the anticipated crowd, this system can scale up or down quickly as needed overcoming the dependencies for a smooth and successful process.

5.3.2 Manufacturing

Manufacturing is an industry that is the epitome of quality and efficiency. Service industries look up to manufacturing to emulate these characteristics while focusing on customer delight. In the manufacturing industry, IoT plays such a significant role that the usage of IR 4.0 technologies in manufacturing has come to be fondly known as Industry 4.0. IoT usage in manufacturing expands across the complete gamut of inventory management, production planning, control, capacity planning, testing, packaging, and shipping. As we all know, inventory needs to be replenished on time and just in time to optimally use the production facilities and minimize storage costs as much as possible. IoT sensor embedded materials have made it easier and faster to organize, know the real-time status and automatically trigger inventory requests considering the reorder levels. Once the production factory procures the required assets, IoT has also made it easier to store and retrieve its components. It helps in maneuvering office layouts in the optimal route by saving costs and preventing mishaps. Every step in the process is an opportunity for error (OPE). As per Six Sigma experts, it is always prudent to avoid error and follow clear and simple steps to ensure quality compliance.

That was just about the manufacturing process. If we step on the products and by-products in the manufacturing sector, the uses of IoT spread beyond the sector to include automotive, 3D printing, aerospace, construction, and a variety of other industries. Autonomous vehicles rule the roost in the auto disruption. Consumers, distributors, insurers are all connected to offer the seamless experience combining the three pillars of cost reduction, expanding growth, and enhancing customer experience. A further step has led to smart homes and smart cities that consist of interconnected devices that work together to offer the users a convenience that has almost become a necessity. Connected cars, connected homes, and connected consumers are offering a complete transformation. Imagine a person is returning home after a long day at work. IoT-based smart cars or smartphones guide the person through the optimal way home, avoiding rush hour hassles. When reaching home, the home is set at the preferred temperature level thanks to the smart home sensors. In India, the electric bulbs that can be turned on or off from the mobile phone are the new ways to ensure the absence of a person at home does not deny any of these regular activities at home. Ordering through Swiggy or the homemade food community ensures the taste buds relish a good dinner. Many cooking ranges support IoT and are programmable to prepare the favorite dish at a specific time. All these devices work together to ensure the safety and comfort of the person. It is no longer a science fiction movie when we watch a refrigerator order the required vegetables or food.

5.3.3 Telecom

Telecommunications is going through a tectonic shift both from mobile technologies' advances and the fusion of IR 4.0 technologies. Telecom providers use IoT for preventive maintenance followed by efforts to improve productivity. More than 30% of the telecom providers globally are at the forefront of applying computer vision and analytics to understand and predict customer behavior (Forbes, 2018).

5.3.4 Energy and Utilities

Smart metering (Tracy, 2016) uses an Internet-capable device that measures the energy, water, or natural gas consumption of a building or home. Generally, meters measure the usage of the resource. However, smart meters also provide usage characteristics such as location, duration, timing, and usage quantity. It helps to provide the necessary resources to enhance the customer experience while reducing unnecessary wastage or overflow.

That was smart metering in general across resources. The most expensive resource is synonymous with the oil and gas sector in energy and utilities. Many countries' economy thrives on the export revenue of oil and gas, and these countries are part of the Organization of the Petroleum Exporting Countries (OPEC) (Tracy, 2016). Narrowing upon the oil and gas sector, the multiple uses of IoT starting from the hunt for the geography and specific region where installing an oil drilling facility will benefit drilling oil, refining, and workers' safety to monitoring the extraction, transport, and delivery.

One of the jobs that have the most significant risk to life is to work in an oil rig. In such extreme situations, it becomes imperative to consider the workers' safety, remotely monitor the rig's conditions, and proactively offer the employed personnel's timely support.

5.3.5 Life Sciences

In life sciences, research and discovery of new drugs to timely diagnosis, disease prevention, monitoring, and treatment are all monitored through IoT. A chip in a pill or smart pill or digital pill transmits images about the patient's internal organs. Patients swallow a pill with an embedded IoT chip. The pill consists of an ingestible sensor as a chip and a logic circuit embedded in the pill. Once the patient swallows the pill, the pill gets dissolved, and the chip transmits the vital details and images about the patient's internal organs.

Radiology is always at the forefront of technology. With IoT, radiology transforms from siloed patient information to a centralized hub from which doctors and caregivers can access the information and provide holistic care. (Figure 5.4)

Beacons have been beacons of hope across industries and value chains and they play an integral part in transforming business models and providing location-based services using BLE (Bluetooth Low Energy) and solar-powered devices. With integrated healthcare, beacons transmit patient information and medical records just in time for the doctor to view, periodic updates of patients' status to the doctor and nurses, management of people and devices, and their interactions within the hospital premises.

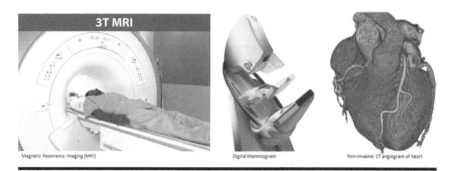

Figure 5.4   Radiology in Healthcare.

IoT-based appliances have been a boon to the differently abled. From assisted wheelchairs using sensor and IoT-based walking stick, there are many devices to aid and assist the needy.

5.3.6 *Banking and Financial Services*

Banking and financial services is known for the increased concern over privacy and security. The industry let certain technology developments pass if the conviction is not enough to "change the bank" or transformational implementations. However, in such an industry, biometric scanners, and usage of mobile phones and tablets have made a formidable entry as pioneers to use IoT and connected devices. This strength has also helped banks to leverage their partnerships beyond banking products. For example, a bank understands the pattern with the customers' cash withdrawals or notices using a ski resort's credit card. It is time for the bank to market its partner's ski insurance when the customer is entering or nearing a ski resort. This specific distribution model is technically known as "Bancassurance", where banks and insurers partner to leverage each other's strengths. Banks extend the partner's products and retain customers through the value-added services while the insurer leverages the partners' client base for its product distribution and innovative new products. The sky is the limit when it comes to the power of IoT-powered business use cases that can leverage technology to disrupt business models.

5.4 Insurance and Healthcare

Insurance and healthcare are two broad areas that touch everyone's lives every day. The plethora of IoT uses in this field is so pervasive that we hardly recognize IoT as external.

Our mobile phones act as our first IoT device that

a. Track our location, the timing of the day, and the duration of time at the location.
b. Track our physical activity, the number of steps that we move, the pace at which we move, whether we move by a vehicle or walk.
c. Our health in terms of our idle phone hours, the pattern of device usage or sleep, the average time that we spend on the mobile, and the apps we use on our mobile.
d. Track our movement and the time we spend in specific locations. It might be fantastic to know that we get a review for a place on Google where we stopped by recently. For example, if that is a gym and a person stops regularly, the healthcare provider could know that the person is visiting a gym regularly. The other business rules of whether it is about dropping and picking up someone or if the person is spending time at the gym can be determined.

These examples show how ubiquitous the technology is. With these everyday examples, we can now delve deeper into the insurance and healthcare industry.

5.4.1 Lines of Businesses in Insurance

Insurance's broad categories are

a. General Insurance
b. Life Insurance

General insurance deals with addressing risks related to all things like car, home, and business. Life insurance deals with the risk of mortality (death), the risk for income due to morbidity (health), and ensuring the means of income after the earning years, such as retirement plans and pensions (Figure 5.5).

Different geographies use different terminologies and nuances for the line of businesses. For example, general insurance in the APAC (Asia Pacific) regions is known as Property and Casualty (P&C) with subtle variations. Health insurance is a part of general insurance in India and the Middle East, whereas health insurance is a part of healthcare and not insurance in the USA and Canada.

If we look at IoT applications in businesses' sublines, we can notice amazing uses as per the needs' subtleties and uniqueness.

1. Personal Insurance
    a. Auto Insurance
    b. Home Insurance
    c. Health Insurance

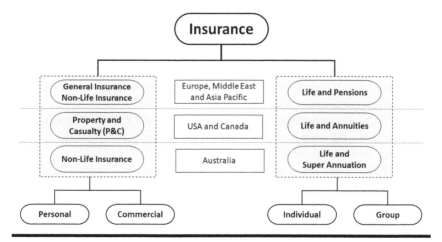

Figure 5.5 Insurance Lines of Businesses.

2. Commercial Insurance
   a. Fleet Insurance
   b. Marine Insurance
   c. Small Business Insurance
3. Life Insurance
   a. Individual Life
   b. Group Life
   c. Investments
4. Healthcare and Health Insurance

5.4.2 Value Chains in Insurance

An insurance company's operations can be generalized and summarized across the business lines in the following manner (Figure 5.6).

5.5 Anatomy of an IoT User Journey in Insurance

Though IoT has touched upon the policyholders, insurers, third-party service providers, agents, and brokers in different ways, we can look at IoT in auto insurance as an example across the value chains.

From applying for a policy, IoT gets into the picture to bring in the vehicle telematics and analytics to know how the prospect policyholder would drive and price the policy accordingly. Various forms of research have happened in collaboration with insurers, auto manufacturers, telecom

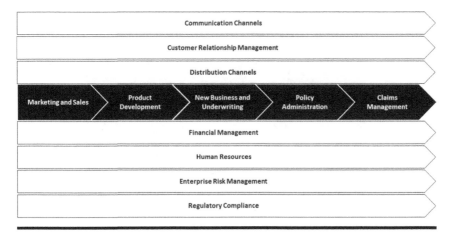

Figure 5.6 Insurance Value Chains.

providers, InsurTech, and academia to bring together vehicle telematics, behavioral analytics to judge Pay-How-You-Drive (PHYD). Insurers began this journey to bring in innovative products where policyholders could pay the premium according to the distance they drive, called Pay-As-You-Drive (PAYD). It is also possible to measure the way the driver accelerates or brakes, the time and duration of driving, the location of driving. Policyholders are also willing to sign up for such policies as they get the advantage of differentiated pricing. Insurers offer discounts to policyholders who agree to share their data on these parameters. The sound drivers get rewarded, while the additional premium only penalizes the drivers who might incur claims from the insurer. It is a proactive process at the time of underwriting and policy issuance. Vehicle telematics, driver behavior, and vehicle data monitored continuously offer value-added services and updates to the premium as needed. Collaborative and social behavior of drivers also earn them redemption points to accumulate and later redeem. All of these change the business model for New Business, Underwriting, and Policy Administration (Figure 5.7).

IoT has an indelible role in claims management. Claims, being the "moment of truth" for the insurer, can help re-create the accident scene from the IoT data.

A. To know the key characteristics of the incident: location and time of the incident, the speed, and direction of the vehicles, the rules of the road and the behavior of the drivers to know the fault percentage of the drivers, the condition of the cars at the time of the incident.

Figure 5.7 Drone Inspecting an Accident Site.

B. Some insurers have also deployed drones to collect the evidence and assess the damage without having the adjuster visit the incident's location in person. More augmented reality tools are also experimented alongside IoT to help adjusters visualize the physical world through their digital gadgets.

C. In emergency cases or where towing the vehicle is needed, the IoT systems have become capable of calling the emergency numbers, towing agencies, and third-party service providers while creating the claim on behalf of the policyholder.

D. Segmentation and adjudication of the claim happen through Straight Through Processing (STP). For example, if it is a fender-bender type of claim and is the first such claim from the policyholder, the system could auto adjudicate the claim and immediately pay the loss.

E. With AI/ML models, the system also learns to classify if a claim could be a fraudulent claim. While insurers continuously improve for sophisticated models to address false positives and combat real claims, they also ensure no negative impact on the customer experience. There is no claim leakage due to payment of inappropriate claims.

F. In addition to all these IoT activities after the incident, the vehicles are becoming more sophisticated to have Machine-To-Machine (M2M) communication and prevent an accident by taking appropriate action while sensing an accident (Figure 5.8).

5.6 IIoT in Healthcare During COVID-19

COVID-19 patients flood hospitals and healthcare workers sacrifice their time and personal health to save patients. In hospitals, increased IoT usage for blood glucose

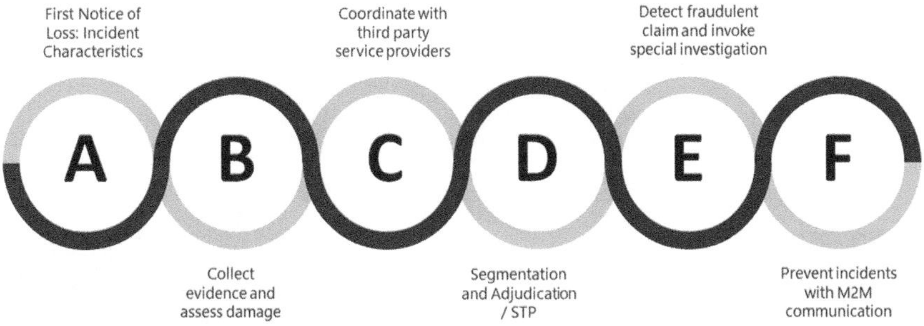

Figure 5.8   Steps in the Auto Claim Process.

monitoring and vitals checks free up healthcare workers' bandwidth to focus on COVID-19 patients. For outpatients monitored from home, mobile device-based monitoring and secure exchange of medical records come in handy for healthcare. In breakthrough cases, artificial intelligence in association with x-rays and scanned images of lungs has proved to be a predictive mechanism to proactively identify how the symptoms could develop and if the symptoms will lead to COVID-19. Maybe the future is not far away from where the laptop would come with an IoT blood scanner, just like the biometric fingerprint scanner. At the drop of blood, the blood results are determined and shared with the physicians paving more tele-medicine and access to world-class healthcare irrespective of the location or time. One of the significant challenges today is the production and delivery of test kits to enable more testing and identification cases. With IIoT advancements in this space in collaboration with medical imaging, diagnostic tests, genetic testing, the future could be the plugging in of the components and installation of apps for various medical procedures combating infections, time, and distance.

5.7 Fusion of IR 4.0 Technologies

The usage of IoT is one of the many technologies in Industrial Revolution (IR) 4.0. The other technologies such as artificial intelligence, machine learning, big data and analytics, blockchain, extended reality (AR/VR), cloud computing, and edge technologies play a significant role in accentuating the benefits. The vast amounts of data (volume) from the IoT devices and the variety and velocity of the data call for big data analytics. In recent days, different businesses want to automate processes and replace human intelligence with automated or augmented decision making through machines. It poses a need for artificial intelligence and machine learning that could span across structured data or unstructured data in the form of docu-ments, images, audio, or videos. This business need gets amplified across the

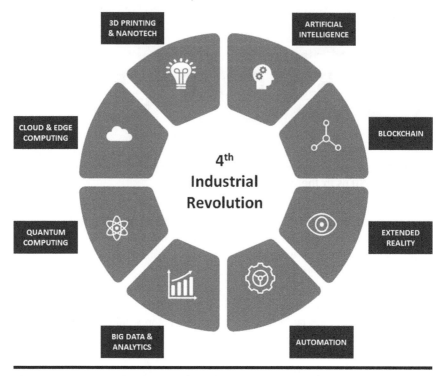

Figure 5.9   Key Technologies of IR 4.0.

business channels as Natural Language Processing (NLP), supervised/unsupervised learning algorithms leading to machine learning, or more sophisticated in-depth learning examples. With that known, IR 4.0 is not impacting industries by bringing the usage of technology; it also offers the possibilities to combine multiple technologies and leverage the benefits manifold. Some of the critical technologies of Industrial Revolution 4.0 in this context are shown (Figure 5.9).

Here are some examples of the fusion of IR 4.0 technologies in the insurance industry. Synechron combines IoT with blockchain capabilities to combat fraud and offer Straight Through Processing (STP). Etherisc (Blockchain) provides crop insurance in combination with IoT. Aerobatics, on the other hand, offers crop insurance in combination with AI on IoT. UBIRCH uses reliable sensor data to provide parametric insurance. Ernst and Young have piloted marine insurance with IoT and blockchain for Lloyds of London. Drones evaluate properties to conduct risk evaluation and property underwriting. Drones/Mobiles and a combination of AR/VR and IoT allow claims adjusters to view the damage and assess the claim from their home office without having to travel to the claim incident location. Finally, it is not only for real time; IoT combined with learning technologies offers experiential learning to adjusters.

5.8 IIoT Implementation Examples in Insurance

Digital ecosystems have become more relevant in recent days. Insurers partner with InsurTech or technology product companies to develop new and differentiated product offerings such as auto insurance, home insurance, life or health insurance, commercial insurance, and reinsurance.

Car insurers are also known as auto insurers: Progressive Insurance in the United States uses a "Snapshot" program to understand how the policyholders drive and adjust the premium amounts accordingly. Vehicle telematics provides the distance and driving behavior of the policyholders. Insurers such as Progressive Insurance use this information to micro-segment the customer base. Knowing the customer segments helps to offer discounts for good drivers reducing their insurance premiums. It is part of rewarding the good behavior of drivers. MetroMile, an InsurTech, has introduced the concept of pay-per-mile so customers can avail or buy Insurance for the miles they need. It is all implemented through IoT and offers a just-in-time servicing and pay per use model.

Home Insurance: liberty Mutual has reduced the premiums of policyholders who have availed of the home insurance offered by Liberty Mutual in partnership with Google to use Google Nest to alert about smoke alarms. American Family Insurance (AFI) partnered with Microsoft to provide home automation and premium reduction for risk mitigation.

Life and Health Insurance: John Hancock partnered with Vitality to monitor fitness levels and offer value-added services to promote healthy living through fitness. Beam Digital, an InsurTech, transmits data from the smart toothbrush to know the oral health and brushing habits. This data helps in determining the insurance premium for dental insurance.

5.9 Challenges and Opportunities

Privacy: Often, technology is ubiquitous, making industries and customers wary and deeply concerned when machines access certain information about people's personal information such as location, whereabouts, social media information, and the like. Industries develop regulations such as the GDPR (general data protection regulation) to address the privacy concerns.

Security: Security cannot be compromised. Overcoming this challenge and ensuring that the data is secure is a topmost concern. Many industries refrain from using cutting-edge technologies if they pose a security risk. It is an opportunity for mushrooming firms that focus on security and offer point solutions in the space, such as Verimatrix, Congent Datahub.

Infrastructure: Initially, all IoT implementations cost heavily for the infrastructure. It deters small and medium businesses from investing though the benefits are well known. The Return on Investment (RoI) is certainly attractive for those who take the plunge.

Expertise: The implementation and maintenance of IoT systems call for specialization. With specialization, the availability and affordability of the appropriate people also become a challenge. Industries are collaborating with academia in hackathons to spot, hire, train, and overcome the challenge.

Lack of Standards: While IoT is gaining widespread acceptance, there is a lack of interconnectivity standards and interoperability. It also makes the availability of expertise tedious as there are no common grounds for maintenance.

5.10 Crystal Gazing into the Future

As we learn i IR 4.0 (Schwab, 2015) and the impacts each Industrial Revolution has created, others think about IR 5.0 and IR 6.0. It is certainly helpful for us to glimpse what the future looks like as we know it today (Figure 5.10).

IR 5.0, also known as the Quiet Revolution, is about personalization. With the advances in 3D printing, the new standard will be product personalization. Products and spare parts no longer need to be manufactured, stored, and delivered, but they can be printed just in time according to the customized features required.

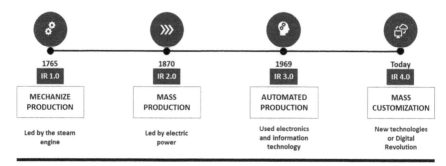

Figure 5.10 Industrial Revolutions.

5.11 IIoT Learning Road Map for Education

In the previous section, we understood the various challenges and opportunities available in applying IoT technologies in the industry. There is a broader gamut of Education 4.0 with nine trends in response to the needs of IR 4.0 (Fisk, 2017; Hussin, 2018). In the context of Education 4.0, the road map for IoT will be as suggested below (Table 5.2).

Table 5.2 Education 4.0 Trends for IoT

#	Trend	Context for IoT
1	Anytime, anywhere	MOOC (Mass Open Online Courses) to get started in understanding the concepts of IoT
2	Personalized	The business domain or the industry determines the practical application of the technology. As mentioned in the earlier section as industries, personalizing the learnings to a particular field is the next logical step.
3	Mode	The mode in which the students want to achieve the outcomes they desire is the next step. It could be through an institution-wide body of knowledge, Special Interest Groups (SIG), or chapters to exchange and collaborate.
4	Project-based	Combining the last three steps of learning, business domain, and expert group in the form of a project provides a planned tangible objective to progress.
5	Field experience	Applying the outcome of the previous step in a real-life environment is proof of the applicability. The choice of the business domain in the personalized learning goes hand in hand with the organization's choice where the project can be applied. It also equips the students with the soft skills needed for corporate careers.

(Continued)

Table 5.2 *(Continued)*   **Education 4.0 Trends for IoT**

#	Trend	Context for IoT
6	Data interpretation	Any learning is like a control system where the feedback loop modifies the inputs and refine the outcomes. The field experience outcomes provide inferences to fine-tune and predict future trends by collecting and interpreting data.
7	Assessment	Assessment will have formal and informal methods that equip the students in both the theory and the practical application and soft skills such as time management, collaboration, teamwork, integrity, and self-motivation.
8	Student's opinion	Like the students' data interpretation to refine their course, the student's opinion forms the feedback mechanism to feed into the curriculum's updates. Based on the previous step's learnings, students will provide their inputs to refine the curriculum.
9	More independent	The teacher's role shifts to a coach while the onus to succeed stays with the student playing an active and vital role in future education.

It is a continuous improvement process that enables academia and industry to collaborate, bringing together the teachers, students, and industry practitioners to implement, sustain and improve the education, and make it relevant and adaptable for future generations.

It is very apt to conclude by remembering the words of Benjamin Franklin:

"TELL ME, AND I WILL FORGET, SHOW ME, AND I MAY REMEMBER, INVOLVE ME, AND I LEARN".

Let the journey of our involvement and learning see successful pinnacles.

References

Accenture, 2015. Winning with the Industrial Internet of Things. [Online] Available at: https://www.accenture.com/t00010101t000000z__w__/it-it/_acnmedia/pdf-5/accenture-industrial-internet-of-things-positioning-paper-report-2015.pdf, [accessed 13 May, 2020].

B. C. G., 2020. Embracing industry 4.0 and rediscovering growth. [Online] Available at: https://www.bcg.com/en-in/capabilities/operations/embracing-industry-4.0-rediscovering-growth.aspx, [accessed 13 May, 2020].

Cano, J.C., Berrios, V., Garcia, B., Toh, C.K., 2018. Evolution of IoT: An industry perspective, *IEEE Internet of Things Magazine* 1(2), 2–7, doi: 10.1109/IOTM.2019.1900002.

Fisk, P., 2017. Education 4.0 ... the future of learning will be dramatically different, in school and throughout life. Available at: http://www.thegeniusworks.com/2017/01/future-education-young-everyone-taught-together

Forbes, 2018. How IoT is impacting 7 key industries today. [Online] Available at: https://www.forbes.com/sites/insights-inteliot/2018/08/24/how-iot-is-impacting-7-key-industries-today/#418e97261a84, [accessed 13 May, 2020].

Gaikwad, G., 2018. Retail IoT: Applications, challenges, and solutions. [Online] Available at: https://www.iotforall.com/retail-iot-applications-challenges-solutions/, [accessed 05 May, 2020].

Hassan, Z. A., Hesham, A. A., Mahmous, M. B., 2015. Internet of Things (IoT): Definitions, challenges, and recent research directions. *International Journal of Computer Applications* 128(1), 37–47.

Hussin, A.A., 2018. Education 4.0 made simple: Ideas for teaching. *International Journal of Education & Literacy Studies* 6(3), 92–98.

IDC, 2019a. According to a new IDC spending guide, steady Commercial and consumer adoption will drive worldwide spending on the internet of Things to $1.1 trillion in 2023. [Online] Available at: https://www.idc.com/getdoc.jsp?containerId=prUS45197719, [accessed 05 May, 2020].

IDC, 2019b. Worldwide connected vehicle shipments forecast to reach 76 Million Units by 2023, According to IDC. [Online] Available at: https://www.idc.com/getdoc.jsp?containerId=prUS45092819, [accessed 13 May, 2020].

Markets and Markets Research, 2020. Research and markets. [Online] Available at: https://www.researchandmarkets.com/reports/5003969/industrial-iot-iiot-market-by-device-and?utm_source=dynamic&utm_medium=BW&utm_code=jj8q97&utm_campaign=1362708+-+Global+IIoT+Market+Expected+to+Grow+at+a+Significant+Rate+from+USD+77.3+Billion+in+2020+to+, [accessed 05 May, 2020].

Marr, B., 2018a. *19 Astonishing quotes about the Internet Of things everyone should read.* [Online] Available at: https://www.forbes.com/sites/bernardmarr/2018/09/12/19-astonishing-quotes-about-the-internet-of-things-everyone-should-read/#4245762be1db, [accessed 05 May, 2020].

Marr, B., 2018b. Forbes. [Online] Available at: https://www.forbes.com/sites/bernardmarr/2018/09/02/what-is-industry-4-0-heres-a-super-easy-explanation-for-anyone/#56662bb19788, [accessed 05 05 2020].

McHaney, R.W., 2002. Selling six-packs of beer with nappies. *Business to Business* 11(12), 1–3.

Schwab, K., 2015. The fourth industrial revolution. [Online] Available at: https://www.weforum.org/about/the-fourth-industrial-revolution-by-klaus-schwab, [accessed 05 May, 2020].

Tracy, P., 2016. IIoT use cases in the oil and gas industry. [Online] Available at: Oil and Gas https://enterpriseiotinsights.com/20160720/oil-gas/use-cases-iot-oil-gas-tag31-tag99, [accessed 05 May, 2020].

Tracy, P., 2017. The top 5 industrial IoT use cases. [Online] Available at: https://www.ibm.com/blogs/internet-of-things/top-5-industrial-iot-use-cases/, [accessed 05 May, 2020].

Wikipedia, 2020. Industrial Internet of Things. [Online] Available at: https://en.wikipedia.org/wiki/Industrial_internet_of_things, [accessed 28 Jan 2021].

Wikipedia, 2020. Industry 4.0. [Online] Available at: https://en.wikipedia.org/wiki/Industry_4.0, [accessed 05 May, 2020].

Worldometer, 2017. Top countries by GDP (2017 NOMINAL GDP). [Online] Available at: https://www.worldometers.info/gdp/, [accessed 13 May, 2020].

Chapter 6

Smart Farming: IoT-Based Plant Leaf Disease Detection and Prediction Using Image Processing Techniques

A. Sakila and S. Vijayarani

Department of Computer Science, Bharathiar University, Coimbatore, India

Contents

DOI: 10.1201/9781003175872-6

Objectives

By reading this chapter, the learner can gain knowledge on the following:

1. IoT in smart farming
2. Advantages of smart farming
3. Precision farming
4. Agricultural drones
5. Application areas of smart farming
6. Service providers of smart farming

6.1 Introduction

India is a farming-based nation. The population relies upon farming directly or indirectly. Food, Water, Fuel is an essential source in the human lives. These are very much important and prime for financial progress. While considering our nation's income, these sources offer the maximum contribution (Lee et al., 2013). In addition to this, agriculture also provides job opportunities to a very high percentage of the population. Our country's climate conditions are iso-tropic; still, people cannot utilize agricultural resources efficiently. The reason behind this is the deficiency of scarcity of water and rains. In traditional farming methods, farmers need to always stay on their land and frequently monitor the plant and crops.

Farmers have difficulty in monitoring manually larger farms and agricultural lands. It is very difficult to identify the portion of the plants in the agricultural land affected by diseases or not. Hence, they used pesticides for the entire land, which might cover healthy plants also. This is mainly used in micro-farming. Micro-farming need only a minimum of land so we can able to perform limited agricultural processes (Lee et al., 2013; iotdunia.com). Currently, the mixture of smart irrigation and local sensors controls the sensing of pH and weather conditions, including insolation and resident temperature (devi 2013,). It is difficult for the farmers to find their experts and sense the problem like amending soil conditions and watering where location and pests on plants. Figure 6.1 illustrates the sample images of a disease-affected mango. Figure 6.2 shows the sample image of a disease-affected orange. Figure 6.3 presents the disease-affected green pepper. Figure 6.4 represents the disease-affected tomato. Figure 6.5 shows a citrus pest leaf disease. Figure 6.6 depicts the air burn leaf disease. Figure 6.7 illuminates the white spot leaf disease. Figure 6.8 shows the oak pest leaf disease.

6.2 Smart Farming and Benefits

Smart farming reduces production costs and uses fewer resources for an accurate monitoring system in all aspects such as water, soil, weather, and vegetation. To determining the crop growth and farming becomes the success of using the above-mentioned factors (http://www.busboard.com/BB400T). Hence, the farmers and landowners have to think to use these newer smart farming systems to monitor their crop fields (). Smart farming systems can reduce waste, save money, and improve the plant cultivation system (Rao et al., 2019). Smart farming includes big data, Internet of Things (IoT), and the cloud for auto-mating, monitoring, analyzing, and tracking operations. Smart farming is also

Figure 6.1   Disease-Affected Mango.

Figure 6.2   Disease-Affected Orange.

Figure 6.3   Disease-Affected Green Pepper.

Figure 6.4   Disease-Affected Tomato.

Figure 6.5   Citrus-Pest Leaf Disease.

Figure 6.6   Air Burn Leaf Disease.

Figure 6.7   White Spot Leaf Disease.

Figure 6.8 Oak Pest Leaf Disease.

named precision agriculture and it is monitored by a sensor and managed by software. Precision agriculture helps reduce waste, whole costs, and improve the products' quantity and quality. It leads to better production, waste management, and cost reduction (Nayyar, 2016). To monitor the anomalies in livestock health or crop growth used to remove the risk of losing yields. Multiple processes can be activated in smart devices for automated services to enhance product volume and quality. Figure 6.9 depicts IoT-based smart farming.

Smart agriculture is utilizing innovative and modern technologies in agriculture to achieve efficient and better results in a crop management system, deploying new techniques and soil analysis to harvest crops and cultivation. By using precision types of equipment like the IoT sensors, models, and geopositioning systems, big data, actuators, drones, robotics, irrigation management, and fertilizers, and so on (Gutiérrez et al., 2013). The farmers can boost their production and harvesting while reducing the time, efforts, and labor required for these tasks. Smart agriculture helps in monitoring every detail related to the production of crops, harvesting and weed management, and soil analysis. Smart farming helps farmers to adjust their nutrition to prevent disease, enhance herd health, and monitor individual animals in their lands. Smart farming benefits are given below (Gutiérrez et al., 2013).

- Sensors (temperature, leaf and soil moisture, nitrates, electrical conductivity, radiation, evapotranspiration, and so on) monitor the plant and soil, resulting in a better environment for plant growth.

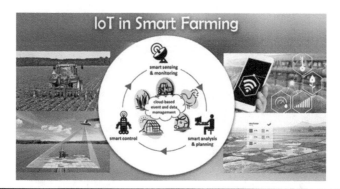

Figure 6.9 IoT-Based Smart Farming (https://data-flair.training/blogs/iotapplications-in-agriculture/).

Greater sustainability and environmental protection   Higher productivity   Economic benefits

Figure 6.10 Smart Farming Benefits.

- Find real-time data: The sensing devices are used to the frequent monitoring system of the agricultural land. It gives real-time crop images, which is used to formers to get information about their crops and plants at all time (Lee et al., 2013).
- Save cost and time: Reduce chemical and fertilizer application costs, hence pollution is reduced.
- It can be integrated with farm management software, like Agrivi, to make all activities on the farm easier and to improve farm productivity.
- Other important benefits are reduction of overlap spraying, less soil compaction, needs less manpower, less fuel use, and time-consuming. Figure 6.10 represents the smart farming benefits (Nayyar, 2016).

6.3 Smart Farming Components

In the present scenario, smart farming is considered a sophisticated and fruitful platform for performing agriculture and it can increase food growth. The growth of technological developments, their applications, and the arrival of numerous connected devices are combined and now these are used in the agriculture industry. Smart forming primarily uses IoT technology and this can tremendously reduce the farmer's severe physical work in the agricultural field. This technology aims to create different possibilities that can be used to improve productivity. The major benefits of using IoT in the agriculture domain are well-planned usage of water, soil identification, type of fertilizers required for the plants, cultivation, and many more (Lee et al., 2013). The agriculture sector fulfills the demand for food of the nation. IoT uses the latest sensor technology for smart farming.

- Sensors assist the mapping fields in recognizing their micro-scale to preserve resources such as soil, water, fertilizer, etc.
- Subsequently mapping crop yields, farmers can apply fertilizer and weed treatments and monitor their land.
- Smart agriculture uses cellular wireless and IoT technologies for remote connectivity.
- Nowadays, in smart agriculture, robots, computer imaging, drones, and remote sensors have played a vital role. These devices will collect the data from the agriculture domain and it carries out the analysis task using various machine learning algorithms and analytical tools and find knowledgeable insights. This will help the farmers to make effective decisions (Suo et al., 2012).

6.4 Smart Farming Application Areas

Agriculture acts as an important role in manufacturing and livelihood. The major application areas of smart farming are described below.

6.4.1 Precision Farming

Precision farming is the procedure of making farming methods easier and it also manages cattle and agronomy growth. Precision agriculture may be a well-known smart agriculture sector. Precision farming offers more precise growing of crops and livestock management system (http://www.cybronyx.com/breadboard-power-suply.html). IoT, various sensors and control systems, robotics, autonomous vehicles, and automatic hardware are used in this method of the farm management system. Figure 6.11 shows precision farming (https://www.sparkfun.com/products/13678). Precision farming improves the productivity, creates a pollution-free environment, and gives profits to the farmers.

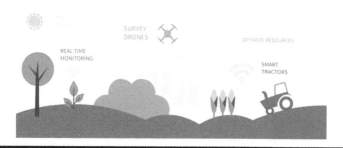

Figure 6.11 Precision Farming (https://data-flair.training/blogs/iot-applicationsin-agriculture/).

6.4.2 Agricultural Drones

In the present situation, the agricultural industry is in development to enhance or improve various farming practices with the help of agriculture drones. Commonly aerial drones are used for land analysis, crop monitoring, planting, crop health assessment, and crop spraying. Sensors and cameras were fixed in the drones to take photography of crop fields and observe the agricultural lands (M.K. Gayatri). The drone monitoring system is a promising technology in the agricultural industry to get information about crop fields. Drones collect the image data from agricultural lands and then send it to the labs to analyze the affected plants and/or corps (Lustiness et al., 2015). Figure 6.12 presents the agricultural drones.

6.4.3 Livestock Management

Smart farming technology is used to quickly find and locate the farmer's pet animals like cattle, goats, chickens, sheep, and pigs in their large agricultural lands very easily. The wireless IoT device is used to simplify this process as mentioned above, i.e., it identifies the sick of cattle and affected cattle will break away from the crowd. It is helpful to control the quick spreading of the disease to the other cattle. Livestock management significantly reduces the time and labor cost as formers can find their animals with the assistance of IoT-based sensor devices. This device gathers data regarding this situation; hence, it will help farmers identify their livestock condition. By getting assistance from the IoT-based sensor devices, the farmers have the feasibility to track their cattle, which can substantially decrease the labor cost (Suo et al., 2012). Figure 6.13 shows the livestock monitoring system.

Figure 6.12 Agricultural Drones (https://www.cropin.com/iot-internet-of-things-applications-agriculture/).

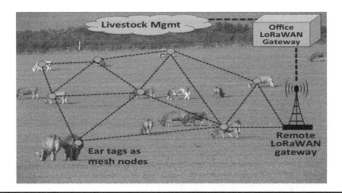

Figure 6.13 Livestock Monitoring System (https://data-flair.training/blogs/iotapplications-in-agriculture/).

6.4.4 Smart Greenhouse

A smart greenhouse is used to enhance agricultural yields, such as vegetables, fruits, greens, flowers, and more. A greenhouse is fully covered by a green sheet on small agricultural land; IoT devices like smart hydroponics, wireless sensors, fan, edge computer, and cameras assist it. These greenhouse system observers the plant growing and eliminating the manual involvement (https://www.arduino.cc/en/Main/arduinoBoardMega2560). Various sensors are used in the greenhouse to control the environment for plant requirements. Hence, the smart greenhouse maintains the climate, energy, saves money from labor charges, and prevents production losses (http://

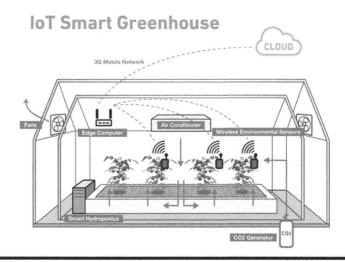

Figure 6.14 Smart Greenhouse (https://jhg.hadiyatransformations.pw/smartgreenhouse-using-iot.html).

www.cybronyx.com/breadboard-power-suply.html). Figure 6.14 illustrates the smart greenhouse.

6.5 Smart Farming in Industries

The advantages of smart farming are to increase productivity and to reduce waste generation. Smart farming can achieve this through the usage of IoT technology. IoT-based smart farming in industrial applications is given below.

6.5.1 Robotics

In the recent development, combined IoT and AI technology used robotics for cultivating the plants in the agricultural industry. Smart agribots, weeding robots, and harvesting robots are used in the smart farming system. Figure 6.15 presents the weeding robots for smart farming and Figure 6.16 shows smart agribots. Figure 6.17 represents the material handling process. Figure 6.18 shows the harvesting robotics.

Weeding robots are combined with image processing technology, which uses the image database to identify the similarity of the plants and spray the pesticides and herbicides (weed out) directly by using robotic hands. Some of

Figure 6.15 Weeding Robots (https://www.cropin.com/iot-internet-of-things-applications-agriculture/).

Figure 6.16 Smart Agribots (https://www.cropin.com/iot-internet-of-things-applications-agriculture/).

the weeding robots are ecoRobotix, SwagBot, Tertill, Naïo Technologies, RIPPA, ASTERIX, AgBot II, Blue River LettuceBot2, and Hortibot.

The tractor is an important piece of equipment in the agricultural industry for organizing the mud for planting. It needs manpower to drive the tractor and it needs lots of time for preparing the soil. Hence, IoT introduced smart agribots for automatic driving technology in agricultural lands. The sensor and GPS are fixed in the agribots; hence, the farmers controlled the agribots in their home. The benefits of agribots is working all the time, reducing labor charges and time-consuming processes (https://www.cropin.com/iot-internet-of-things-applications-agriculture/).

Figure 6.17 Material Handling (https://www.cropin.com/iot-internet-of-things-applications-agriculture/).

Figure 6.18 Harvesting Robotics (https://www.cropin.com/iot-internet-of-things-applications-agriculture/).

The smart agribots are used to collect fruits, greens, and vegetables from agricultural lands. It minimizes the human resources; it operates all day and night. The image processing technique is used to store the fruit and vegetable extracted features in the database. Based on the similarity, this robot identified the fruits and veggies and collected.

6.5.2 *Remote Sensing*

IoT is performed based on sensors; these sensors are used in remote sensing for gathering data. Sensors are devices sensitive to irregularities. An analytical dashboard is used for farmers; with this they can perform the crop monitoring tasks. The decisions are taken based on the insights of these analytical tasks. Figure 6.19 represents remote sensing.

Crop Monitoring – The significant features considered for observing the crops are size, shape, light, humidity, and temperature. The sensor cameras monitor the dissimilarities of these features. Normally, the sensor cameras are placed in various places on the farm. If the sensor analyzed any difference in the plant, it notified the former.

Weather Conditions – Different parameters of weather data are temperature, precipitation, and humidity. Sensors are used to collect these parameter values in agricultural lands.

Soil Quality – To analyze the mud quality is an important factor in growing plants in crop fields. Mud quality is determined by the nutrient value of soil, farms or acidity, and soil sewerage capacity. Hence, farmers can know how to improve their cultivation with changing the needed fertilizer and watering for crops (www.cropin.com).

6.5.3 *Computer Imaging*

Sensors cameras are installed in divergent places on the farm. In addition to this, drones are also used and these drones are strengthened with cameras for capturing the images of plants. Then the images are stored in the image database and it will be processed by image processing technique. The fundamental definition of image processing is to process the raw input images using computer algorithms. The input image database is processed using image processing

Figure 6.19   Remote Sensing (https://www.cropin.com/iot-internet-of-things-applications-agriculture/).

Figure 6.20   Drone Camera.

algorithms to identify the disease in plants. Image post-processing (recognition), classification, feature extraction, segmentation, edge detection, and pre-processing are important steps in plant disease prediction. Figure 6.20 shows the drone camera.

6.6 Service Providers of Smart Farming

6.6.1 Mothive

Mothive (https://www.plugandplaytechcenter.com/resources/10-precision-agriculture-companies-watch-2019/) helps farmers to improve their likelihood and regulate the crops, maximize efficiency, and decrease the waste in automatic agronomy services. Mothive ladybird is a device that gives the farmers an affordable and simple solution to extract information about crop fields. Figure 6.21 illustrates Mothive.

6.6.2 CropX

CropX developed a cloud-based software solution company integrated with wireless sensors. This system increases crop yield and cost savings and saves energy and water while conserving the atmosphere. This company provides an automatic solution to crop fields for water management in the same crop field in various parts and it makes irrigation maps. Figure 6.22 shows the CropX.

6.6.3 Arable

Arable is an analytics-based company, which is embedded with IoT for the smart farming management system. This tool is used to monitor the crop field and weather station. It is a reliable decision-making system to save customer money,

Figure 6.21   Mothive.

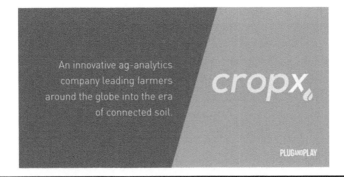

Figure 6.22   CropX.

reduce risk, and preserve natural resources (www.plugandplaytechcenter.com). Figure 6.23 illustrates Arable.

6.6.4 Ceres Imaging

Ceres is an imaging company that uses an aerial spectral image to grow crops, fertilizer, and optimize water. This system uses low-flying planes to take multispectral super-resolution images. These images are processed by using innovative image processing techniques for crop fields. The images produce higher accuracy information about every plant and crop field. Figure 6.24 illustrates Ceres Imaging.

Figure 6.23   Arable.

Figure 6.24   Ceres Imaging.

6.6.5 Gamaya

Gamaya was developed for smart farming in diagnostics services in Brazil. This company using patented-imaging technology to capture crop images inefficient way. Gamaya monitored the growth of fertilization optimization and provided quick detection of crop disease like pests and diagnostics of stresses such as water stress, mechanical damages, soil compaction, and nutrient deficiency (www.plugandplaytechcenter.com). Figure 6.25 presents Gamaya.

6.6.6 AgriData

AgriData provides digitalized agriculture for tracing permanent crops (vines and trees, high-value crops). Farmers using this product to predict their yields, detect

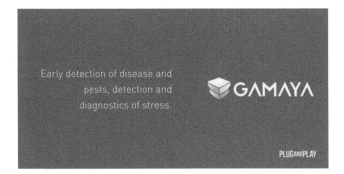

Figure 6.25 Gamaya.

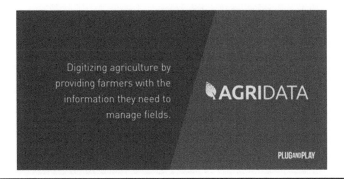

Figure 6.26 AgriData.

pests, and time their harvests (www.plugandplaytechcenter.com). Figure 6.26 illuminates AgriData.

6.6.7 Agrowatcher

For the identification of crop diseases like pests, water stress, and infestation Agrowatcher uses multispectral imaging and computer vision technology. This system uses a digital camera to record multiple bands with higher re-solution. After the raw input image was processed by using computer vision and machine learning algorithm for analysis for finding the disease in the crop field. This system is fully automated, using expensive equipment and replacing labor-intensive processes. Figure 6.27 shows Agrowatcher.

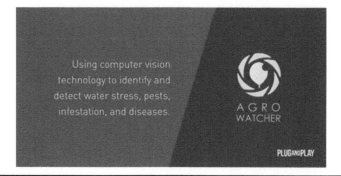

Figure 6.27   Agrowatcher.

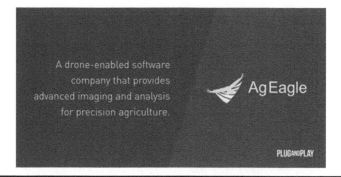

Figure 6.28   AgEagle.

6.6.8 AgEagle

The main aim of the AgEagle was developed for the precision agriculture industry. This company used advanced little Unmanned Aerial Vehicles (UAVs or Drones) and distributed technology for the crop management system. Figure 6.28 illustrates AgEagle.

6.6.9 PrecisionHawk

PrecisionHawk is combining remote-sensing technologies, advanced data analytics, and aerial system to improve the smart farming system in the business sector. An information delivery company offers aerial data gathering analysis and processing to give illegal information across an extensive choice of data-intensive civilian industries (https://www.plugandplaytechcenter. com/resources/10-precision-agriculture-companies-watch-2019/). Figure 6.29 shows PrecisionHawk.

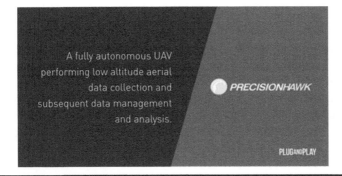

Figure 6.29 PrecisionHawk.

Figure 6.30 Aker Technologies.

6.6.10 Aker Technologies

Smart in-season crop management was developed by Aker Technologies to quicken the adoption of precision farming applies across the industry. Patented biometric sensors and computer vision techniques were applied to develop the Aker. It used to classify, detect, measure pest pressure, crop diseases, fertility issues, and airborne in every plant in the crop fields (www.plugandplaytechcenter.com). Figure 6.30 presents Aker Technologies.

6.7 Conclusion

In the classical way of farming, the farmers find it difficult to monitor larger farms and agricultural lands. It is difficult for farmers to find their experts and sense the problem like amending soil conditions and watering location and pests on plants. To overcome the traditional system, IoT introduced smart farming to increase production, reduce production costs, and use fewer resources for an accurate monitoring system in all aspects such as water, soil, weather, and vegetation. The drone monitoring system is a promising technology in the agricultural industry to get information about crop fields. Smart agribots are used for automated driving technology in agricultural lands. This chapter reviews basic concepts of IoT in smart farming, the advantage of smart farming, precision farming, agricultural drones, application areas of smart farming, and also service providers of smart farming are discussed.

References

Gayatri, M.K., Jayasakthi, J., Anandhamala, G.S., 2015. Giving smart agriculture solutions to farmers for better yielding using IoT. IEEE International Conference on Technological Innovations in ICT for Agriculture and Rural.

Gutiérrez, J., Villa-Medina, J.F., NietoGaribay, A., ÁngelPortaGándara, M., 2013. Computerized irrigation system using a wireless sensor network and GPRS module. *IEEE Transactions on Instrumentation and Measurements*, 0018–9456.

http://blog.agrivi.com

http://honartabiat.ir/plant-disease/

http://internetofthingsagewnda.techtarget.com

http://iotdunia.com

http://www.biz4intelllia.com

http://www.busboard.com/BB400T

http://www.cybronyx.com/breadboard-power-supply.html

http://www.iotforall.com

https://biology.usu.edu/recruitment/who_we_are/Nischwitz%20lab%202021.pdf

https://organicgardeningeek.com/how-to-avoid-fungus-during-summer/

https://treediseases.cfans.umn.edu/sites/treediseases.cfans.umn.edu/files/leaf_rusts_2014_0.pdf

https://ufstonefruit.wordpress.com/2019/02/22/peach-nectarine-and-plum-management-guide/

https://www.arduino.cc/en/Main/arduinoBoardMega2560

https://www.cropin.com/iot-internet-of-things-applications-agriculture/

https://www.maximintegrated.com/en/products/analog/sensors-and-sensor-interface/DS18B20.html

https://www.plugandplaytechcenter.com/resources/10-precision-agriculture-companieswatch-2019/

https://www.researchgate.net/publication/313804002_Smart_farming_IoT_based_smart_sensors_agriculture_stick_for_live_temperature_and_moisture_monitoring_using_Arduino_cloud_computing_solar_technology

https://www.sparkfun.com/products/13322

https://www.sparkfun.com/products/13678

https://www.tarunbharat.net/Encyc/2019/2/13/Artical-of-Vibhag-pramukh.amp.html

Lakshmisudha K., Hegde, S., Cole, N., Iyer, S., 2011. Good particularity most stationed cultivation spinning sensors. *State-of-Theart Weekly Going from Microcomputer Applications* (0975-8887).

Lee, M., Hwang, J., Yoe, H., 2013. Agrarian protection system based on IoT. IEEE sixteenth International Conference on Computational Science and Engineering.

Lee, M., Hwang, J., Yoe, H., 2013. Agricultural production system based on IoT. In: IEEE 16th International Conference on Computational Science and Engineering (CSE), pp. 833–837.

Lustiness, R Nandurkar, Thool, Slant R., Thool R. Tumor, 2015. Plan together with situation coming from rigor horticulture technique executing trans-missions sensor network, *IEEE World Consultation Toward Tele Mechanics, Regulate, Intensity also Wiring (ACES).*

Meena, Ashvin & Meena, Ram & Meena, Ajay. 2019. Use of Precision Agriculture for Sustainability and Environmental Protection.

Nalajala, P., Hemanth Kumar, D., Ramesh, P., Godavarthi, B., 2017. Design and Implementation of Modern Automated Real Time Monitoring System for Agriculture using Internet of Things (IoT) *Journal of Engineering and Applied Sciences* 12, 9389– 9393.

Nayyar, A. 2016. An encyclopedia coverage of compiler's, Programmer's & Simulator's for 8051, PIC, AVR, ARM, Arduino embedded technologies. *International Journal of Reconfigurable and Embedded Systems (IJRES)* 5(1), 18–42.

Patil, V.C., Al-Gaadi, K.A., Biradar, D.P., Rangaswamy, M., 2012. Internet of Things (IoT) and cloud computing for agriculture: An overview. Proceedings of Agro-Informatics and Precision Agriculture, India, 292–296.

Rao, S., Nalajala, P., Sangeetha, Y., Balaji, O., Navya K., 2019. Design of a smart mobile case framework based on the Internet of Things. *Advances in Intelligent Systems and Computing* 815, 657–666.

Smith, I.G., 2012. The Internet of Thing 2012: New horizons. *Internet of Things – New security and Privacy Challenges, Computer Law & Security Review* 26(1), 23–30.

Suo, H., Wan, J., Zou, C., Liu, J. 2012. Security in the Internet of Things: A review. In: Computer Science and Electronics Engineering (ICCSEE), 2012 International Conference on, 3, pp. 648–651.

Vidyadevi Kumari, M. 2013. Continuous mechanization along with patrol process under the authority of most aerodynamic agriculture. Universal Newspaper Made from Appraisal Furthermore Probe Contemporary Scientific Knowledge Together with Structures (IJRRASE), 3(1), 7–12.

Chapter 7

Artificial Intelligence and Internet of Things: The Smart City Perspective

A. Sangeetha[1] and T. Amudha[2]

[1]*Ph.D Research Scholar, Department of Computer Applications, Bharathiar University, Coimbatore, India*
[2]*Associate Professor, Department of Computer Applications, Bharathiar University, Coimbatore, India*

Contents

DOI: 10.1201/9781003175872-7

7.1 Introduction

Digital transformation plays a significant role in the development of the smart city, over the past decades. The nine essential technologies associated with digital transformation are represented in Figure 7.1. These technologies help to improvise the decision making based on advanced analytics, customer experience, automation of manual activities, the innovation of products, and risk optimization. Among these, artificial intelligence (AI) and the Internet of Things (IoT) are the two most important technologies that play a primary role in developing smart city applications. A combination of connected devices, software, network connectivity, platform applications, and various stakeholders' data are expected to emerge in all real-time processes.

7.1.1 Artificial Intelligence

The name "artificial intelligence" was named by John McCarthy, a scientist at Stanford University in the mid-1950s and described AI as the "Science of building intelligent machines". It is a branch of computer science that has the ability to extract intelligence and creates new intelligent machines that perform certain tasks associated with intelligent beings. AI refers to a set of computational tools aimed to emulate human-like intelligence to perform tasks in different sectors such as healthcare, manufacturing, retail, banking, and so on. AI system involves learning, reasoning, and auto-correction. AI systems can understand human speech; recognize objects, faces and voices; and process natural languages. It can be applied in the gaming industry, defense and military, automotive industry, healthcare, and so on. A report by PwC (PricewaterhouseCoopers) suggested that the evolution of AI happens along with a band from assisted

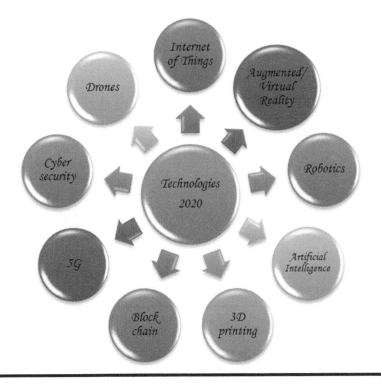

Figure 7.1   2020 Technologies.

intelligence, via augmented intelligence, to autonomous intelligence (Leveraging the upcoming distributions from AI and IoT) represented in Figure 7.2.

7.1.2 Internet of Things

Internet of Things (IoT) is described as the Internetworking of physical objects such as sensors, cars, homes, electronic devices, virtual objects, actuators, and many others that are able to communicate among themselves and with external devices over the Internet. IoT-enabled objects will observe, identify and recognize the surroundings without the help of humans and have an ability to move independently (An Introduction to the Internet of Things). IoT applications are moving forward to a network of intelligent objects, capable of addressing the interaction between self-governing systems and humans. IoT can be widely used in remote patient monitoring, retail marketing, wearable devices, driverless cars, and the motorized industry. IoT is also referred to as the fourth Industrial Revolution or Industry 4.0. In order to acquire the benefits of IoT,

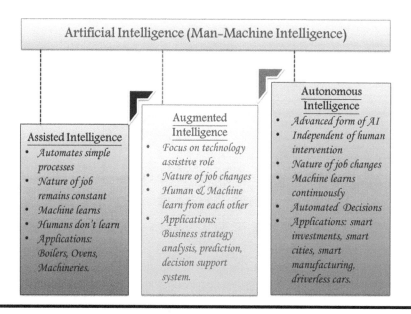

Figure 7.2 AI Evolution Continuum.

data, speed, and accuracy of the data analysis need to be improved. IoT-enabling technologies are illustrated in Figure 7.3.

AI and IoT are standalone expertise and can be applied together to provide a smarter way in real-world applications. A number of devices can be connected over the network and generate an enormous amount of data and those data has the potential to deliver amazing insights but how to analyze those data is always uncertain. To overcome this uncertainty, AI is a perfect application for making sense of those huge amounts of data and produce significant results. AI is the engine that facilitates analytics and decision-making for the data collected by IoT devices. AI also provides solutions, predictions, rapid response, and re-commendations when linked with IoT. Amazon's Alexa, apple's Siri, and Google Home are some of the working systems based on AI and IoT.

7.2 Convergence of AI and IoT

The combination of AI and the Internet of Things (IoT) will dramatically increase the benefits of digital transformation for end-users, industrial, en-terprise, and government market segments. The main purpose of combining AI and IoT is to avoid downtime through predictive capabilities, to improve

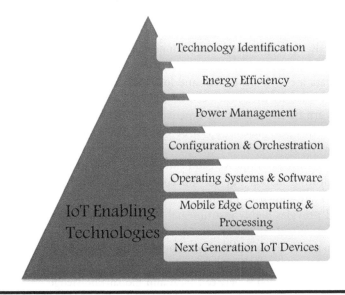

Figure 7.3   IoT-Enabling Technologies.

operational efficiency, and to make additional sense to IoT data. AI coupling with IoT will make stronger security, reduce fraud, and safeguard resources. AI and IoT can be referred to as "Artificial Intelligence of Things" (AIoT), whereas IoT improves the value of AI-based on connectivity and data exchange and AI enhances the importance of IoT data through machine learning and decision making. AIoT is defined "to connect IoT devices with sensors and make them perform intelligent tasks with help of AI capabilities." AIoT makes life easier by providing intelligent automation, predictive analytics, and proactive intervention. The working mechanism of IoT and AI is shown in Figure 7.4.

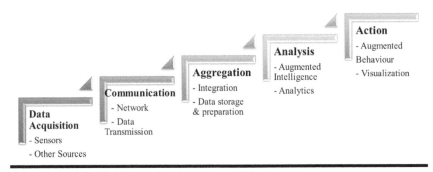

Figure 7.4   Working Mechanism of IoT and AI.

7.3 Need for AI-Enabled IoT

An IoT deals with different sensors connected with devices over the Internet and generates an enormous amount of data in day-to-day life, whereas the captured data are time-dependent and lose their value within milliseconds. As the data provided by the sensors can be analyzed with AI, while AI enables the device to learn from the data and experience. With the help of AI-enabled IoT, innovative intelligent machines can be crafted that mimic the smart behavior and support decision making with little or no human intervention. AI and IoT together can deliver an improved and entirely new product and services not only for the industrial market but also for consumer markets. The benefits of AI-enabled IoT are shown in Figure 7.5.

The AI provides highly instrumental solutions to IoT data to [e],

    a. Manage, analyze, and create meaningful perceptions
    b. Assure accuracy and speed in data analysis
    c. Maintain a balance between local and global knowledge
    d. Provide custom-made privacy with data
    e. Enhance security, to defend from threats and cyber attacks

The potential benefits of the convergence are:

    a. Intelligent decisions
    b. Enhanced operational efficiency

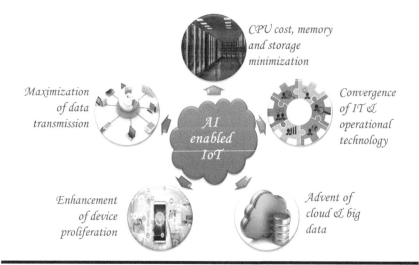

Figure 7.5 AI-Enabled IoT.

c. Improved risk management analysis

d. Better products and services

e. Scalability

f. Reduced unintentional interruption

The presumed challenges of this convergence of AI and IoT are:

a. Compatibility

b. Complexity

c. Privacy/Security

d. Safety

e. Ethical and legal issues

f. Artificial stupidity

7.4 Application Domains of AI-Enabled IoT

AI and IoT applications are expanding steadily and several industries are investing in AIoT applications. This section explores the different real-time AIoT applications.

a. **Smart homes** – Smart homes are also referred to as "home automation or domotics". It allows the owner to control devices like entertainment systems, lights, thermostats, and other home appliances remotely using a system, tablet, or smartphone via the Internet (Leveraging the upcoming distributions from AI and IoT). The devices in the network may have wired or wireless connections. Zigbee and Z-Wave are the two major radio networks that play a prominent role in home automation. They enable monitoring and management of utilization, alarm system for security purposes, and energy efficiency. AI and IoT help to reduce costs, conserve energy, and increase the convenience of the inhabitants.

b. **Smart farming** – It refers to the irrigation automation system, precision farming, agricultural drones, livestock monitoring, water management, and fertilizer minimization. It makes use of high-technology systems to enhance small- and large-scale production and reduces waste by using temperature, soil moisture, humidity, light sensors, and actuators (Alliance for Internet of Things Innovation (AIOTI)). To ensure the crop healthiness and harvesting automated equipment and advanced robots are used in agricultural fields.

c. **Autonomous vehicles** – A vehicle that is able to optimize its own operations using on-board sensors, intelligence, and connectivity (Wang and Wang, 2019). It is going to be the next revolution in the automobile industry. Such systems are fully integrated, highly adaptable, and function independently by perceiving the environment and by taking dynamic actions. The aim is to control traffic congestions and avoid accidents.

d. **Industrial IoT** – Empowered by industrial engineering with sensors, software, and AI techniques to create intelligent machines. The data from the IoT devices are collected and analyzed by AI to provide meaningful insights (Alliance for Internet of Things Innovation (AIOTI)). IIoT has the capability to enable energy management, optimize the resources for manufacturing, maintenance prediction, early warnings, optimization of processes, self-organized logistics management, and quality control enforcement.

e. **Smart cities** – It makes use of information and communication technology (ICT) to improve quality, operational efficiency, and performance of urban services. AI together with IoT addresses the challenges possessed by the urban population and helps in traffic management, water management, energy management, environmental monitoring, and many more (Saba et al., 2020).

f. **Wearables** – Wearable devices like smartwatches, smart clothes, Google glasses, bracelets, and health monitors facilitate self-monitoring and self-management through sensors, actuators, and IoT platforms (Alliance for Internet of Things Innovation (AIOTI)). These components are lightweight, easy to wear, and assist the user in real time. The tiny microchips embedded in the wearable devices enable data collection, data integration with other devices or applications, device management, interoperability, security, and so on.

g. **Cognitive systems** – Creates a novel method which is applicable to the user's sense of taste, generates an optimized menu for every individual, and adapts to local requirements automatically. It involves three components namely understanding, reasoning, and learning (Cognitive IoT). Understanding refers that "a model can be developed by means of an enormous volume of structured and unstructured data". The reasoning makes the model derive solutions for a specific or related problem without having the solutions. Learning automatically discovers new knowledge based on the understanding from the obtained data.

h. **Smart retail** – IoT and AI empower retail stores as "smart retail". It improves retail management and provides an opportunity for the retailers to connect with the customers to improve the in-store experiences. The real-time data gathers information about customer's requirements based on their searching criteria and delivers the products or services (Alliance for Internet of Things Innovation (AIOTI)). Insights developed via inquiries, customer service communication, purchase history, and profile details will be useful for personalized campaigns and predict future trends.

i. **Smart grids** – These are data communication networks incorporated with the power grid. The power and information flow are bidirectional between the generation and transmission phases. The grids are interconnected with sensors and devices to collect an enormous amount of data in real time. The information obtained from distribution stations and sub-stations, transmission lines, and end users are analyzed. It helps in allocating the proper resources and reduces the risk. In power management, smart grids are used to predict the power supply and demand (Hossain et al., 2019).

j. **Predictive analytics** – It is defined as an analysis of historical data or existing data to find a pattern or user behavior for future outcomes. AI enables self-learning techniques to process data from IoT systems and projects the future based on the learning inputs and targets (Leveraging the upcoming distributions from AI and IoT). Accurate predictions can assist in making decisions for various real-time applications like harvesting a crop, smart retail, environmental monitoring, airplane scheduling, and so on.

k. **Healthcare** – AI and IoT empower the machines to diagnose, analyze, and predict several types of diseases, monitor the patient's health conditions such as tracking of heartbeat rate, temperature, physical activities, and so on. It also helps scientists in exploring new drug findings and medicine development, which helps people to effectively handle health-related concerns (Alliance for Internet of Things Innovation (AIOTI)).

7.5 Smart City Environment

A smart city environment is referred to as "a city that is digitally enabled". IBM smarter city-states "Universe is becoming instrumental, interconnected and intelligent". A smart city is powered by lots of technologies, whereas AI-enabled IoT plays a major role in making the city "smarter". A report by the International Data Corporation has stated that the smart city projects are likely to increase to almost $158 billion USD by the year 2022, due to the rising investment in strengthening the infrastructure for improved services and connectivity to facilitate IoT capabilities. The smart city environment comprises a huge number of IoT devices, user interfaces, software solutions, and communication networks connected with different devices over the Internet and enriched with AI technologies to support decision making without human

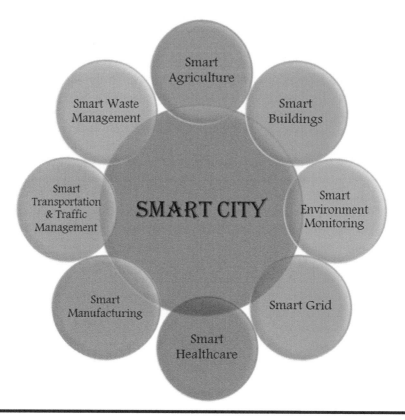

Figure 7.6 Smart City Components.

inference. It optimizes the city functions and drives economic growth which improves the quality of life based on data analysis combined with different technologies. Smart city development aims to facilitate improved delivery of services to inhabitants with less infrastructure and cost. Smart city applications involve in boosting financial gains. The government, technical experts, and urban organizers are the works to transform an ambitious idea into reality. Figure 7.6 specifies the several components used in the development of a smart city (Bawany and Shamsi, 2015).

7.5.1 Smart City Initiatives Worldwide

The major highlights of worldwide smart city development acquired from the "Smart cities – Thematic Research" report by GlobalData are represented in Table 7.1.

Table 7.1 Smart City Initiatives – Worldwide (History of Smart Cities Timeline)

Year	Country/City/Organization	Initiatives
1974	Los Angeles, United States	Big data was used to build a smart city. To make the policy decisions, Los Angele's Community Analysis Bureau uses the technologies such as cluster analysis, computer databases, and infrared aerial photography.
1994	Amsterdam, Netherland	Amsterdam digital city promotes the use of the Internet for individuals referred to as "De Digitale Stad (DDS)"
2005	Cisco Systems	Invested up to $25 million over five years on smart city research
2008	International Business Machines Corporation (IBM)	IBM smarter planet vision focused on three I's—Instrumentation, Interconnectedness, and Intelligence.
2009	IBM	Initiated the promotion of smart cities, extensive support for the smooth functioning of the cities, reduce expenditure and effectively utilize the available resources.
2009	American Recovery and Reinvestment Act (Recovery Act)	It provides the Department of Energy (DOE), the US$4.5 billion to modernize the electric power grid.
2009	European Union (EU)	Electricity directive requires EU member states to ensure deployment of 80% smart metering systems for consumers by 2020.

(Continued)

Table 7.1 *(Continued)* **Smart City Initiatives – Worldwide (History of Smart Cities Timeline)**

Year	Country/City/Organization	Initiatives
2010	Yokohama, Japan	Japanese government has identified Yokohama, a Japanese city south of Tokyo, to establish "Next-Generation Energy Infrastructure and Social System Demonstration Area".
2011	IBM	IBM selected 24 cities as smart cities universally from 200 applicants. IBM intended to spend around $50 million to make the city smarter.
2011	Smart City Expo World Congress (SCEWC 2011), Barcelona	SCEWC 2011 brought together around 6000 visitors from 50 different countries and 300 presenters from 30 different countries shared their knowledge, experience, and vision-related to a smart city.
2012	Barcelona, Spain	A city deploys a responsible data-driven urban system, including public transit, parking, waste management, and street lighting.
2012	Ministry of Housing and Urban Rural Development (MOHURD), China	Proclaimed 90 cities to be the first batch of pilot smart cities.
2013	Smart London Board, London	London smart cities vision and investment plans were devised by the board.
2014	MOHURD, China	Launched 103 cities as second batch pilot smart cities
2014	Vienna, Austria	Smart City Wien Framework Strategy (SCWFS), Vienna is projecting its development towards becoming a "smart

(Continued)

Table 7.1 *(Continued)* Smart City Initiatives – Worldwide (History of Smart Cities Timeline)

Year	Country/City/Organization	Initiatives
		city". The first and foremost aim of SCWFS is resource preservation.
2015	MOHURD, China	MOHURD along with the Ministry of Science and Technology announced 84 cities as third-batch pilot smart cities.
2015	Ministry of Urban Development, India	"100 smart cities mission" launched by India's Prime Minister Narendra Modi. A US $14 billion was approved for the development of 100 smart cities.
2016	Columbus, Ohio	Secretary of the U.S. Department of Transportation (DoT) announced that Columbus won the smart cities challenge. The city received a grant of about $50 million.
2017	Department for Digital, Culture, Media & Sport, United Kingdom (UK)	Announced 5G Testbeds and Trials Programme – a nationally coordinated program of investment in 5G
2017	Special Administrative Regions (SAR) department, Hong Kong	SAR delineated the smart city blueprint of Hong Kong.
2018	Sidewalk Labs	Google's sibling company, Sidewalk Labs, revealed its plan to redevelop a stretch of Toronto's waterfront with "smart" features.
2018	Smart London Together, London	It is the London mayor's goal to see London as the top class smart city.
2018	IESE Business School Cities in Motion Index	IESE Business School's Department of Strategy and the

(Continued)

Table 7.1 *(Continued)* **Smart City Initiatives – Worldwide (History of Smart Cities Timeline)**

Year	Country/City/Organization	Initiatives
		Center for Globalization and Strategy have initiated the IESE Cities in Motion Strategies. According to IESE 2018, the top three highly developed smart cities are London, New York, and Amsterdam.
2018	Smart City Expo World Congress, Barcelona	Singapore awarded as Smart City of 2018 in Smart City Expo World Congress held at Barcelona. The country was recognized as a "Smart Nation" as it transforms the country, through technology.
2019	World Economic Forum (WEF)	WEF collaborates with G20 nations, which leads to a new worldwide effort to establish global norms and guidelines for implementing smart city technologies.
2019	Federal Communications Commission (FCC), US	US FCC authorized Salt Lake City and the West Harlem neighbourhood of New York City as "innovation zones". The cities act as test-beds for network technology experiments and wireless communications, including 5G, across a range of spectrum bands.
2020	Vietnam	Vietnam kicks off a $4.2 billion smart city project in Hanoi's Dong Anh district, in partnership with BRG Group and Sumitomo, a Japanese finance house and targets to complete by 2028.

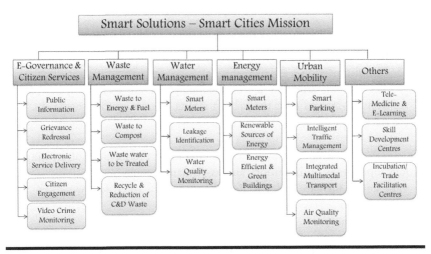

Figure 7.7 Smart City Applications (Smart Cities Mission Statement & Guidelines Report).

7.5.2 *Smart City Initiatives in India*

In India, the "100 smart cities mission" was launched by the honorable Prime Minister Narendra Modi in June 2015. For the enhancement of 100 smart cities under the ministry of urban development US$14 billion was approved. The smart city mission promotes cities to deliver core infrastructure and a better quality of life to their citizens. The elements included in the smart city core infrastructure are sufficient water and electricity supply, management of waste, well-organized urban mobility, public transport, affordable housing, robustness, IT connectivity and digitalization, e-governance, sustainable environment, and safety and security of citizen's, health, and education. It also focuses on a clean and sustainable environment and makes use of several applications of "smart" solutions shown in Figure 7.7. The application of smart solutions involves the use of data, information, and technology for better services and infrastructure. It promotes area-based developments that involve city retrofitting, redevelopment, and green-field development. Pan-city development initiative envisions the application of smart solutions to the existing city-wide infrastructure (Smart Cities Mission Statement & Guidelines Report).

Smart cities development gets energies through the technologies such as machine learning, IoT, and automation. The four phases of smart city environment are represented below:

1. Collection of data
   Smart sensors throughout the city collect data in real-time.

2. Analysis
   Data acquired from the smart sensors are accessed in order to draw meaningful insights.
3. Communication
   The insights initiated in the analysis phase are communicated to the decision-makers with the help of strong communication networks.
4. Action

Cities use those insights drawn from the data for the purpose of creating solutions, operations optimization, and asset management.

The key challenges in developing the smart city are as follows:

a. **Infrastructure**

To analyze and gather real-time data, the smart city makes use of sensor technology. For installation and maintenance of the sensors, expensive and complicated infrastructure is required, whereas the sensors are powered by solar energy, batteries, or hard-wiring. Also, broadband wireless services need to be enhanced for data transmissions.

b. **Security and Privacy Issues**

Internet-connected devices will transmit an enormous quantity of data in real time which has many privacy concerns. The acquired data will be helpful in providing efficiency at metropolis functions, but it also offers some security risks that cannot be ignored. Data generated from the parking zone, CCTV camera footage, charging stations, GPS, and many more contains confidential information of inhabitants (Tokoro, 2016). As of now, every connected device is not cyber-resilient and hence the offenders can easily access the data and use it with illegal intention. Therefore, necessary software solutions are mandatory to strengthen the security borders of smart devices and the supporting infrastructure.

c. **Educating and Engaging the Community**

Smart cities need their citizens to be smart, should actively use the new technologies, and adapt to the environment. The major part of the smart city implementation process is to educate the community through meetings, campaigns and online education platforms which keeps citizen updated.

d. **Social Inclusion**

Smart city planning must equally consider all groups of people, not involving only technologically advanced and high-income groups of the society. Technological developments should lead people to work together, rather than dividing them based on income and education levels.

7.6 AI-Enabled IoT in Smart City Development

In smart city development, IoT infrastructure enables an intelligent way to manage buildings, energy usage, environment monitoring, health assistance, transport, and much more. Smart city development is dependent on millions of IoT devices that need to be connected together and managed by wireless sensor networks (WSN). The combined role of AI and IoT along with the generated big data in the smart city environment is shown in Figure 7.8.

This section explains the smart city layers and various real-time applications used in the development of the smart city. Figure 7.9 specifies the key layers involved in a smart city. The core layer is the ICT infrastructure, which consists of physical devices, sensors, communication networks, high-end data centers, and so on. E-governance is the next layer that lies between infrastructure and services and facilitates the development of public-sector administration. It

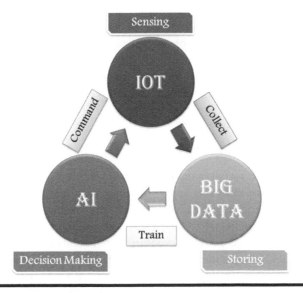

Figure 7.8   Role of AI and IoT in Smart Cities.

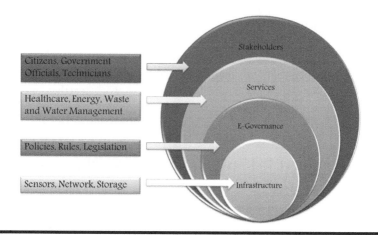

Figure 7.9   Smart City Layers (Bawany and Shamsi, 2015).

formulates the policies, rules, and legislation to enhance the performance of government organizations by which citizens are benefited. The next layer is services; it relies upon infrastructure and e-governance layers. Various public services will be provided to citizens to improve their quality of life. Finally, stakeholders are benefited in an efficient and effective manner.

7.6.1 Smart Environment

This phase deals with the preservation of natural resources. It includes environmental protection, sustainable resource management, monitoring climatic conditions, and pollution. AI and IoT play a major role in protecting environmental sustainability. The key applications of AI and IoT in environmental sustainability are monitoring of air and water quality, renewable energy production.

7.6.1.1 AI and IoT in Air Quality

Air is the basic need for all living organisms to survive on the earth. A World Health Organization (WHO) report specifies that nine out of ten people around the globe breathe polluted air, which causes varied respiratory problems. The AI and IoT technologies provide a smart way to know about the pollutants in the surroundings and personal exposure to pollutants through smartphones or smartwatches. Small-scale air quality sensors are used to measure common pollutants such as ozone (O_3), carbon dioxide (CO_2), particulate matter ($PM_{2.5}/PM_{10}$), nitrogen oxides (NO_x), and many more. The data will be communicated to the public through mobile applications that hold observed and modelled data. The real-time data from sensors, devices, and satellites are combined to perform environmental analytics using AI techniques and to upgrade data accuracy and reliability. It facilitates researchers, environmental scientists, and municipal administrations to understand air quality. Based on these outcomes, air quality prediction is done to provide preventive measures as well as framing guidelines and policies to maintain a healthier environment (Alaoui et al., 2019). Smart air quality management in office buildings, industrial plants, and urban environments will lead to an improved level of environmental protection.

The benefits of air quality monitoring are as given below:

a. Helpful in assessing the impacts caused due to poor air quality
b. To determine whether the air quality standards have adhered
c. Identification of pollution level and the air quality level at different regions
d. Assessment of long-term and short-term disorders due to air pollution
e. Taking preventive measures for the protection of health and the environment

7.6.1.2 AI and IoT in Water Quality

Water is one of the precious resources on the earth for survival. In the early days, chemical test strips were used to check the water quality, as detection of contaminants in water was found to be a very difficult and challenging task. According to WHO, around 2 billion people are still being affected by water contamination. AI and IoT technology play a major role in water quality protection and preservation. An AI-enabled IoT device makes use of PH, ultrasonic and water-flow sensors along with a PIC microcontroller to continuously detect the water quality and flow. It also classifies dangerous bacteria and harmful particles present in the water. The system can also be used in lakes, ponds, reservoirs, and rivers to monitor and assess water quality. Smart water management can also be done using AI-enabled IoT; it allows resources to be assigned based on the demand without compromising the quality. Smart cities can install AI-enabled IoT devices across different water sources by which continuous water quality assessment becomes easier. The sectors that benefit from smart water quality monitoring are water utilities, research laboratories, agriculture activities, aquaculture, wastewater treatment plant, and manufacturing units.

The benefits of water quality monitoring are as follows:

a. Improved human health
b. A real-time revelation about the contaminant composition in ponds, lakes, and rivers
c. Minimization of surface water pollution
d. Minimization of water overflow
e. Environmental protection

7.6.1.3 AI and IoT in Renewable Energy Production

The rapid growth in urbanization leads to exponential energy consumption. Majorly, the energy is produced using fossil fuel combustion and it leads to harmful substances in the atmosphere and pollution in the environment. To overcome the energy demand and emission-free environment, energy production can be maximized by using renewable resources like solar, wind, hydropower, and traditional biofuels. The use of AI-enabled IoT devices in renewable energy production efficiently satisfies the energy demand of smart cities. The sensors are attached to generation, transmission, and distribution units. The connected devices are used to monitor and control equipment workflow remotely in real time. These systems are highly automated, cost-efficient, enhance energy management, and enable distributed environment (Sanchez-Miralles et al., 2014). The collected data are used to make decisions about network configuration, energy production capacity, triggers alert regarding interruption of services in real-time, and switch off the powers while transferring via damaged connections.

The benefits of smart renewable energy management are as follows:

a. Increased accessibility and availability of energy
b. Expands the energy supply
c. Emission-free environment
d. Bio-waste disposal minimization
e. Optimized energy consumption
f. Possibility to store and share the energy in future

7.6.2 Smart Healthcare

In the healthcare sector, AI and IoT are standalone expertise that provides multiple functions such as patient monitoring via different sensors, digitizing the clinical records, telemedicine, data analysis, surgical robots, wearables, diagnosis, and so on. AI and IoT can provide better patient monitoring towards treatment protocols and enhances the clinical outcome. This technology transforms physical devices to smart systems that help the patient and doctor to connect in a new manner, transfer data in real-time, and diagnose the life-threatening events earlier than before (Sangeetha and Amudha, 2019). The mission is to provide "anywhere, anytime healthcare services". Figure 7.10 illustrates smart healthcare based on AI and IoT.

The key steps involved in coupling AI and IoT are data collection, data analysis, control, optimization, and model automation. The technologies incorporated are deep learning, natural language processing (NLP), context-aware processing, and intelligent robots. The applications involved are drug discovery, early detection of diseases using clinical records, critical disease diagnosis, virtual assistant, hospital management system, medical imaging diagnosis, therapy, and discovers solutions for early aging (Jiang et al., 2017). Chat-box is another application that acts as a health assistant and personal trainer.

The notable advantages of smart healthcare are as follows:

a. Remote patient monitoring
b. Ubiquitous health monitoring

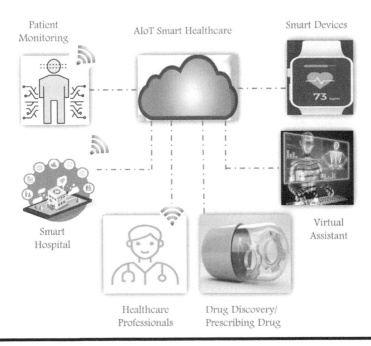

Figure 7.10 Smart Healthcare Using AI and IoT.

c. Delivers a patient-centric service
d. Timely treatment to patients
e. High accessibility of medical specialists
f. Secured data transfer between patient and healthcare professionals
g. Continuous monitoring of implanted devices on human

7.6.3 Smart Agriculture

Over a decade, farming practices are becoming harder due to climate change, natural disasters, extreme weather conditions, and other environmental factors. To assist and enrich the farming practices, the agricultural devices are equipped with different IoT sensors like temperature, humidity, soil moisture, etc. Based on the acquired data, crop yield, irrigation, and land management can be optimized. Farming practices need to be enhanced in order to compete with the growing population and improve productivity levels based on the demands. The blend of AI and IoT enables real-time data collection, analysis, and decision making for constant improvisation. AIoT also incorporates the insights and predictions obtained from the analytics of collected data for planning the agricultural activities. In the future, farmers will widely make use of crop and soil monitoring, ground-based wireless sensors, agricultural robots referred to as "agribot", predictive analytics, driverless tractors, and drones to monitor the growing conditions of the crop in the field. Other areas of focus involved in the smart agriculture revolution are weather prediction, livestock monitoring, precision farming, and smart greenhouses. Table 7.2 specifies the organizations which are currently building up AI-enabled IoT platforms to achieve smart agriculture processes.

The notable advantages of smart agricultural practices are as follows:

a. Increase in production and profit via automation
b. Enhancement in quality and volume of products
c. Optimal allocation of resources
d. Minimization of cost and waste
e. Crop disease and weed identification at an earlier stage
f. Minimization of pesticides and fertilizers

7.6.4 Smart Buildings

A smart building is an automated process that automatically optimizes utility parameters, safety, and security. To optimize these operations, the smart building makes use of numerous sensors, actuators, communication connectivity, and microchips. Initially, sensors and actuators are used to collect the

Table 7.2   AI and IoT Applications: Smart Agriculture

Application/ Organization Name	Functionality Provided
Smartfarm by Cropin	i. Complete digitization of farm. ii. An intelligent, intuitive, self-evolving system provides farming solutions to the entire agricultural sector.
Greensense by Yuktix	i. Accurate farm monitoring using wireless sensor devices. ii. Nodes with a dashboard provide an effective tool for crop monitoring and DPI (disease, pest, and irrigation) management.
Daisy.si	i. Smart plant watering suitable for indoor and outdoor plants. ii. Measures soil humidity, temperature, brightness, and irrigates through an unconventional algorithm, capable of defining the optimal water amount the plant requires.
smartAMCU by stellapps	Transforms the dairy supply chain with help of higher-end technologies and sensors.
mooOn by stellapps	A herd management application that contributes recommendations to optimize herd performance (livestock management).
Agribotix	Develops a drone-enabled cloud-based analytics platform for precision agriculture.

data, then the data sharing between the devices are done using wired as well as wireless connections, and the collected information are processed to make insights.

The categories of smart buildings are given in Figure 7.11 and the components are represented in Figure 7.12. Smart buildings require different types of sensors and devices such as smoke sensors, temperature sensors, humidity sensors, heating ventilation and air conditioning (HVAC), cameras, charging stations, lighting, and smart meters. The collected data from the sensors need to be processed in the implementation phase, which holds device management and connectivity to provide access and control to the connected devices, data

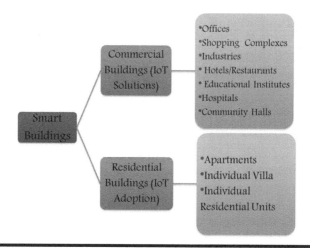

Figure 7.11   Categories of Smart Buildings.

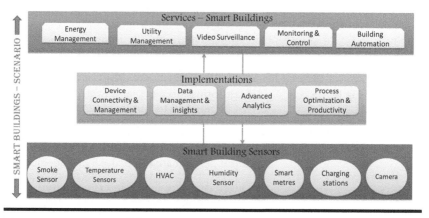

Figure 7.12   Smart Building Components.

management, and insights to enhance the operational efficiency and to make decisions, advanced analytics to anticipate problems in advance, prevent them and also plan for new value-added services, and process optimization and productivity. Based on the perceptions, better services such as energy and utility management, video surveillance, monitoring and control, and building automation will be provided to the citizens for improved quality of life.

The notable advantages of smart buildings are mentioned below:

a. To create or transform a building into a smart building will be beneficial to the proprietor and the organization.

b. It delivers a scalable, secure, and interoperable environment.

c. It can be scaled according to the requirements of the stakeholders.

d. It decreases energy cost, enhances productivity, and improves living.

e. Identifies used and unused areas and leads to optimal space utilization

f. Planned and proper usage of energy and their resources

g. Eliminates the carbon emissions

7.6.5 Smart Manufacturing

AI and IoT have dramatically changed the activities of the industrial sector. Globally the industrial sector is moving towards digital transformation and Industry 4.0. Figure 7.13 illustrates the revolution from Industry 1.0 to Industry 4.0. Industry 4.0 is well-defined as "The fourth industrial revolution applies the principles of AI, IoT, cloud computing, virtual reality, cyber-physical system (CPS), digital twin, autonomous robots, edge computing, augmented reality, additive manufacturing, and cognitive computing". Smart city enforcement is the heart of Industry 4.0. In particular, manufacturing undergoes a massive change as AI and IoT technologies are more acceptable, accessible, and affordable by business and consumer markets. In smart manufacturing, industrial robots and automation processes are used to improve the core operations of the industries.

Figure 7.14 shows how the digital transformation occurs from sensors to new business services in Industry 4.0. Intelligent systems play a vital role in making business decisions like ordering of raw materials, planning of production, scheduling, resource planning, etc. The automated system can collect the data immensely, and based on the data, AI systems can provide highly informative insights to the use cases of smart manufacturing such as facility

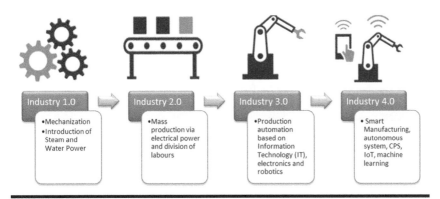

Figure 7.13   Industrial Revolution.

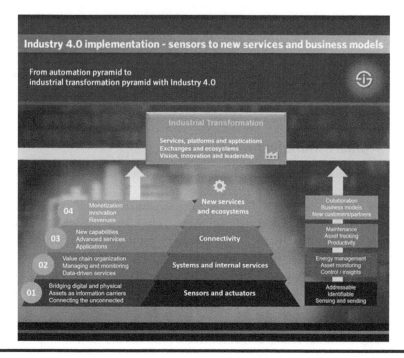

Figure 7.14 From Automation Pyramid to Industrial Transformation with Industry 4.0 [Source: Industry 4.0: Fourth Industrial Revolution – Guide (Industry 4.0: Fourth Industrial Revolution-Guide)].

management, inventory management, digital factory, production flow monitoring, packaging optimization, plant security and safety, logistics and supply chain management, and quality control (Anthopoulos, 2017). Industry 4.0 has the capability to transform anything to be smart includes smart energy, smart grid, smart logistics, and so on.

The novel advantages of smart manufacturing are as given below:

a. Optimizes the energy consumption
b. Enhances the equipment performance
c. Increased operation speed
d. Cost reduction
e. Enhancement of operational equipment uptime and availability
f. Improves the performance and quality of product
g. Equipment failure prediction
h. Identify anomalies and triggers alert/warnings
i. Enhances the business opportunities

7.6.6 Smart Transportation

The IoT devices and AI applications transform the transportation system into an intelligent transportation system (ITS), another essential component in smart city development. ITS uses a network of objects connected through sensors, actuators, and other devices to collect and transfer data in real time. ITS involves traffic data collection, data transmission, traffic data analysis, and information. Autonomous vehicles, connected cars, public transport management, traffic management system, smart roads, and smart parking (Wang and Wang, 2019) are ITS applications used in the development of smart cities.

a. **Autonomous vehicles**

These vehicles are capable of sensing the environment and control their movement without human involvement at any time. Sensors, actuators, machine learning systems, complex algorithms, and powerful processors to execute the software are embedded in the different parts of the vehicles to keep them smart enough.

b. **Connected cars**

Cars are equipped with a network of antennas, sensors and actuators, embedded software, and communication technologies. The integration of connected cars with city traffic management system is known as "Vehicle to Infrastructure" (V2I) technology.

c. **Public transport management**

Sensors used in public transport sends the traffic data to the city transportation management software. The data will be processed and information shared in real-time using mobile apps. It helps in the optimization and automation flow of public transport.

d. **Traffic management system**

It combines the information from toll booths, traffic lights, parking, and smart roads. Based on the analysis, real-time information about traffic conditions is provided to the drivers and city, which can optimize traffic flow, reduce emissions and congestion on road.

e. **Smart roads**

Smart roads are part of the modern transport infrastructure. The existing roads are to be embedded with IoT sensors, communication, and transmission technologies for improved safety, monitoring road conditions, traffic management, and energy efficiency.

f. **Smart parking**

Smart parking uses sensors and actuators, security cameras, and Internet connectivity. By using the information provided by the devices, cities can optimize the problem of parking in congested urban areas by transferring data about available parking slots to the citizens with the help of mobile apps (Artificial Intelligence for Smart Cities - Becoming Human: Artificial Intelligence Magazine).

The notable advantages of smart transportation are as follows:

    a. Improvement in quality of life
    b. Low levels of atmospheric pollution
    c. Increased safety
    d. Reduction in energy usage and congestion
    e. Optimal operational cost
    f. Improvised vehicle tracking

7.6.7 Smart Waste Management

A waste management system is an essential component in smart city development. In existing systems, Municipal Corporation collects the waste manually in a predefined route on daily basis and replaces it with empty receptacles whether it is fully filled up or not. The replacement of receptacles when it is not completely filled leads to unnecessary usage of fuel and city resources. The current system is highly reliable on resources. With the help of IoT systems, waste management can be transformed into a data-driven process.

Smart waste management uses ultrasonic sensors which are fixed in receptacles to measure the level of waste and alerts the city corporation services when receptacles are completely filled and can be emptied. This process leads to avoid the overflow of waste bins. Data collected by the sensor over a time period will be used by experts to identify the filling patterns, redefine the schedules and routes, and optimizes the operational costs. Along with ultrasonic sensors, other sensors like IR sensor, moisture sensor, and DC motor can be attached with waste bins to segregate the dry and wet waste.

IoT-based waste management systems alone cannot smartly deal with tons of waste generated by the urban population every day. AI can be coupled with IoT to automate the waste management process of disposal and recycling, as illustrated in Figure 7.15. AI uses radio frequency identification (RFID) tags along with IoT devices to determine the types of waste and transfer the information for analysis. Based on the information obtained, the main server compares the categories of waste and provides which category to be disposed of or recycled. Intelligent trash can and robots can be used in smart waste management systems for better segregation, disposal, and recycling.

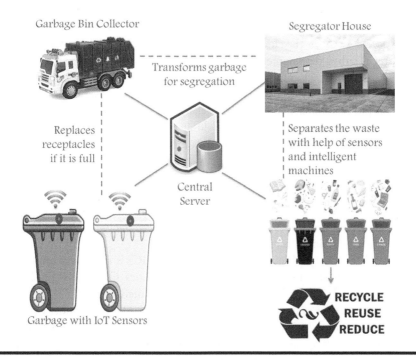

Figure 7.15   AIoT Smart Waste Management System.

The notable advantages of smart waste management are as follows:

a. Clean and hygienic environment
b. Reduced carbon-di-oxide (CO_2) emission
c. Effective waste management
d. An improved lifestyle of citizens
e. Route optimization

7.7 Case Study: Coimbatore City

Coimbatore city is the second-largest in the state of Tamil Nadu and the 16th largest urban agglomerated city in India (Coimbatore City Municipal Corporation). Local bodies in Coimbatore district are categorized into one corporation (Coimbatore Municipal Corporation) referred to as Coimbatore city, which consists of 72 wards, three municipalities, one district Panchayat, 12 Panchayat Unions, 37 Town Panchayat, and 227 Village Panchayats (Coimbatore District-Local Bodies Administration). In June 2015, under the "100 Smart Cities

Mission" initiative by honorable Prime Minister Narendra Modi, Coimbatore city was selected as one of the cities to be developed as a "smart city" supported by the ministry of urban development. It stands first amongst the 11 urban cities in the Tamil Nadu state, in completion of projects under the Government of India's Smart Cities Mission directive. The corporation is implementing the Smart Cities Mission projects under two categories – namely "pan-city" to be executed across the city and "area-based development" limited to specific areas. Area-based development (ABD) revamps the existing area including slums, into a healthier area which improvise the liveability of the city and quality of life. Around the cities, novel areas will be developed in order to provide accommodation for the expanding population in urban zones. "Pan-city" goal is to promote the existing city-wide infrastructure by means of smart solution applications. The smart solution application pulls up cities to move towards using technologies, information, and data to improvise infrastructure and services.

Coimbatore City Municipal Corporation (CCMC) is engaged with 49 projects, costing about ₹ 1,014.8 crores. As per the statistics, CCMC has finished 18 projects worth ₹ 72.67 crores, 21 projects to be executed worth ₹ 755.56 crores, four projects tender evaluation in on-going worth ₹ 7.28 crores, tender called for a project value of ₹ 15.7 crores and five projects with a value of ₹ 163.59 crores. Installation of air quality monitoring devices, construction of digital display boards on specified locations, two solar power plants assembly with a capacity of one MW each are the few projects completed by CCMC. Some of the projects to be implemented are 24x7 drinking water distribution, multi-level car parking, and lake development. The projects yet to be called for the tender are the development of a race course as a model road, renovation of Narasampathy and Kurichi water containers, biomining of collected waste in Vellalore dump yard, and purchasing light commercial vehicles for gathering waste.

7.7.1 Smart City Architecture for Coimbatore City

Generally, a smart city has a layered architecture consisting of a data sensing layer, data transmission layer, data management layer, and service layer (Saba et al., 2020). Each layer in the architecture has its own responsibility and security components. Figure 7.16 specifies the projected layer architecture for Coimbatore city and its components.

a. **Data Sensing Layer**

It is the primary layer in smart city architecture and plays a significant role in controlling the various operations in the physical environment. The data collection from sensors, devices, and systems was done through the data sensing

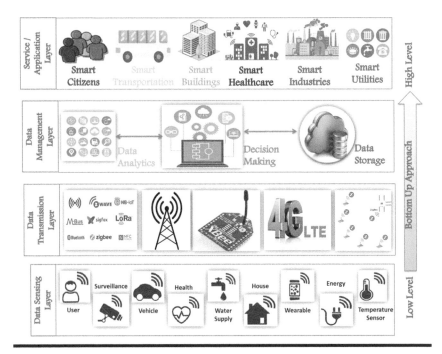

Figure 7.16   Projected Smart City Architecture for Coimbatore City.

layer. To implement a smart city, numerous sensors and devices are inter-connected over the network. The streaming data from various devices need to be collected for further analysis, which is considered a challenging task because of the heterogeneous devices and data. The data can be acquired from each device and system operating in the smart city such as wearables, public trans-port, air quality monitoring, waste accumulation, energy consumption by means of commercial and residential buildings, and so on.

b. **Data Transmission Layer**

It is the second layer in the smart city architecture and lies between the data sensing layer and data transmission layer. The data communication between individual devices occurs through wired, wireless, or satellite communication. There is a need for robust communication technology to handle the enormous volume of data collected across a widespread geographical area. The users can be connected with wired broadband connections like Passive Optical LAN (POL), Fiber to the x (FTTx), Asymmetric digital subscriber line (ADSL), or mobile broadband connections like 3G, 4G/LTE, or Wi-Fi. The technologies used to connect the short-range infrastructure coverage are Wireless Personal Area Network (WPAN), Bluetooth, M2M, RFID, Zigbee, and Z-Wave. Likewise, Low-Power Wide Area Network (LPWAN) can be used for wide infrastructure coverage in the transmission layer.

c. Data Management Layer

It is the third layer in the smart city architecture and lies between the data transmission and service layer. It acts as the brain for smart city applications. This layer performs various tasks such as data analysis and analytics, data organization, data manipulation, storage of data, and decision making for further analysis. The techniques like AI, ML, and statistical methods are used for the purpose of data analytics. The AI algorithm uses historical data present in cloud storage or big data warehouse for identifying trends and creates a model. Automation can also be achieved based on valuable insights. The predicted model helps in obtaining smart solutions for smart city development.

d. Service Layer

It is the topmost layer in the smart city architecture, also referred to as the "application layer". This layer connects all the public services such as e-governance, air, and water quality monitoring, public transport, waste management, healthcare, and so on with citizens by means of web portals or mobile applications. The data will be shared among the public, organizations, and corporations and they can be made aware of the operations of the smart city. Citizens in the smart city are gradually moved towards the adaptation of intelligent services such as smart healthcare, smart transportation, smart waste management, smart environment, smart metering, smart lighting, and smart buildings.

7.8 Summary

Globally, the smart city concept has been widely established because the cities in a country play a substantial role in energy consumption, economic activities, and greenhouse gas (GHG) emissions and hence, city development authorities come up with various project initiatives for the transformation of a city into a smart city. The goal of a smart city is to provide a multitude of services to "all the people at anytime and anywhere". There is no wonder if everyone agrees that smart technologies will rule the world in the forthcoming years. Revolutionizing technological advancements paved the way for cities' progression and also supports through novel ways of managing resources and distribution of services. The combination of persistent communication, smart healthcare, ITS, connectivity, security, and digitization were highly useful in the promotion of economy and the society. Cities with huge populations need to focus on reduction in their carbon footprints and carbon-free environment. It will help to improve the ecosystem, control climate change, and protect human health.

AI and IoT technologies hold a major part in the development of smart cities. These technologies are involved in tasks such as data acquisition, data transmission, data storage and management, and decision making. The next generation is moving towards urban evolution by combining smarter things and connected infrastructure. It includes citizens, businesses, municipalities, corporations, and government. The information obtained will be communicated and shared with all the people around the city through one unified portal system. The information access can be made using mobile phones, desktops, laptops, tablets, or smart TVs. The integration of system utilities and public services with interconnected networks transforms the city "smarter". In the upcoming days, the cities will be more upgraded with sensor technologies, infrastructure development, automation, connectivity, and data analysis using AI for better management of smart applications. Smart city development is responsible for a better quality of life to survive, a clean and sustainable environment, and holistic growth of the country.

References

Alaoui, S.S., Aksasse, B., Farhaoui, Y., 2019. Air pollution prediction through Internet of things technology and big data analytics. *International Journal of Computational Intelligence Studies (IJCISTUDIES)* 8(3), 177–191. doi: 10.1504/IJCISTUDIES.2019.102525.

Alliance for Internet of Things Innovation (AIOTI). Research and Innovation Priorities for IoT. https://aioti.eu/wp-content/uploads/2018/09/AIOTI_IoT-Research_Innovation_Priorities_2018_for_publishing.pdf, [accessed 03 April, 2020].

An Introduction to the Internet of Things. https://www.iotforall.com/free-intro-ebook-on-the-Internet-of-things/, [accessed 03 April, 2020].

Anthopoulos, L.G., 2017. Smart city in practice. In: Reddick C.G. (Eds.) *Understanding Smart Cities: A Tool for Smart Government or an Industrial Trick? Public Administration and Information Technology*, Springer International Publishing, San Antonio, TX, USA, vol. 22, pp. 47–185. doi: 10.1007/978-3-319-57015-0.

Artificial Intelligence for Smart Cities - Becoming Human: Artificial Intelligence Magazine. https://becominghuman.ai/artificial-intelligence-for-smart-cities-64e6774808f8, [accessed 03 April, 2020].

Bawany, N., Shamsi, J., 2015. Smart city architecture: Vision and challenges. *International Journal of Advanced Computer Science and Applications* 6, 246–255. doi: 10.14569/IJACSA.2015.061132.

Cognitive IoT. https://www.ibmbigdatahub.com/blog/what-cognitive-iot, [accessed 03 April, 2020].

Coimbatore City Municipal Corporation. Available on the link. https://www.ccmc.gov.in/ccmc/index.php/about-us

Coimbatore District-Local Bodies Administration. Available on the link. https://coimbatore.nic.in/local-bodies/

History of Smart Cities-Timeline. Published on 02/02/2020. https://www.verdict.co.uk/smart-cities-timeline/

Hossain, E., Khan, I., Un-Noor, F., Sikander, S.S., Sunny, M.S.H., 2019. Application of big data and machine learning in smart grid, and associated security concerns: A review. *IEEE Access* 1-1, 2169–3536. doi: 10.1109/access.2019.2894819.

Industry 4.0: Fourth Industrial Revolution-Guide. https://www.i-scoop.eu/industry-4-0/, [accessed 17 April, 2020].

Jiang, F., Jiang, Y., Zhi, H., et al., 2017. Artificial intelligence in healthcare: Past, present and future. *Stroke and Vascular Neurology* 2: e000101, 230–243. doi: 10.1136/svn-2017-000101.

Leveraging the upcoming distributions from AI and IoT. www.pwc.com, [accessed 17 April, 2020].

Saba, D., Sahli, Y., Berbaoui, B., Maouedj, R., 2020. Towards smart cities: Challenges, components, and architectures, In: Hassanien, A., Bhatnagar, R., Khalifa, N., Taha, M. (Eds) *Toward social Internet of Things (SIoT): Enabling technologies, architectures and applications. Studies in Computational Intelligence 846*, Springer Nature Switzerland, pp. 249–286. doi: 10.1007/978-3-030-24513-9_15

Sanchez-Miralles, A., Calvillo, C., Martín, F., Villar, J., 2014. Use of renewable energy systems in smart cities, In: Sanz-Bobi, M.A. (Ed.) *Use, Operation and Maintenance of Renewable Energy Systems, Green Energy and Technology*, Springer International Publishing Switzerland, pp. 341–370. doi: 10.1007/978-3-319-03224-5_1.

Sangeetha, A., Amudha, T., 2019. Pervasive healthcare system based on environmental monitoring, In: Sangaiah A.K., Shantharajah, S., Theagarajan, P. (Eds.) *Intelligent Pervasive Computing Systems for Smarter Healthcare*, John Wiley & Sons Inc, pp. 159–178.

Smart Cities Mission Statement & Guidelines Report. http://smartcities.gov.in/upload/uploadfiles/files/SmartCityGuidelines(1).pdf, [accessed 20 April, 2020].

Tokoro, N., 2016. Co-creation of value through initiative of a leader company and collaboration of participating companies—Case study of Fujisawa sustainable smart town, In: *The Smart City and the Co-creation of Value-A Source of New Competitiveness in a Low-Carbon Society*, Springer Briefs in Business, Springer Japan, pp. 55–74.

Wang, Q., Wang, S., 2019 Application of intelligent transportation system in intelligent network environment, In: Zeng X., Xie X., Sun J., Ma L., Chen Y. (Eds.) *International Symposium for Intelligent Transportation and Smart City (ITASC) 2019 Proceedings. ITASC 2019. Smart Innovation, Systems and Technologies*, vol 127, Springer, Singapore, pp. 39–48. doi: 10.1007/978-981-13-7542-2_4

Chapter 8

Internet of Nano Things: An Amalgamation of Nanotechnology and IoT

G. Srividhya[1] and N. Ponpandian[2]

[1]*Ph.D. Research Scholar, Department of Nanoscience and Technology, Bharathiar University, Coimbatore, India*
[2]*Professor and Head, Department of Nanoscience and Technology, Bharathiar University, Coimbatore, India*

Contents

Objectives

The objective of the chapter is to introduce and familiarize the concepts of the Internet of Nano Things technology to the reader. This chapter focuses on nano-fabrication and nano-communication to develop nano-machines for the Internet of Nano Things technology. At the end of this chapter, the readers are expected to have an understanding of the basic concepts of the technology, various approaches to fabricate nanodevices, different nano-communication paradigms and network architecture, applications, and challenges associated with the technology.

8.1 Introduction

8.1.1 Internet of Things: Making Things Smarter

Due to tremendous technological development, the home and working environment has adapted to a smart lifestyle with the interconnectivity of things and application. This resulted in the emergence of the Internet of Things (IoT), which enables every living and non-living thing to communicate with its environment smartly for easy automated working. IoT is a network of "things" that are made responsive to the circumstances or the environment by collecting and sharing data between them. IoT connects a countless number of devices to the Internet and makes them respond with a service, suitable for the situation, without the need for intervention from humans.

Computer scientists and engineers have conceptualized the contemporary ideas of IoT as a system that encounters the physical world without the need for external intervention. The term "Internet of Things" was coined by Kevin Ashton of AutoID Center of MIT, describing it as a system that connects to the physical things in the world through ubiquitous sensors. Generally, IoT can be defined as a system of interconnected microsensors and microprocessors with necessary power electronics embedded with software and network connectivity that can enable data collection and transfer between devices and any physical thing in the world. The power of IoT is that almost all things in the world can be made a part of IoT to serve a system or environment from/to which the data is shared through the Internet.

The "things" mentioned in IoT not only comprise electronic gadgets that are made for communication like computers and mobile phones. Instead, the "things" in IoT refer to any physical living or non-living thing in the sensible domain. For example, the "thing" can be a home, a building, a manufacturing machine, an automobile, a person or a pet, and so on. Auto-security monitoring a building or a campus that auto-alarms us of intruders, smart home with appliances connected to a central virtual assistant, smart automobiles that can sense proximity and traffic conditions, a smart band that tracks the physical activity and location of a person, smart manufacturing units in factories and industries that can check and dispose of defect products automatically without the need of human labor, are a few of many realizations of IoT technology. In an IoT system, the data can be transferred and inferred to and fro between

1. Human to Human (H2H)
2. Human to Thing (H2T)
3. Thing to Thing (T2T)

The applications of IoT is extended to a multi-dimensional platform including healthcare, agriculture, smart cities, environment screening, device to device communication, unmanned vehicles, and military. IoT can be seen as a heterogeneous network of diverse devices, places, environments, and persons. Figure 8.1 shows how IoT can be understood as a giant network of different, distinct networks connected together with security and management directions.

With advanced wireless communication technologies such as Radio Frequency Identification (RFID), cloud computing, embedded systems, and adaptive AI systems, IoT now takes over the most important technology. By 2008, the number of devices connected to the Internet overcame the number of people on the Earth. The number of devices connected is predicted to be

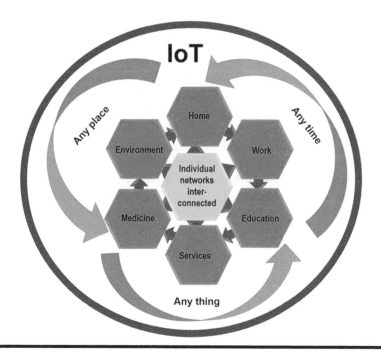

Figure 8.1 IoT Is a Network of Networks that Connects Anything at Any Time at Any Place.

50 billion by 2020. With such growing popularity, IoT has an enormous impact on us and our environments. And protocols for communication, technologies for data processing, storage, and data security are being developed to accomplish the complete usefulness of IoT.

8.1.2 Internet of Nano Things: Making Smarter Things Smaller

Internet of Nano Things (IoNT) is the different dimension of IoT in which the basic concepts remain the same, except that the devices interconnected are of the nanoscale in size. By connecting nanoscale devices to the Internet, accessing data from places that are inaccessible to the bulk devices, can be achieved. However, IoNT is only about the size miniaturization of micro into nanodevices. It also extends its purpose to form nanonetwork to establish communication among the nanodevices. Akyildiz and Jornet proposed graphene-based nano-antennae operating at terahertz frequency for utilization in IoNT. They describe IoNT as a networking paradigm based on the interconnection of nanoscale devices with existing communication networks and the Internet.

The main components of an IoT system are i) sensors and actuators and ii) communication and data processing. The sensor is an electronic device that detects one form of input signal like light, sound, pressure, movement, etc., and converts it into a digital output to be read on a screen by a user. The actuator is responsible for controlling the mechanism. Finally, the data collected are put to the user or stored in a cloud as per protocols. With the technological advancement of materials fabrication and designing, the last decades see a rise in designing piezoelectric, chemical, and biosensors. By implementing such nanosensor devices for the tasks of sensing and actuation, IoNT can serve medicine, energy, and other areas of IoT applications with better detailing and cost-effectiveness. The main challenging task of IoNT is new standards are required to establish communication among nanodevices and to interface them with existing micro and macro devices.

Thus, in a nutshell, IoNT is the miniaturization of IoT. IoNT uses nanosensors, connected to one another by nanonetworks for data collection and transfer, opening up dynamic opportunities for research in nanodevices and nano-communication (Miraz et al., 2018). Thus broadly, nanodevices and nano-networking are the two main aspects of IoNT, which will be discussed in detail in the next sections of the chapter.

8.2 Nanotechnology and Nanomaterials

Nanotechnology is the study, design, and control of matter on the scale of 1–100 nm to construct novel structures and systems with whole new physical and chemical properties attributable to their smaller size. The concept of nanotechnology was put forth by Dr. Richard Feynman in 1959 in his popular lecture "There's plenty of room in the bottom", in which he emphasized the imminent commencement of design and production of tinier yet effective devices to perform a specified task. It gained widespread attention with the discovery of fullers and the development of a scanning electron microscope to visualize matter in such a small scale. For understanding the scale of a nanometer to a meter, one can think of the size of a marble compared to the size of the earth. Nanoscience and nanotechnology provide the insight to build materials atom by atom, molecules by molecules to produce molecular-sized matter to be applied for industrial use.

The interesting phenomenon that happens at the nanoscale is that the materials show different, sometimes completely opposite, properties to their bulk counterparts. Quantum mechanics and quantum size effect become more pronounced at the nanoscale. And as a result, scientists have been able to produce new materials that unique properties that can be harnessed in various

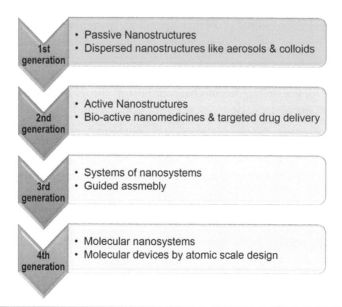

1st generation
- Passive Nanostructures
- Dispersed nanostructures like aerosols & colloids

2nd generation
- Active Nanostructures
- Bio-active nanomedicines & targeted drug delivery

3rd generation
- Systems of nanosystems
- Guided assmebly

4th generation
- Molecular nanosystems
- Molecular devices by atomic scale design

Figure 8.2   Generations of Nanotechnology, as Organized by Mihail Roco of NNI, U.S.

applications such as energy production and storage, environmental monitoring, biomedical engineering, agriculture, and so on. Owing to the rapid progress in the techniques to synthesize and characterize nanoparticles, the field of nano-technology has acquired a colossal advancement.

Scientist Mihail Roco of the U.S. National Nanotechnology Initiative (NNI) categorized the improvement of nanotechnology in different generations as de-picted in Figure 8.2 to understand its evolution. The first generation of nano-technology falls into the period 2000 and earlier, from the discovery and earlier commercialization of nanomaterials. The first-generation nanomaterials were passive structures that could enhance the properties of existing materials. For example, reinforcement of carbon nanotubes (CNTs) brought in water resistance and strength in cement and steel. In the next five years, the emergence of active nanomaterials gave rise to the second generation of nanotechnology. Porous nanostructures filled with anti-cancer drugs act as nanomedicine to deliver the drug into the target area. This phase also saw the development of multi-tasking Micro-Electro-Mechanical Systems (MEMS) that enable the fabrication of highly effectual sensors and actuators in microchips. The evolution of self-assembled nanosystems paved the way for third-generation nanotechnology, where the na-nomachines constructed from the assembly of nanosystems can perform desig-nated tasks. The final and fourth generation of nanotechnology is based on molecular nanosystems, where the control to prepare precise molecule by molecule assembly of nanostructures can be achieved.

8.2.1 Processing Nanomaterials for IoNT Applications

Devices and machines for IoNT are designed based on i) nanomaterials-based design and ii) bio-inspired design. The study of nanotechnology has powered the designing and engineering of nanomaterials so that they can fit in the small-scale MEMS and NEMS (Nano-Electro-Mechanical Systems) with function effectiveness. The fabrication and printing techniques not only benefit the miniaturization of the materials, but also the cost-effective production of the materials. Miniature nanodevices can be effectively printed by processing nanomaterials into nano-inks. 3D printing, transfer printing, and lithography techniques are becoming more popular and more feasible these days and this paves the way for easy fabrication of nanodevices for IoNT applications (Moinudeen et al., 2017). The ability to control the dimensionality of the nanomaterials has led to the synthesis of zero-dimensional (0D), one dimension (1D), and two dimension (2D) nanomaterials, each of which has unique properties and functionalities.

A range of polymer materials offers flexibility to the nanomaterials and acts as a substrate for printing flexible electronics. Moreover, flexible, conductive nanofiber polymers incorporating nanomaterials can be produced by the electrospinning method, which leads to the production of smart fabrics for pollution filtering, anti-bacterial, and wearable electronics applications. Novel hierarchical architecture of molecular complexes that can react to specific chemical markers can be created with electronic intelligence and network connectivity on such flexible substrates by low-cost printing techniques, thus fulfilling the requirement to produce tiny, connectible functional devices for IoNT applications (Nayyar et al., 2017). There are numerous techniques to fabricate nanodevices of which techniques that are widely employed in MEMS and NEMS are categorized in Figure 8.3 and will be discussed in brief in this session.

Lithography: Lithography is a widely used method for fabricating electronic systems and by mechanism, it transfers a pattern onto a substrate with the thin film coating is etched. There are a variety of lithographic techniques employed to fabricate MEMS and NEMS systems and photolithography, electron-beam, and x-ray lithography are the widely adapted methods. The desired material such as silicon dioxide is deposited on a substrate such as glass by spin coating or drop-casting, upon which a thin layer of photo-resist is deposited. A computer-generated layout of a photo-mask in the desired pattern is designed and is laid over the photo-resist. Then, the UV light or e-beam or x-ray is exposed, which etches the photo-resist other than the area which is protected by the photo-mask.

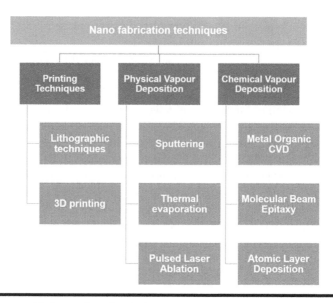

Figure 8.3 Widely Employed Fabrication Technologies for MEMS and NEMS.

The photo-resist is then hard baked and washed away to reveal the material layer etched easily to the desired pattern.

3D printing of nanomaterials: 3D printing of nanomaterials is a recent addition to the MEMS and NEMS fabrication techniques. Generally, it prints the material layer by layer in 3D space. The design in which the material has been printed is modeled using a computer (generally using CAD) and then the printer prints the material in the preserved template. Processing of nanomaterials before printing is important. The nanomaterial is made into ink with the addition of polymers. Polymers help in the curing of the printed layer with the help of UV or visible light. Each layer is cured before the next layer can be deposited on that layer. Inks can be of any materials like metals, dielectrics, and polymers. 3D printing enables the printing of substrate-free fabrication.

Chemical Vapour Deposition: chemical vapor deposition (CVD) is a thin film deposition technique in which the thin film is brought by the reaction of chemicals in the gas phase. It is carried out at very low pressures (0.1–1.0 Torr). The energy required for the occurrence of the chemical reaction is provided by heating the substrate. The temperature of the substrate depends on the material that needs to be deposited as the film. Typically, oxides and nitrides deposited using low-pressure CVD (LPCVD) are at the temperature range 450–900 °C. In case of situations where the substrate or the materials require low temperature, alternative energy sources like plasma excitation are used. In a method called plasma-enhanced CVD (PECVD), radio frequency (RF) induced plasma is used to create high-energy species that react with lower temperatures (150–350 °C). In LPCVD a large numbers of wafers can be processed simultaneously, while in the case of PECVD, only a limited number of wafers can be processed. Epitaxial growth of thin films can also be brought about by CVD techniques. Vapor phase epitaxy (VPE) and molecular beam epitaxy (MBE) are the common methods to grow high-quality thin films. VPE also called metal-organic CVD (MOCVD) uses vapors of metal-organic compounds and metal hydrides. The reaction of the precursor gases at the surface of the heated substrate results in the formation of epitaxial layers. In MBE, molecular beams, produced by thermal evaporation of the source, are used and carried out at an ultra-high vacuum.

Atomic Layer Deposition: Atomic layer deposition (ALD) is a modified CVD process in which the deposition of two or more vapor phase reactants can be done in a self-limiting fashion. The important feature of ALD is its excellent control over the thickness of the films deposited. Thin films of about one atomic thickness can be deposited using ALD. The reactant vapors are serially introduced into the chamber. Once the first reactant vapor is deposited in a self-limiting monolayer, the excess vapor is flushed out and the second reactant vapor is introduced for self-limiting deposition followed by excess vapor flush-out. It offers not only control over the thickness of the film, but also the composition of the films. A variety of materials like semiconductors, metals, oxides, sulphides, and nitrides can be deposited into thin films using this technique.

Physical Vapour Deposition: in the physical evaporation (also known as thermal evaporation) technique, the source is held in a crucible. The evaporation of the materials achieved by either induction of high currents over coil or electron beam bombardment. The crucible is placed at the bottom of the chamber and the substrate is usually near the ceiling of the chamber so that the evaporated vapors from the source are deposited on the substrate. Compared to CVD and lithography, this is a less complicated process. However, the coverage of deposition is poor in this method.

Sputtering: In sputtering, the target material to be deposited is bombarded with high-energy inert gas ions (plasma) and as result atoms or clusters of atoms are ejected from the target surface and get deposited over the substrate. Direct current (DC) or radio frequency (RF) current passed through a magnetron vacuum tube is used to produce plasma (high-energy ions of an inert gas such as argon). The atoms are ejected from the target by the exchange of momentum from the inert gas ions. Sputtering can be used to deposit thin films of metals, metal oxides, semiconductors, semi-conductor oxides, and alloys. The oxides are deposited by introducing reactive species (oxygen gas) inside the sputtering chamber. Insulators can be deposited through RF magnetron sputtering.

Though the coverage step is high, the deposition rate is lower than that of thermal evaporation, but not as low as CVD techniques.

Laser Ablation: Laser ablation is the process of removing materials from the target surface by irradiating them with a laser. In Pulsed laser deposition (PLD) technique uses high intensity, short duration UV laser pulse to ablate the target material. Typical pulse intensity and duration are of the range 1 GW and 25 ns. With such high laser flux, the target is turned into plasma form which is then deposited onto the substrate. PLD is very useful to deposit thin films of complex materials and also to control the thickness of the deposited thin film.

8.2.2 Roles of Nanomaterials in IoNT

Nanomaterials possess novel characteristic traits. As a result, "nano things" in IoNT serve multiple purposes. A few of their roles are listed below:

1. Targeted drug delivery is a commercial success in delivering drugs to the target area in the body using nanomaterials as drug carriers. This helps in reducing the dosage of the drug and minimizes the side effects significantly. A variety of nanomaterials like lipid-based drug delivery systems, micelle nanoparticles, nano-valves are employed to carry drugs for treating various diseases.

2. Nanoparticles also have therapeutic ad anti-microbial properties. Gold, silver, and other inorganic nanoparticles show therapeutic properties to cure deadly diseases like cancer.

3. Besides medicines, nanomaterials are widely used as implants, bone substitutes, and dental curatives. For example, calcium carbonate and hydroxyapatite coatings are highly biocompatible and stimulate the growth of bone for reparation. The endurance and the life span of the implants can be very much improved by the incorporation of nano-materials such as carbon nanotubes. Nanotechnology upholds the near future of tissue engineering and regeneration.

4. Further, nanotechnology inspires the invention of nano-scale needles, tweezers, and other surgical tools that could allow the tissue and cellular level precision surgeries with lower risks of errors. Also, the idea of inventive nano cameras and nanobots proposes the improved visualization and regulation of surgeries.

5. Nanomaterials and quantum dots are extremely useful in MRI and other imaging techniques because they facilitate accurate imaging of damaged cells that helps in the early diagnosis of cancers and tumors.

6. Apart from using nanomaterials for imaging techniques, one thoughtful way to prevent and early diagnose various diseases and bio-conditions is

to monitor and detect the usual and unusual number of biomarkers of those ailments. Keeping this as motivation, an extensive number of researches is carried to develop nano-bio sensors that can actively track the levels of biomarkers in a biosystem. Many successful efforts have been made to fabricate real-time, wearable biosensors, that could assess the number of specific biomarkers and communicate the numbers to the users through mobile phones. On venturing the impediments in realizing them, it is only a matter of time for them to become commercial. Once realized commercially, these sensors will revolutionize the healthcare system.

7. Nanosensors are also functionalized to monitor different environmental factors such as the temperature and level of toxic gases in a manufacturing unit, carbon emission in an industry. They are also employed in other environmental applications such as purification and desalination of water, owing to their porosity and size. Moreover, nanotechnology holds the prospect of using nanobots to remove plastic debris and oil spills in oceans.

8. Other than biomedical sensing and environmental monitoring, nanosensors that are based on mechanical and electromagnetic principles and developed on MEMS systems can efficiently detect any change or movement in the physical realms. Such sensors are highly useful in automated systems to respond to a change in the physical system like auto-inflation of airbags in a car, automated door security system in a building, auto-watering of plants depending on the moisture level, monitoring traffic in an area, tracking physical activity and location of a person, RADAR, proximity checking, and illegal prosecution of opponent vehicles in the army, sample collection in space missions, etc. In fact, the future of automation highly depends on nanosensors and embedded systems.

9. In addition to all the above, there is an essential need to develop high-performance nano-power systems such as batteries and supercapacitors to power up the nanodevices so that they can work stand-alone. Enormous efforts are being made to construct nanoscale power devices that can deliver high performance, have longevity, and require little or no maintenance/replacement.

10. Ultimately, the role of nanotechnology in next-generation electronics is revolutionary. Nano transistors, nano FETs, programmable nanowires in the scale of tens of nanometres have already been realized by enterprises like Intel and Nano VIA. The nano processors will empower the manufacture of smaller and thinner computing machines, modernizing the whole world of computers and electronics.

Nanomedicine enables the nano-level accurate performance of specific tasks in biological systems using a range of diverse nanomaterials. Employing nanomaterials and nanotechnology in biomedical applications takes the medical field to the next phase of upgraded and effortless healthcare. The development and implementation of nanosensors and other nanodevices are crucial for the improvement of several environmental, energy, and other detection/automation applications. In all the above-discussed roles of nanotechnology, the connection of the nanodevices to a network is indispensable to take the real advantage of nanotechnology to mass usefulness. IoNT empowers the nanotechnology to be easily accessible to the end-user through communicating the data collected by the nanodevices regarding the state of the system being monitored.

8.3 Nanomachines

IoNT requires miniaturization of IoT components into a final product called "nanomachines". A nanomachine is an assembly of several nanoscale components capable of performing a required task like sensing, computing, communicating, and data storing. The nano-components are made by the arrangements of molecules, driven by the molecular-level interactions and affiliations, into organized structures in nanoscale. A nanomachine is provided with a set of instructions embedded within its molecular assembly units to perform the intended task. A single nanomachine performs a simple and uncomplicated task confined to its adjacent environment, owing to its smaller size. The different components of a nanomachine are coordinated so that the various components function as a single organized and synchronous unit.

8.3.1 Architecture of Nanomachines

As discussed previously, a nanomachine may consist of one or more nano-components that are linked with one another. The integration of components in a nanomachine may vary depending upon the weight of the task to be carried out. For example, the level of integration of components in a nanobot would be more complex than in a simple molecular switch. However, the basic components that produce the general structural design of a nanomachine, whether it is a nanobot or a molecular switch, are the same. The components of nanomachines architecture are given in the block diagram (Figure 8.4) and are explained as follows:

1. Control Unit: The control unit is the central unit that controls all the other components for the overall functioning of the nanomachine. It is responsible for accomplishing the labeled task by executing a set of instructions. It also

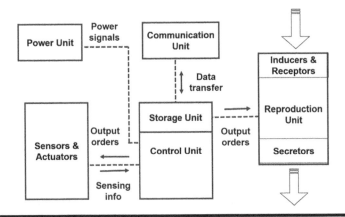

Figure 8.4 Block Diagram of the Architecture of Nanomachines.

serves as the storage unit to save the data collected by the nanomachine for user consumption.

2. Communication Unit: The communication unit liable for transmitting and receiving data at the nano level using nano-transceivers.

3. Reproduction Unit: The reproduction unit reproduces the components of the nanomachines at the expense of external elements. It replicates the nanomachine successfully by assembling the nano-components that make up the nanomachine. The set of codes to copy itself from the external elements are provided within the reproduction unit.

4. Power Unit: The power unit lights up the components of the nano-machine by reaping power from external sources like light, temperature, etc. The power unit also stores energy for future needs.

5. Sensors and Actuators: Sensors and actuators, included in the nano-machine, act as the interface between the nanomachine and the environment. Sensors are the key part of IoNT systems, as they provide means to sense and collect data from the system without any external intervention.

8.3.2 Development of Nanomachines

There are mainly three different approaches to develop a nanomachine – top-down approach, bottom-up approach, and biohybrid approach. Though a stand-alone, working, wholesome nanomachine is yet to be made, the rapid development of fabricating techniques, also supported with naturally occurring self-assembly will soon expedite the achievement of real-world nanomachines. Figure 8.5 shows the different approaches to develop nanomachines as depicted by Akyildiz et al.

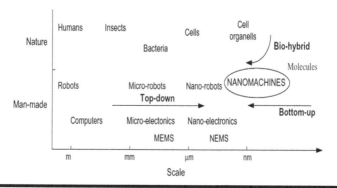

Figure 8.5 Approaches to Develop a Nanomachine, as Depicted by Akyildiz et al. (Source: Akyildiz et al. (2008)).

1. Top-down approach: In this approach, the nanomachines are fostered by trimming down the existing microelectronic and MEMS technologies by advanced fabrication techniques like electron beam lithography and microcontact printing. Certain nano-components like NEMS have been produced by these techniques, but they are in the infancy of development.

2. Bottom-up approach: This approach endeavors to assemble the individual building blocks such as molecules to develop a nanomachine. This method is also known as molecular manufacturing, as it is based on assembling several discrete molecules to produce a nanodevice. This technology is not a reality thus far. However, theoretical studies have suggested the development of nanomachines like molecular differential gears and pumps through this tactic. Presently, simple nanodevices like molecular switches have been developed by self-assembling properties of molecules.

3. Biohybrid approach: One notable feature of the biological systems of living organisms is that there exist self-supported biological nanodevices like molecular motors which can sense, actuate, store and communicate data to other living cells by molecular signaling. Complex activities like immune system response, cell division are possible in living organisms due to the network of interconnected multiple cells with actively working nanomachines. The biohybrid approach exploits these already existing nanodevice models in biological systems to develop nanomachines. These subsisting biological nano archetypes which are optimized in terms of working and communication inspires the invention of a new generation of nanomachines.

8.4 Communication and Networking of IoNT

8.4.1 Nano-Communication Paradigms

A nanomachine needs to communicate among its components and with other external microdevices to establish a smooth and synchronous performance in a cooperative working environment. Setting up a connection in nanomachines requires more than just a simple augmentation of conventional communication routes. It requires the development of an entirely new communication standard.

There are two ways are communication in nanomachine:

1. Internal communication – between the two or more nanodevices
2. External communication – between the nanodevice and an external device like a microelectronic device

There are a few communication processes proposed for nano-communication like electromagnetic communication, molecular communication, and acoustic communication. Electromagnetic communication is the transmission of electromagnetic waves where molecular communication is the transmission of coded information in molecules as in DNA, peptides, proteins, etc. These are the two dominant ways of establishing nano-communication. Acoustic communication uses ultrasonic waves for data transmission using ultrasonic transducers. Nano-mechanical communication uses nano-scale mechanical transducers to transmit the data. Though acoustic and nano-mechanical communication systems operate in a much lower frequency (megahertz) when compared to an electromagnetic communication system (terahertz), they require a high-power source which restricts their use in nano-communication.

a. Electromagnetic communication: Novel nanomaterials are capable of stipulating communication by transmission and reception of electromagnetic (EM) waves in nanodevices. Graphene and CNTs based nano-antennas and nano-transceivers have been proposed for nanoscale communication, which is highly dependent on the operating frequency band of the nano-antennas and nano-transceivers. Graphene-based or CNT-based nano-antenna of 1 μm length radiates energy in the terahertz (THz) band. Graphene is a two-dimensional material with high electrical and thermal conductivity. It shows plasmonic effects and allows propagation of THz surface plasmon polariton (SPP) waves, as shown in Figure 8.6. Applying a voltage between drain and source of high electron mobility transistor causes electrons to accelerate in the channel producing SSP wave on the graphene gate. In the receiving end, the process is reciprocated.

EM Wave

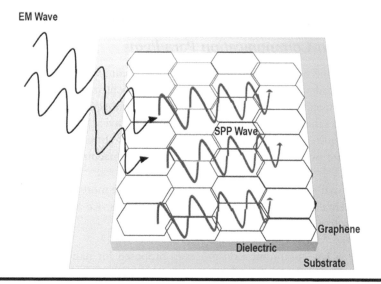

Figure 8.6 Tetrahertz Communication for Nanomachines Using the Plasmonic Effect of Nano-Antenna Graphene.

Molecular communication: Molecular communication is a whole-new communication model that is inspired by the communication processes occurring in nature between living cells. The information encoded in the molecules can be transmitted and received by the transceivers in the nanomachines as depicted in Figure 8.7. The size compatibility of the molecules facilitates the easy integration of molecular transceivers in nanomachines. Enthused from the natural way of communication in biological systems, this paradigm of communication promises to be an effective form of nano-communication.

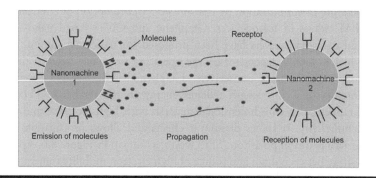

Figure 8.7 Molecular Communication between Nanomachines. The Data Is Contained in the Molecules That Are Transmitted.

8.4.2 IoNT Network Architecture

Akyildiz et al. first presented the network architecture for IoNT in two different applications and to be exact, they are as follows:

1. An intrabody nanonetwork of nanosensors implemented inside the human body and controlled remotely by an external healthcare service provider using the Internet.
2. An interconnected office where every single object is connected to a network using nano-transceivers for smart management of the location and status of the object.

They determined that the basic components of the network architecture for IoNT are the same, as shown in Figure 8.8, irrespective of the kind of application involved.

Components of IoNT @@Network Architecture:

1. **Nano-nodes:** Nano-nodes are nanomachines that can execute very simple and basic tasks like unsophisticated computation, limited storage, and very short-range communication. They are the simplest and smallest units in IoNT networks. They have only limited memory and so can perform only the basic chores. They are also constrained in terms of communication capacity and energy consumption.
   a. Examples: Nanomachines that can be attached to books, keys, files, and nanosensors that can be implemented inside the human body.
2. **Nano-routers:** Nano-routers are relatively larger nanodevices with much higher computational capacities. They are used to gather the information

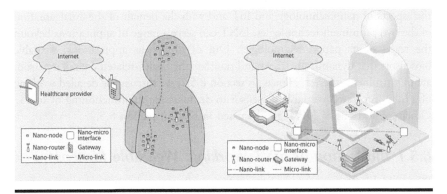

Figure 8.8 Network Architecture of IoNT for Intrabody Network for Healthcare Application and Interconnected Office, as Illustrated by Akyildiz et al. (Source: Akyildiz et al. (2015)).

from the less capacitive nanodevices. They are also used to control the nano-nodes by sending command signals like on/off, read, sleep, etc. However, the capability of the nano-routers is reliant on their size. Bigger nano-routers have increased capabilities but have the disadvantage of more intrusive deployment.

3. **Nano-micro interface devices:** Any data collected by the nano-routers need to be communicated to the end user in feasible ways to serve the purpose of the application. Hence, nano-micro interface devices act as the interface between the nano-routers and the electronic units such as a mobile phone, an electronic wrist band, or a computer that uses microprocessors. Hence, nano-micro interface devices are hybrid devices that can communicate in both micro and nano realms. They utilize either electromagnetic or molecular communication techniques to communicate on the nano-scale and utilize traditional communication techniques in conventional networks.

4. **Gateway:** Gateway enables the entire system to be remotely controlled over the Internet. For instance, in the case of the intrabody network, the information provided by the nano-micro interface devices can be forwarded to the healthcare service provider through a sophisticated wrist band or an advanced cell phone. Similarly, in the interconnected office, a modem-router can carry out the same function.

8.5 Applications of IoNT

With a future foreseen with miniaturization, complete automation, and device to device communication, IoNT will serve in numerous domains of applications (Cruz Alvarado and Bazán, 2018). IoNT is an advanced technology that combines the aspects of nanotechnology and IoT and with the benefit of the amalgamation of the two prominent technologies, IoNT can serve a range of applications beyond the reach of its parent technologies. Out of numerous applications, wearable biosensors that dynamically tracks and transfers the health-related data of a person, are of prominent interest. Hence, in section 8.5.1, we discuss the detailed working of a fully integrated wearable biosensor to demonstrate the functioning of IoNT. Other applications of IoNT are discussed in brief in section 8.5.2.

8.5.1 Illustration of IoNT Working: Wearable Biosensors

Wearable biosensors are electronic devices that can be worn as a band or coupled with dresses or skin and can continuously monitor the activities and vital signs of a person. A biosensor is mainly composed of a sensor system, a transducer, and an output system, to sense a particular biomarker or vital signs and convert it into digital and analog signals and finally the output system is responsible for communicating the result to the user, a remote healthcare provider using an interface. Electrochemical, electromagnetic, ultrasonic, and fluorescence sensors can detect the unusual presence of certain biomarkers like glucose, cholesterol, and tumor biomarkers from biofluids like blood, sweat, urine, and tears. Instead of lab-based tests that are usually lengthy and variable, wearable biosensors do not require sample collection processes and can effectively track the vitals continuously, providing a vivid understanding of the changes in the patient's biosystem.

This section deliberates the fully integrated sensor array (FISA) developed by Gao et al. as an example to illustrate the working of IoNT of how the data is collected and communicated by the sensor to the end-user. Gao and Emaminejad et al. developed a wearable FISA for the active simultaneous screening of various metabolites in human sweat perspired during various physical activities like indoor exercising and outdoor activities like running. The FISA was capable of sensing various biomarkers in human sweat effectively. It was also capable of signal transduction, amplification, filtering, conditioning, processing and data transfer. The wireless transmission of data was achieved by using existing integrated circuit technologies since nano-communication is very much their beginning stage.

Firstly, the FISA was fabricated by depositing the electrodes which were chosen to be chromium/gold (Cr/Au), by photolithography and electron beam deposition techniques in clean, flexible polyethylene terephthalate (PET) substrates. To ensure reliable sensing and avoid metal line contacts with the skin an insulating parylene layer was deposited by plasma etching, after which silver (Ag) is deposited by electron beam deposition method. This Ag layer is etched on the Cr/Au working electrodes and chlorinated for working as the reference electrodes. A flexible printed circuit board (FPCB) fused with integrated circuit components was employed to feature the signal processing and wireless transmission of data. The sensor array was of a size of a coin and flexible. When integrated with the FPCB, it could be worn as a wristband or a headband as can be seen in Figure 8.9. (The enumerated components of the FCPB given in Figure 8.9(c) are particularized in Figure 8.10 (a)).

The FISA could reliably and efficiently monitor the levels of glucose and lactate and also the body temperature of the subjects. Concerning the excess levels of metabolites, the sensor arrays independently produce corresponding current signals. The self-reliant and selective operation of discrete sensors in the array was ensured by multiplexing the measurements. The block diagram illustrates the system-level multiplexed measurement, signal transduction, conditioning, processing, and wireless transmission.

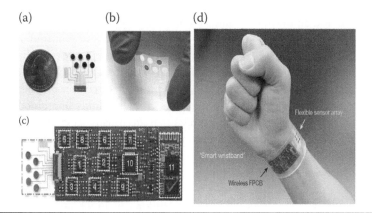

Figure 8.9 Demonstration of the Multiplexed Array Sensor's (a) Size and (b) flexibility. Photographs of (c) the Flattened FISA and d) on a Subject's Wrist. (Source: Gao et al. (2016)).

The Ag/AgCl electrode acts as a shared reference electrode and counter electrode for both the glucose and lactate amperometric sensors. Ion-selective electrodes (ISEs) are employed to measure the levels of sodium ions and potassium ions to stabilize the potential level. Cr/Au metal micro-wires enable the chemi-resistive sensing of the body temperature.

The current signals from the distinct sensors after amplification through amplifiers, are sent for signal conditioning for filtering and then fed into the analog to digital converter. The microcontroller calibrates the conditioned signals corresponding to the transduced signal and conveys them to the onboard wireless transceiver. The transceiver transmits the data through wireless Bluetooth technology to a mobile phone. With the help of a custom-developed mobile application with a user-friendly interface, the data can be viewed, shared and uploaded to the cloud servers as shown in Figure 8.10. The FISA was put to test in both indoor and outdoor-based activities, in both of which the device was able to sense and communicate efficiently.

8.5.2 Other Application

8.5.2.1 Internet of Bio-Nano Things (IoBNT) and Biomedical Applications

   a. A huge number of researches concentrate on merging the benefits of synthetic biotechnology with nanotechnology tools. Such interests result in the rise of the Internet of Bio-Nano Things (IoBNT), which is a

(a)

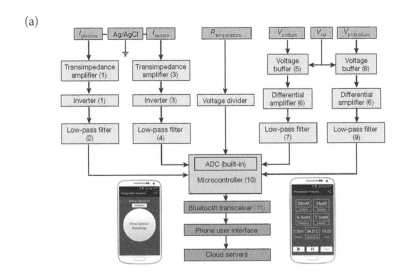

(b)

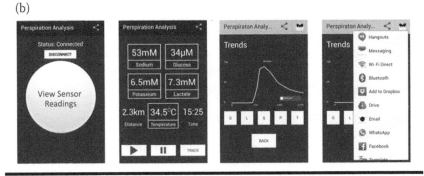

Figure 8.10 (a) Block Diagram of FISA, (b) Custom Developed App for Data Display, Real-Time Progress Viewing and Data Sharing/Uploading. (Source: Gao et al. (2016)).

subfield of IoT and IoNT. The main purpose of IoBNT is to develop bio-inspired nanoscale devices that can connect with each other and the surrounding environment (Maksimović, 2017).

b. Nanodevices can be employed for intrabody sensing and actuation for collecting health-related information, send them to a healthcare provider, and auto-initiate the release or preparation of drugs in the targeted area inside the body. IoBNT can be very useful in supporting the immune system by triggering an immune response when a foreign element of a pathogen invades the body.

c. IoBNT will be able to control the intrabody connectivity and can prevent and repair communication failures among the internal organs like nervous systems, thus preventing various diseases.

d. Nanosensors when coupled with IoNT can actively detect various biomarkers and send the record of them to the consumer and the healthcare provider. This helps in the prevention and early detection of various fatal diseases and promotes a healthy lifestyle for the people.

8.5.2.2 Industrial Applications

a. Nanosensors enabled with electromagnetic communication can considerably improve the quality control and check-in industries. With nanomachine and nanobots connected to a network, the products can be produced with nano-level precision and the number of defective products can be reduced, thus helping in less wastage of source materials.

b. In a manufacturing environment, it is of utmost necessity to monitor the temperature, humidity, and release of toxic gases. Advanced IoNT system keeps such threats monitored.

c. Functionalized fabrics can be potentially used for filtering harmful gases and other pollutants. IoNT will enable the nano actuators in the functionalized fabrics to communicate with the nanosensors so that a control reaction can be performed to improve the airflow.

8.5.2.3 Environmental Applications

a. Improper waste management severely affects the environment. The main challenge with waste management is the inappropriate disposal of wastes. Nanosensors communicated with nano actuators and external devices can actively help to tag, segregate, and locate non-biodegradable wastes from biodegradable ones. This will result in plastics ending in recycling facilities rather than in oceans.

b. IoNT can help monitor the wildlife by deploying nanosensors in animals and plants. This will prevent illegal animal trafficking and help study the animals and ecosystem with ease. IoNT can enable the transmission of data such as temperature and humidity levels in the forest to the control offices so that a mishap of wildfire can be timely detected and prevented.

c. The implementation of IoT in agriculture will enable many precision agricultural techniques like crop monitoring, observing field conditions, scrutinizing the level of usage of the pesticides and their effectiveness, and intrusion of animals and other crop destroyers.

d. With the employment of IoNT, the hygiene levels of public places like railway stations, hospitals, schools, and public offices can be supervised. The monitoring of traffic conditions and air pollution can be more effectively and simply done by employing IoNT and nanosensors.

8.5.2.4 Military and Spacespace Applications

With the rapid development of fabrication and printing techniques, highly advanced nanobots and nano-drone can be developed which will be of extreme usefulness in military and space applications where the risk of human life is high.

8.6 Challenges of IoNT

IoNT is a cutting-edge technology that allows nanodevices to be connected to a network using nano-communication protocols. It is highly adaptable to the environment in which it is applied and hence provides a range of applications with higher advantages. However, there are some serious inconveniences and challenges associated with it. For IoNT to become a reliable technology to be safely introduced in all sectors of society, the following challenges should be addressed with intensive research:

■ Establishing communication is crucial for IoNT and difficulties in communication part such as routing, energy consumption, and interfacing are need to be overcome for the complete implementation of IoNT (Mezaal et al., 2018).

■ The key challenge of IoNT is to ensure the security and privacy of user data. When IoNT becomes a part of life, a bunch of vulnerable and personal data like a person's health details, professional details, and other legitimate information will be handled by the technology which involves the frequent transfer of data. A regimented security mechanism that safeguards user data from hackers and accesses the only user-approved data is still to be developed.

■ The next major challenge involved with IoNT is data processing. With every nanodevice connected to the Internet, a lot of data is produced by it. Even a simple fitness tracker produces a huge amount of data such as activity tracking, location tracking, calorie levels, sleep data, and heartbeat levels. Apart from the data generated at the user end, there are other sets of data from the industry and service provider end. A standardized data handling methodology using technologies like cloud storage is necessary for the active functioning of IoNT.

■ Most of the applications provided by IoNT are healthcare applications. However, a universal understanding of the toxicity of nanoparticles has not yet been acquired. Many studies show that the nanoparticles are toxic when administered beyond a recommended amount. Nanodevices are fabricated by the assembly of such nanoparticles. Hence, they should be tested for environmental affability and safety before putting into prevalent use.

■ There is a lack of standardized regulation in software coverage, communication protocols, and network architectures for IoNT systems. This demands rigorous researches and studies in these areas to bridge the knowledge and technology gap.

8.7 Conclusion

To draw a concluding outline, IoNT wide opens the capability of nanotechnology to reach different levels of application, by connecting nano things to the Internet. On the other hand, by incorporating nanomachines, IoNT has the potential of reaching the nooks and corners of several applications that were once inaccessible to IoT. Miniaturized nanodevices institute new ways of communication in the nanoscale. The general network architecture of the IoNT, irrespective of the type of application, provides an undisputed comprehension of the nanonetworks. However, IoT suffers from several challenges like data security, privacy, data processing, lack of software development and communication protocols. To overcome these obstacles, a multi-disciplinary approach is required, as developing IoNT requires knowledge from diverse resources like materials science, device engineering, network and communication engineering, and software development. Though it will take some time for the complete practical realization, IoNT will have a huge impact in all fields and lives in the society in the near future.

References

Akyildiz, I.F., Brunetti, F., Blázquez, C., 2008. Nanonetworks: A new communication paradigm. *Computer Networks* 52(12), 2260–2279. doi: 10.1016/j.comnet. 2008.04.001

Akyildiz, I.F., Pierobon, M., Balasubramaniam, S., Koucheryavy, Y., 2015. The Internet of bio-nano things. *IEEE Communications Magazine* 53(3), 32–40. doi: 10.1109/ mcom.2015.7060516.

Cruz Alvarado, M.A., Bazán, P.A., 2018. Understanding the Internet of nano things: overview, trends, and challenges. *E-Ciencias de La Información* 9. doi: 10.15517/ eci.v1i1.33807.

Gao, W., Emaminejad, S., Nyein, H.Y.Y., Challa, S., Chen, K., Peck, A., Fahad, H.M., Ota, H., Shiraki, H., Kiriya, D., Lien, D.H., Brooks, G.A., Davis, R.W., Javey, A., 2016. Fully integrated wearable sensor arrays for multiplexed in situ perspiration analysis. *Nature* 529(7587), 509–514. doi: 10.1038/nature16521

Maksimović, M., 2017. The roles of nanotechnology and Internet of nano things in healthcare transformation. *TecnoLógicas* 20(40), 139–153. doi: 10.22430/22565337.720.

Mezaal, Y.S., Yousif, L.N., Abdulkareem, Z.J., Hussein, H.A., Khaleel, S.K., 2018. Review about effects of IOT and Nano-technology techniques in the development of IONT in wireless systems. *International Journal of Engineering and Technology (UAE)* 7(4), 3602–3606. doi: 10.14419/ijet.v7i4.21741.

Miraz, M.H., Ali, M., Excell, P.S., Picking, R., 2018. Internet of Nano-Things, things and everything: Future growth trends. *Future Internet* 10(8). doi: 10.3390/fi10080068.

Moinudeen, G.K., Ahmad, F., Kumar, D., Ahmad, S., 2017. IoT applications in future foreseen guided by engineered nanomaterials and printed intelligence technologies a technology review. *International Journal of Internet of Things* 6(3), 106–148. doi: 10.5923/j.ijit.20170603.03.

Nayyar, A., Puri, V., Le, D.-N., 2017. Internet of nano things (IoNT): Next evolutionary step in nanotechnology. *Nanoscience and Nanotechnology* 7(1), 4–8. doi: 10.5923/j.nn.20170701.02.

Chapter 9

Blockchain and Cybersecurity

R.S. Gopalan

Deputy Director General, UIDAI Regional Office, Bengaluru, India

Contents

DOI: 10.1201/9781003175872-9   **221**

Objectives

By reading this chapter, a student will gain knowledge in the following:

1. Definition of blockchain and the need for blockchain
2. Hash functions and their usage
3. Application of hash function in blockchain
4. Advantages of using blockchain and disadvantages of blockchain
5. How blockchains are used to provide a more secure cyberspace

---

9.1 Introduction to Blockchain

A **blockchain** is a distributed (decentralized) register of transactions or records that is continuous, immutable, and validated by multiple peers. It is a replacement for centrally guarded databases. It uses the tools of cryptography to achieve its immutability. It can be either public or private. Blockchain provides a database with public access that is also secure.

Normally, databases are centralized; they can be physical or digital; a register of tax assessment and payments written and maintained by an ancient tax collector or land records maintained by the Tahsildar, are examples of centralized physical databases; bank ledgers maintained in a computer server are an example of a centralized digital database. A database can be private or public;

the account of a private company is a private database; Tahsildar's land records, or the sale deeds registered in a Registrar Office, are public databases.

A database has to be secure against tampering; otherwise, it is unreliable. Physical databases achieve this by ensuing secure custody, paper trials of the movement of registers between place to place and person to person ("logbook"), samples of handwriting and signatures and attestation. Digital databases achieve this by passwords, cryptography, tracking the changes ("logs") and timestamping the transactions. Only authorized personnel can modify or add to the database. In addition, they are protected by layers of physical and digital security.

Centralized databases suffer from one major drawback, namely, **trusting the custodian**. Irrespective of all the precautions and security measures, a centralized database can be tampered with by its custodian. Any centralized database needs to have at least one person who has complete access to it. If that custodian modifies the database without authorization, it cannot be detected easily; usually, this is avoided by distributing this responsibility among many persons and keeping a log of their access and modifications in a file, which will be inaccessible to the custodian. However, even this file has to be under someone's custody, and hence it can be tampered with, or the entire group may be compromised. In short, however long the chain of custody may be, or however much it is distributed, a centralized database is theoretically vulnerable to manipulations.

Blockchains take a different approach to this problem. They solve this problem by making the data tamper-proof at every stage, and adding blocks of immutable data continuously, hence the name blockchain. Since the data is immutable, data security is no longer a problem – i.e., this data does not need layers of security. Thus, blockchains are said to be **trustless**.

The concept of blockchain was first discussed in the whitepaper released by **Nakamoto (2008)**, the anonymous inventor of Bitcoins, in 2008, though he did not use the term blockchain. Blockchains are hosted in a network of computers. Those machines that host the distributed database are called **nodes**; they are all peers, and all of them host the same software to run the node. They all store replicas of the same ledger; these ledgers are append-only, and all transactions appended here are digitally signed. These nodes maintain the ledger through consensus, that is, by synchronizing it at intervals.

A blockchain can be private or public; a public blockchain is open for anyone to join; it provides a small incentive to the nodes, to attract participants; usually, this incentive is a small commission for every transaction and an incentive for finishing a block. A public blockchain needs to spend a lot of time ensuring that the nodes are in sync, through a proof-of-work task that consumes much time and energy. In contrast, in a private blockchain, a central authority authorizes nodes to participate, either through traditional methods of authentication or through the blockchain itself.

However, this data security comes with a price – it needs to be distributed over many machines in a network, and therefore consumes more power than a centralized database.

Let us understand how a blockchain makes the data tamperproof.

9.2 Cryptographic Hash Functions

Blockchains use an algorithm called the **cryptographic Hash function**. It is a mathematical function that takes inputs of variable length and converts them into an output of uniform length. This function has the following properties:

1. It is a **one-way function** – the input cannot be determined from the output
2. It is **deterministic** – the same input always produces the same output
3. It is **unpredictable** – not possible to get the output by using any other algorithm
4. It produces a **unique output** – no two inputs produce the same output, as much as possible
5. It is **highly variable** – even changing a single character in the input produces a completely different output

SHA -1, SHA -2, SHA -3, SHA – 256, SHA -384, SHA -512, AES, BLAKE2, and Whirlpool are some of the Cryptographic Hash Functions.

SHA 256 ("Secure Hashing Algorithm – 256") is a widely used hash function; it gives an output of 256 bits, irrespective of the input; the increase in processor speeds has rendered it unusable for security purposes anymore; however, it can still be used for verifying the integrity of data, etc. Here are some examples of SHA 256 hashing:

Plain Text	SHA 256 hash
1	6b86b273ff34fce19d6b804eff5a3f5747ada4eaa22f1d49c01e52ddb7875b4b
India	abd149214539d9f222d25de6358735b9fa0efd3956f66102b2c119ae2d9f6348
INDIA	f8929fed8f0112944163064bce39c020eeefaee2a78515fcf2ac006b8317daf2
INDAI	20dda2a7c9e309621ff5e09c4a1a2e0c40239c8452fbc43cd056b80f58b4c78e
InDIA	122cb37cc59e98c52b5f9d6f4384ba2fd4a6f268e25799c38cc355336aa865bb

Even a small change in the input produces a completely different output. The output is of uniform size – 256 bit – 32 bytes. This has since been superseded by SHA 384, SHA 512, etc. These algorithms are available in open source.

Cryptographic hash functions are one way – they are **irreversible**; these can be compared to a juicer that crushes fruits and produces juice and pulp. It is not possible to reverse this process and recover the fruit; or a paper shredder, where the shredded pieces cannot be put together again. Thus, hashing is different from encryption; in encryption, a message is encrypted with the public key of the recipient; the recipient can use his private key to decrypt the encrypted message. The decrypted message will be exactly the same as the original message before encryption. In hashing, it is not possible to recover the original message from the hash.

Ideally, in a hash function, no two inputs should produce the same output; however, given that there is an infinite number of inputs but only a limited number of outputs, this property is difficult to achieve; in practice, there are occasions when two inputs may produce the same output; in such situations, there are fixed rules on how to resolve a collision in every hash function – where two different inputs produce the same output.

Hash functions are used for verifying the integrity of data, files, and communications, the safety of passwords, digital signatures, proof-of-work, etc. Blockchains use hash functions for verifying the integrity of data; cryptocurrencies use proof-of-work to generate new coins.

9.2.1 Uses of Hash Functions

9.2.1.1 Integrity of Data

The integrity of a file downloaded from a website may be doubtful; it may so happen that malicious changes have been made in the file, without the knowledge of the author. Therefore, the author may also publish the **hash digest** of the file (the result of hashing the file) along with it. A user can download the file, hash it, and compare the result with the hash digest provided by the author. Any change in the file will produce a different hash.

9.2.1.2 Protecting Passwords

Many websites allow users only after authentication; the most common method of authentication is using a **password**. The website administrator has to store the usernames and passwords; however, storing them in plain text is not desirable, as it may get hacked; or even the administrator may use the credentials to enter the user accounts. Therefore, both the username and password are hashed using a hash function, and the resultant string is stored instead.

However, there is a drawback in this method too; since these hash function algorithms are openly available, a good number of commonly used words, names, and phrases can be hashed, and the hash results can be stored in a table; such tables can be used to find the original text ("**preimage**") of the hash string. Therefore, certain selected words or strings ("**salt**") are added at random to the username or password, and the resultant string is hashed; this makes the recovery of the username or password virtually impossible.

9.2.1.3 Proof-of-Work

This concept is used to ensure that the resources of the service provider are not abused, and to reward a user for the work. To prevent a user from overusing the resources, the service provider imposes a task on the user; the task is such that it is feasible but moderately hard for the user, but the service provider can easily verify the solution. Therefore, while the user has to spend some time and effort on solving the task, the service provider need not spend the same time and effort to verify the solution. For example, an email service may want to prevent spam mail; it may impose a task on the user before he can send each mail; this is not a burden for a bonafide user who sends one or two mails, but a user who wants to send thousands of spam mails must spend considerable time and energy.

The typical task is to ask the user to provide a hash result that contains a specified string of characters. For example, the user may be asked to provide a text whose hash result starts with three continuous zeros or ones. This will force the user to spend time and energy in solving the problem. But the service provider can easily verify it and need not spend the same amount of time and energy as the user. The user may have to attempt a thousand times to find the text that produces the necessary hash, but the service provider needs to check it by hashing the answer only once.

This property is used in cryptocurrencies to create new coins as a reward. In Bitcoins, the rewards are reserved for the node which comes up with a hash that starts with n number of zeros. The winner is rewarded a certain number of Bitcoins by the algorithm itself. This will be discussed in detail subsequently.

9.3 Hash Functions in a Blockchain

A blockchain is a public ledger, hosted in many nodes. Every transaction is broadcast to all the active nodes, and all the nodes record the transactions they receive. It can be visualized as a group chat in WhatsApp or Telegram; the same message is received in every member's handset and recorded in its memory. In a blockchain, once this data reaches a predetermined size ("**block**"), it is time-stamped and hashed, and the hash digest is taken as the header for the next block. Thus, every block contains the hash of its previous block. If someone tries to change an entry in a block, its hash result will immediately change, and his block will be different from all other blocks, and other nodes can reject it. The blocks are added one by one, with the hash of the previous block forming the link with the next block. The whole record is comparable to a chain of blocks, hence the name blockchain.

The difference between a group chat in WhatsApp and a blockchain is that in a group chat, there is a central server, from which all handsets receive data. In a blockchain network, there are no central servers; instead, each node is broadcasting to all other nodes.

In a WhatsApp group chat, its members post messages, and these messages are the contents. In the blockchains, any data that is incrementally built over time can be recorded; for example, in the blockchains of a cryptocurrency, all the transactions of that cryptocurrency are recorded. Let us understand how a blockchain is formed in the Bitcoin network, the oldest network of blockchains.

9.3.1 Blockchain in Bitcoin Network

Let there be a peer-to-peer network of nodes; each node is uniquely numbered, each Bitcoin is uniquely numbered, and each address that holds bitcoins is also uniquely numbered; wherever there is a transaction, that is, whenever a Bitcoin is exchanged between two addresses, that transaction is broadcast to all the nodes; the nodes record the transaction with time; a node takes a block of items recorded, hashes it, adds a timestamp, and broadcasts the result. The next node takes up that hash, adds it to its block, hashes it, adds a timestamp, and broadcasts the result (Figure 9.1).

For a private blockchain, this is sufficient; however, the Bitcoin network is a public blockchain; therefore, it adds a proof-of-work to implement a distributed timestamp server on a peer-to-peer basis. It demands that the hash result obtained through the process described in the last paragraph should begin with a certain number of zeros. To make this happen, the timestamp server takes up the hash of the previous block, adds the data in the current block, and adds a random text ("**nonce**") and hashes it; usually, natural numbers are taken as nonce; if the result does not begin with the requisite number of zeros, it changes the nonce incrementally by adding one, and hashes again; this process is repeated until the resulting hash begins with the requisite number of zeros. It must be noted that only nonce is changed in every attempt. Once such a nonce is found, that whole block (previous hash + timestamp + transactions +nonce) is

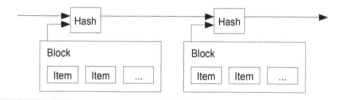

Figure 9.1   Blockchain (Nakamoto, 2008).

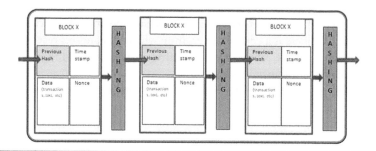

Figure 9.2   Continuous Blockchain.

broadcast over the network to other nodes. Other nodes hash the block, and confirm that the hash indeed starts with a requisite number of zeros; this process is very easy, as it involves hashing only once (Figure 9.2).

This method of finding a hash with the requisite number of zeros for a given block, by adding a nonce, constitutes the **proof-of-work** for the node. As every node has to work to find a requisite hash, once a node finds such a hash, then it is deemed that that node has spent time and effort on that task; hence, it is called proof-of-work.

Once a node confirms that another node has created a new block, whose hash begins with the requisite number of zeros, it accepts the hash of that block and starts a new block by adding transaction data to it. This process of re-cording the transactions, adding a timestamp, adding a nonce, and hashing it repeatedly until a new hash with necessary zeros is obtained, is called "**mining**". Once the nonce is found, the block is said to be "**finished**". Normally, mining is a very processor-intensive process that generates a lot of heat. It is not possible for a single CPU to take up the huge computations; therefore, many processors are connected in parallel, to take up the task simultaneously. Such collective efforts are called mining pools. Whatever rewards they get, by mining new blocks and through transaction fees, is divided among the owners of the pro-cessors. As the mining process became resource-intensive, GPU-based specia-lized mining equipment was built; later on, dedicated hardware, called ASIC

("Application-Specific Integrated Circuits") rigs, were built for the purpose of cryptocurrency mining.

The very first transaction in the new block is a reward to the node that successfully created the last block – by releasing a certain number of new Bitcoins to the creator. For example, if ten nodes confirm a newly created block (by verifying that its hash starts with a necessary number of zeros) they all start a new block of their own, with the hash of the last block as its header (the very first line of the block); they all record further transactions, wait until their block reaches the stipulated size (2 MB for Bitcoin blocks), and then add the time-stamp, add a random nonce, and start hashing. All of these ten nodes will form blocks with different transactions, but the first transaction in all the new blocks will be the reward to the creator of the last block. This transaction is also included in the header of the baby blocks. Except for this one transaction, the transactions recorded in these newly started ten blocks may be very different. Of these ten blocks, the first one to be finished will form the next block in the blockchain. Now the remaining nodes will pick the hash of this new block, and start hashing again.

Thus, the principles of the Bitcoin blockchain network can be summarized as follows:

1. New transactions are broadcast to all nodes. These transactions are temporarily held in a memory pool (**mempool**); the size of the memory pool varies from node to node.
2. Each node chooses some new transactions from the mempool into a block.
3. Each node works on finding a difficult proof-of-work for its block – by adding a nonce, and hashing it, repeatedly, until getting a hash that begins with a requisite number of zeros.
4. When a node finds a proof-of-work, it broadcasts the block to all nodes. All other nodes verify the proof-of-work and base their next block on that hash.
5. Nodes accept the block only if all transactions in it are valid (if an address tries to spend more coins than it has or to spend the same coin twice, by trying to send it to two different addresses (**double spending**) that transaction will be rejected; any block that includes such a transaction will also be rejected by other nodes. Therefore, even if a node finds the requisite hash for a block, if that block contains an invalid transaction, it will be rejected by other nodes, and the time and effort spent on hashing that block is wasted. Therefore, all the nodes have an incentive to include only valid transactions in their blocks).

6. Nodes express their acceptance of the block by working on creating the next block in the chain, using the hash of the accepted block as the previous hash (header).
7. If two nodes find the next block simultaneously, both will be broadcasted; those two blocks will be different; all other nodes will receive both the blocks, record them but each will choose the hash of only one block as a header for their next block.
8. Thus, there will be two branches of the same blockchain; each may continue to grow; however, the moment one chain becomes longer, all nodes will abandon the other chain, and take the last hash of the longer chain as the header for their next block. The longest chain is always preferred.
9. New transaction broadcasts do not necessarily need to reach all nodes. As long as they reach many nodes, they will get into a block before long.
10. Block broadcasts are also tolerant of dropped messages. If a node does not receive a block, it will request it when it receives the next block and realizes it missed one (Nakamoto, 2008).

9.3.2 Private Blockchain

A Private Blockchain is where the entry to the network is controlled by a central authority; the central authority decides the participating nodes. Unlike a public blockchain, a private blockchain can demand **varying levels of proof-of-work**, and may raise or lower the requirement; thus, its reliability is reduced; however, it does not consume as much energy as a public blockchain.

Private blockchains are employed within a closed network of members, where each member is familiar with others, and they add the blockchain protocol only as an additional safeguard.

9.4 Advantages of Blockchains

Blockchains are **immutable**; data can be stored without getting modified.

The host computer's security does not have any impact on the blockchain; thus, nodes can be hosted even on a compromised computer affected by a virus, worm, etc.

Since the hosts can remain anonymous, it is not possible to identify the location of the host computers. This ensures complete protection from snooping.

Similarly, since the transactions are recorded only as between addresses, and not as between users, the identity of the users can be protected.

9.5 Disadvantages of Blockchains

Blockchains need many nodes to run; this makes blockchains more expensive than conventional centralized databases. To work with the same size of data, a blockchain consumes energy many times that of a centralized database, even a hundred times more.

There is an apprehension that the introduction of quantum computers can make blockchains vulnerable to manipulation; in theory, a sufficiently powerful computer can take a finished block with a particular hash, change an entry in the data, and then find a nonce that produces the same hash; thus, the chain is not disturbed but data in the block is tampered with. However, since the transaction could be recorded in many blocks, the consensus of the whole network may be towards the untampered data.

Blockchains are vulnerable to **51% of attacks**.

9.5.1 51% Attack

Even a public blockchain is vulnerable to a type of manipulation called the 51% Attack. In a blockchain network, all the nodes continuously hash the blocks, looking for the desired hash result. The collective capacity of the network to hash is called **hash rate** or **hash power**. All the transactions of crypto coins are temporarily held in a mempool. If a single person or a group of persons control more than 51% of hash power, they can ignore certain transactions in the mempool and keep those transactions away from the blocks they are hashing. Suppose address X has sent 100 coins to address Y; the malicious miner who controls 51% hash power can ignore this transaction out of the blocks they are hashing; other honest nodes may include this transaction in their blocks. Since the malicious miner controls more than 51% of the hash power, he hashes blocks faster than the rest of the network; but he chooses not to broadcast the blocks he mined, and continues to add new blocks to his chain. After some time, he reveals the whole chain to the network; since his chain is the longest, all nodes will abandon other blocks they were working on, and switch to this chain. Since this malicious chain does not include the transaction of address X in any of the blocks it has mined, now, as per the whole network, the above transaction between X and Y has never happened, and those 100 coins are still with address X. Thus, address X can send those coins again to some other address, spending them again (double spending). This is called a 51% Attack.

In practice, a 51% Attack is almost impossible to carry out if the network is sufficiently large. Since private blockchains demand much less onerous proof-of-work than public blockchains, the possibility of a 51% Attack in a private blockchain is more.

9.5.2 Examples of 51% Attacks

The very first 51% Attack was on Feathercoin, a Litecoin clone, in June 2013 when 16,000 coins were double-spent. This led to a fall in the value of this crypto coin.

In May 2018, a very large double-spending worth $18 million occurred in a cryptocurrency called Bitcoin Gold. Even though the exchanges were notified of the theft (a cryptocurrency being spent by the same node a second time amounts to stealing it from the first recipient), and the exchanges tried to stop the transactions, in the end, they could not stop the double-spending.

Coinbase, a very large exchange, noted a double spend in the Ethereum Classic blockchain in January 2019; the value was not disclosed. Another exchange, Gate.io, identified seven transactions of double-spending related to the same attack.

Two big mining pools of Bitcoin Cash, a hard-forked crypto coin out of the Bitcoin chain, carried out a 51% Attack in May 2019, on an unknown miner who was trying to steal some newly created Bitcoin Cash coins.

9.6 Blockchains and Cybersecurity

Blockchains are far stronger than centralized databases; it is true that advances in computing may produce computers that can unravel a hash function, but the same developments can compromise the security of a centralized database very easily. Therefore, for a given capacity of the processors, it is always easier to hack a centralized database than unravel and redo a blockchain.

Blockchains can be used to record any series of transactions, like transactions of a stock exchange (transfer of financial instruments like shares, debentures, etc.) or transfer of movable and immovable properties, or health records of patients, etc. In all these cases, the underlying principles are the same.

Theoretically, blockchains can replace all centralized databases; however, since blockchain needs power many times that of a centralized database, it is used only where it can provide a significant advantage over the centralized database. Blockchains solve some of the complicated problems encountered in classical cyberspace through their radically different approach. Let us see how blockchains are used to provide a more secure cyberspace.

9.6.1 Cryptocurrency

Even though the digital currency is used since at least the 1990s it suffered from a classical drawback: it required a trusted third party to function as a ledger keeper of transactions. This involved maintaining a centralized database of transactions, protecting it against malicious attacks and guarding its access through usernames and passwords. Even then, the problem of **double spending** remained difficult to solve: What if a person sends the same digital currency unit to two different persons successively, before the first transaction is recorded in the database? As sending a digital currency unit is not the same as sending a physical object because the sender can still have a copy of the digital currency unit in his computer even after sending it, it becomes necessary to have a trusted third party to keep track of the movement of all digital currency units. If the same digital currency unit is sent to two different parties, this third party will accept only the earlier transaction as genuine and reject the later one. Practical difficulties in this approach include the delays in networks in reporting to the central server that keeps the transaction register (ledger), the trustworthiness of the third party, security measures around the central server, etc. Due to these reasons, the only successful digital transactions were those carried out by banks over their private networks.

Nakamoto (2008) solved the problem of double spending without resorting to a central server or a trusted third party. His 2008 paper introduced the concept of using cryptographic hashing to establish the immutability of the records of transactions. The resulting digital currency is called a **cryptocurrency**.

A cryptocurrency is a digital asset created with cryptography, that can be used as a medium of exchange, either in cyberspace or in the real world. Cryptocurrencies are decentralized, and autogenerated by the nodes after they submit a proof-of-work to the network. It is based on a digital signature and is uniquely numbered. In this aspect, they differ from centrally managed digital currencies and banking systems.

A centrally controlled digital currency suffered from one more drawback, namely, new currency units are introduced only by the central authority; these new units can be allotted arbitrarily to any member, and other members have no say in it. A cryptocurrency resolves this drawback awarding the nodes which keep the ledger, by distributing new cryptocurrency units as rewards to submitting a proof-of-work.

A cryptocurrency network has the following characteristics:

a. It is decentralized; there is no central server or authority.
b. The nodes collectively keep records of the transfer of cryptocurrency units between addresses.
c. The nodes charge a small fee for recording these transactions, which is deducted out of the transferred amount.
d. The number of cryptocurrency units and how they are created is determined by the system; new units can be created as a reward to the nodes for successfully completing a new block, or can be created at fixed quantities either one time or at intervals.

234 ■ *Securing IoT in Industry 4.0 Applications with Blockchain*

All software related to a cryptocurrency is published as open source in some public domain, thus open for inspection.

A cryptocurrency node does three functions simultaneously: a. it records the cryptocurrency transactions between addresses, b. it bundles these transactions into a block, adds the hash of the previous block, and adds a nonce, hashes the resultant block; if the hash starts with the necessary number of zeros, the new block is complete, and this node claims its reward; and c. it confirms the claims of other nodes by hashing and comparing the result.

Crypto coins are stored in a wallet; it is a program that keeps pairs of public and private cryptographic keys; these are used to generate an **address** that is given out to the sender; the sender can send crypto coins to this address. Only the receiver can unlock it with his private key. Thus, every transaction will have a sender address and a receiver address. These addresses are recorded in the nodes, along with the number of crypto coins; however, it is not possible to determine which wallet owns which address; thus, crypto coin transactions are anonymous as to the ownership of the coins, but not as to how many coins were transacted and between which addresses. Some wallets come with their hardware.

Cryptocurrencies generally use two methods to distribute the newly created cryptocurrency units (**"crypto coins"** or simply **"coins"**). In the **proof-of-work** method, a node has to submit a finished block, consisting of a set of transactions data, the hash of the previous block and a nonce, the hashing of which should produce a hash that begins with a requisite number of zeroes. The difficulty of this work is increased exponentially, by demanding an increased number of zeroes at the beginning of the hash. In the **proof-of-stake** method, the cryptocurrency wallets send proof to the network that the addresses in the wallets held a certain number of coins on a particular date; the network awards new coins to these addresses proportionately. Proof-of-stake is used to attract wallet owners to new coins that are clones or hard forked out of an existing crypto coin. Thus, when Bitcoin Cash was hard forked out of the Bitcoin blockchain, every address that held Bitcoins was rewarded an equal number of Bitcoin Cash.

The very first cryptocurrency is **Bitcoin**, introduced in 2010; it uses SHA-256 Hash Function; soon it was followed by Namecoin, Litecoin, and Dogecoin; at present there are more than 2000 such cryptocurrencies. Various cryptocurrencies use various cryptographic hash functions; a few of them use a mix of more than one hash functions.

Bitcoin blockchains are published on many websites; Blockchain.com is a popular website, which publishes the completed blocks at the URL www.blockchain.com/explorer (Figure 9.3) (Blockchain, 2021).

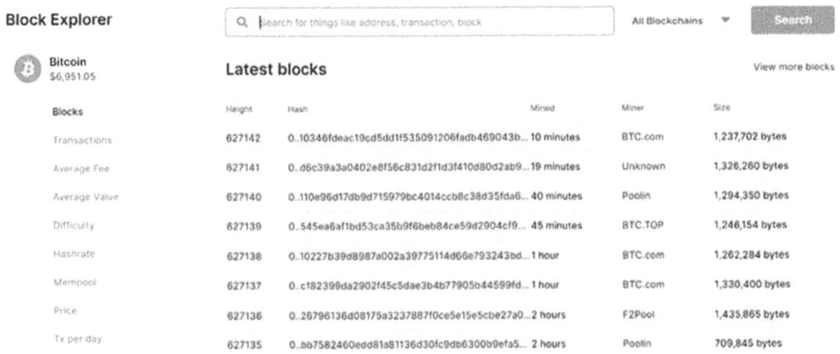

Figure 9.3   Blocks in Blockchain.

Let us look at a typical block; here is a block:

https://www.blockchain.com/btc/block/00000000000000000000021
e6062cc0290b3313e7c601ea901277d58892b21e38a
Hash: 00000000000000000000021e6062cc0290b3313e7c601ea
901277d58892b21e38a Timestamp: 2020-04-22 12:11
Height: 627133 (position in the longest blockchain)
Miner: AntPool
Number of Transactions: 1,777
Difficulty: 15,958,652,328,578.42
Nonce: 2,425,980,328
Transaction Volume: 4328.80228168 BTC
Block Reward: 12.50000000 BTC

From this, we understand that this block was mined (completed, that is, the hash with the requisite number of zeroes at the beginning was found) on 22nd April 2020, at 12:11 UTC; it contains 1,777 bitcoin transactions, the total volume of these transactions is 4328.8 Bitcoins. This hash was found by forming a block (that is, taking the previous hash value of 627132nd block, appending these 1777 transactions details, and adding 2,425,980,328 as nonce) and hashing it. On that date, the required hash must start with 18 zeros at the beginning; this defines the level of difficulty for the nodes. When a node finds out such a hash, it is deemed that that node has worked for a certain amount of time on the task; hence, finding this hash is deemed to be a "proof-of-work". Since there could be a countless numbers of hashes that start with 18 zeros, even if two blocks find hashes for the same block, and even if both hashes start with 18 zeros, the nodes could have used different nonces, and therefore their hash value will be different. In other words, even if two blocks use the same hash from one previous block as their header, and add the same set of data to that since their nonces are different, their end result of hashes will also be different.

It must be noted that not all nodes need to spend the same amount of time in finding the hash. It is possible that a node may find out the requisite hash at the very first attempt itself. However, on the average, the work done by the nodes to mine a block at any given level of difficulty (18 zeros at the beginning, 15 zeros at the beginning, etc.) is taken to be the same, all the nodes are rewarded the same amount of coins on mining a block (Bitcoin, 2021).

The transactions in this block are listed below these details (Figure 9.4).

Cryptocurrencies normally have a ceiling of how many coins can be created; Bitcoin has a ceiling of 21 million coins. Most cryptocurrencies award newly created coins as rewards to those who run the nodes. However, some cryptocurrencies issue all the currency units at the beginning, in the very first block ("genesis block"). Such cryptocurrency units are called tokens instead of coins. In such a cryptocurrency, the nodes do not create new coins; instead, they record the transactions in blocks in return for a small fee. In a Bitcoin blockchain, the difficulty of hashing is increased every four years, and the reward size is reduced by half. When the Bitcoin network was started in 2010, the reward for a successful block was 50 bitcoins, it has subsequently been halved to 25 bitcoins in 2012, and 12.5 bitcoins in 2016.

There are specialized platforms for buying and selling cryptocurrencies, called **cryptocurrency exchanges**; they work along the lines of stock exchanges, although there is no specific law to regulate their functioning. Coinbase is one of the largest cryptocurrency exchanges. Some of the drawbacks of Bitcoin are discussed in the whitepaper of Monero, another cryptocurrency (Whitepaper database, 2021).

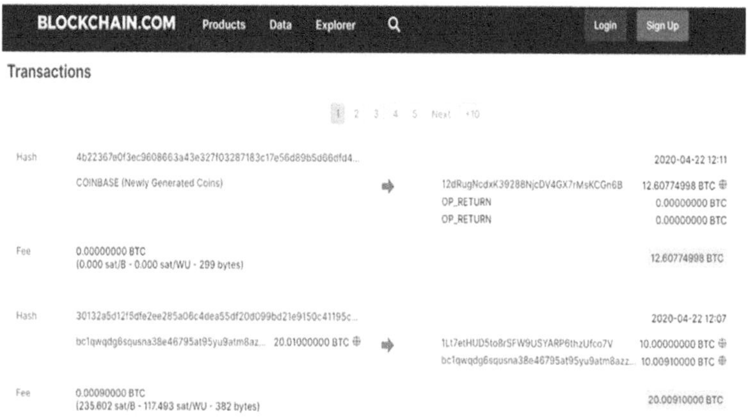

Figure 9.4   First Page of a Block.

Cryptocurrencies are useful in payments across national borders. Since they can be sent from anywhere to anywhere over the Internet, there is no need for banks to act as intermediaries, or convert one currency into another. For this reason, countries have made laws concerning the use of cryptocurrencies.

9.6.2 Smart Contracts

A contract needs a trusted third party to enforce the contract; if a party to a contract fails to adhere to the contract, a trusted third party becomes necessary for dispute resolution and enforcing the terms against the defaulting party. Under the contract laws, courts play the role of this trusted third party; sometimes the law provides for appointing an arbitrator who can adjudicate between the contracting parties. Sometimes, even when there is no dispute, a trusted third party becomes necessary; for example, if two parties from two countries enter into a contract for supplying goods, the seller may demand a trusted third party to stand surety for the buyer, to avoid disputes in payments. These are called escrow services. Normally, banks provide such escrow services for a substantial fee.

Smart contracts are software programs that eliminate the need for a trusted third party; they play the role of the trusted third party. This term was coined in 1994 by **Nick Snabo**; however, he envisaged only a classical contract enforced through a computer program instead of a third party. Smart contracts can be described as programs enforcing a contract; however, they are now extending beyond the classical forms of contracts. The most widely used smart contract platform is the Ethereum blockchain (Ethereum, 2021).

Ethereum is a public blockchain that has its own scripting language; in addition to creating and managing a cryptocurrency called **Ether** (ETH) and its associated blockchain, Ethereum nodes also act as a Virtual Machine; it is a Turing complete software that can run any program. Ethereum-based smart contracts can be written in many languages (Wood, 2021).

An example can show how Ethereum smart contract works. Suppose there is a contract between A and B about selling 100 shares of a company on a future date, subject to an agreed price per share; that is, A will sell to B 100 shares on 1st August 2020 if the market price of the shares is not less than Rs 150 per share. If the price is less than that, the sale is off. Both A and B agree that the price of the shares as quoted on the website of the National Stock Exchange to be binding. The smart contract is written; A sends his 100 shares to the contract; B sends payment Rs 15,000 in Ether to the same contract. The URL of the website of the National Stock Exchange is also coded into the contract. On 1st August 2020, the smart contract will check the price of the shares with the URL; if the price is more than Rs 150 per share, it will send the shares to B and

Ethers worth Rs 15,000 to A; if the price is less than the agreed price, then the sale is off, and the smart contract will return shares and cryptocurrency to A and B, respectively.

This simplified example shows the potential of Ethereum smart contracts, to provide escrow services. Escrow services is a huge international market, with large growth prospects. Smart contracts issued by bankers can speed up international business transactions. Any buyer who needs a Letter of Credit from a bank for an export may instead opt to send cryptocurrencies of equivalent value to a smart contract; as these smart contracts are also open-source software, they can be inspected for hidden malware. Smart contracts can completely replace future trading. They can prevent short-selling, by ensuring that either the digital form of shares is appended to the smart contract, or by attaching an encrypted password to a hardware locker.

Smart contracts may suffer from **code bugs** that may cause unexpected and unintended adverse actions that cannot be stopped.

NEO is another popular smart contract platform; Hyperledger project, an endeavor by the Linux Foundation, is also a type of smart contract platform.

9.6.3 Transferring Financial Instruments: Uses in Stock Exchanges

At present, most stock exchanges store the transaction data in centralized servers. To obviate the problems associated with centralized databases, stock exchanges are now switching to blockchains in part. **NASDAQ**, the second-largest stock exchange in the world in terms of capitalization, is using blockchains for certain types of shares. London Stock Exchange and Moscow Stock Exchange are also introducing blockchains in their system.

Blockchains can be used for recording the transactions of a stock exchange. Since a blockchain can record data in chronological order, it is possible to stipulate that blocks must contain all transactions as they occurred in time; this will necessitate forming more blocks, but the difficulty of proof-of-work can be reduced accordingly, to make it easier for hashing.

Let us see how a blockchain can be used to record transactions in a stock exchange. Every user gets a **wallet** with unique addresses, every **financial instrument** (shares, debentures, swaps, etc.) gets a unique identification number; all financial instruments are issued only by the authorized companies listed in the stock exchange. When a user buys a financial instrument from the company, that instrument is sent to an address in his wallet, and that transaction is broadcast to all nodes; similarly, when a user buys from another user, the financial instrument is sent from the sellers' wallet to buyers' wallet. All nodes must record all transactions, unlike a Bitcoin blockchain, where the nodes may choose some transactions out of a memory pool, and leave others. All nodes are set down to the task of hashing the block by adding nonce; soon, a node discovers the right hash, and broadcasts it to all nodes; all nodes verify the claim, and if the claim is true, abandon the block they are working on, and take up the next block for hashing. Since all nodes are owned by the stock exchange, there is no reward for the node that finished the block. The level of difficulty of hashing (number of zeros at the beginning, or any such criterion) can be increased periodically, to compensate for the increasing processor power over time. In addition, companies can issue their financial instruments in the form of **tokens**. Stock exchanges use private blockchains (Figure 9.5).

It is also possible for a company to issue shares directly to the investors without going through a stock exchange. Such offers are called Initial Coin Offering (ICO). These tokens are directly sold to investors; their subsequent sale and purchase transactions can be recorded in a public blockchain. The nodes that maintain this blockchain may also create new crypto coins as a reward, or a small fee can be charged per transaction; alternatively, the company may redeem these coins at a profitable price. At present, ICOs are used mainly by companies planning to enter into cryptocurrency markets. However, in the future, companies may opt to directly raise money from the public without going through stock exchanges and registrars.

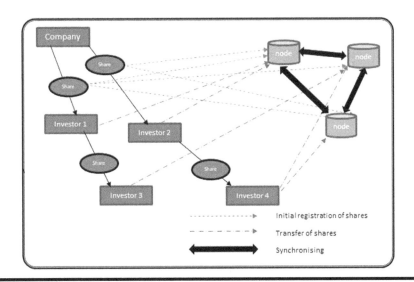

Figure 9.5   Blockchains in Stock Exchange.

9.6.4 Namecoin: Distributed DNS

Namecoin is a clone of Bitcoin; it also has a maximum of 21 million coins, rewards halving every 210,000 blocks, same proof-of-work protocol; it forked out of Bitcoin blockchain in 2011. Namecoin has its own Top Level Domain (TLD).bit which is similar to other TLDs like.com,.net, etc., but it does not fall under the purview of ICANN; therefore it cannot be subject to censoring by any government (Fromknecht, 2014).

9.6.5 Public Key Infrastructure: Playing the Role of Certificate Authorities

Public Key Infrastructure is built for verifying the authenticity of websites and users. It relies on the traditional Private/Public Key and a **Certifying Authority** (CA), which acts as a Trusted Third Party. Websites apply for a certificate with the Certifying Authority and register their public keys with the CA. The CA's responsibility is to sign these public keys digitally and distribute them to the users via their browsers. A PKI can revoke certificates if a public key becomes compromised, whether it be by loss of the secret key or implication of the associated individual as malicious.

The CA stores the list of public keys in a database called the **Central Registry**. This database is made available to the users. When a user accesses a website, his browser obtains the public key of that website from the CA, and the user's communications with the website are encrypted with that public key; the website, in turn, decrypts the incoming message with its private key. Thus, the communication becomes encrypted and secure.

The Central Registry suffers from the usual drawbacks: the CAs do not have legal status; their Central Registries are vulnerable to hacking; if the private key of the CA gets compromised, then the reliability of the Central Registry becomes questionable; if a hacker gets the private key of the CA, he can build a phishing website, and replace the public key of the original website with that of the phishing site, and it cannot be easily detected; if a key is compromised, the website has no option but to apply for another certificate. It was confirmed on 3rd September 2011 that the Dutch CA DigiNotar was hacked, and many fraudulent certificates were issued with its keys.

A blockchain-based Central Registry will obviate these difficulties. CertCoin, is an example of Domain Registrar using blockchains. CertCoin also emits a crypto coin at the completion of blocks. Remme, a blockchain-based password replacement solution, uses SSL certificates to devices instead of usernames and passwords. The certificates are stored in a blockchain (Remme capital Ltd., 2021).

9.6.6 Anonymizing Data: Uses in the Healthcare Industry

Blockchains can be used for anonymizing data, thus protecting the privacy of a person, allowing only limited access; this control can be left to the individual. Such a network uses a peer to peer-encrypted data storage solution to store electronic health records and stores access keys on the blockchain, maintaining a single true version of the user's data. This enables users to provide access to their personal health data to any doctor while still maintaining transparency, auditability, and security. This data can be sold and bought at the data marketplace enabled by the network.

At present, the data in the health sector is fragmented, it is not under the control of the patient, the healthcare provider can monetize the data without the knowledge of the patient, increasing the cost of insurance, etc. A distributed platform based on blockchain with access to doctors, patients, insurers, pharma, and other healthcare-related services, can solve most of these problems, enabling the patient to share the data with anyone for a cost. The Swiss company **Sana** is experimenting with a similar product called **Medblocks**; it is a private blockchain that stores the medical records of a patient. It can be created by a registered user; it is encrypted and sent to the nodes. Each block carries different levels of permissions, as per the choice of the owner of the block. The level of monetization by the clinic, insurer, or government can be determined by the user.

9.6.7 Blockchains as Repositories of Public Registers

Governments maintain many public databases. These are protected at huge costs, since the value of the transactions and properties recorded in these databases are very vital to the economy and the country. In spite of all the protection, it may be still vulnerable to unethical hacking, or abuse of trust. Blockchain eliminates the need for trust, as we saw, by recording the data with adequate cryptography that renders it immutable. Therefore, blockchains are highly suitable for maintaining publicly accessed databases.

Let us see an example of the use of hash functions in ensuring the authenticity of data. More often, governments issue many certificates and documents; there is often the question of checking their authenticity. Normally this is achieved by physical protections, like hologram stickers, stamp papers, preprinted stationery, rubber stamps, etc. Increasingly, the certificate carries a link to the database where the relevant data is recorded. For example, birth certificates issued in Tamil Nadu carry a link to the database of births. However, this feature is limited by access to the database, and also depends on the integrity of the database.

Providing a simple hash digest of the data carried on the certificate on the certificate itself is another step towards the immutability of data. Hashing can be carried out off-line and the result can be compared with the digest provided. However, even this feature can be circumvented.

Blockchains prove useful at this point. Since blockchains are distributed databases, all the transactions of a government office can be recorded in it; the nodes could be maintained by individual offices; since the purpose of this blockchain is to store records, the proof of work can be kept at a fairly difficult level, and there is no necessity to reward the nodes on mining a block.

Let us consider the use of blockchains in the Registration Department. The Registration Department registers all public documents like sale deeds, mortgage deeds, power of attorney, wills, partnership deeds, etc. It also has the responsibility to keep the copies of these documents under safe custody, and to allow public access to these documents. The documents can be scanned, and the images can be included in the blocks for hashing. Alternatively, the text of the agreement can be included in the block. This prevents any attempts at tampering. In an advanced system, each property can be issued a digital token as its identity key, and each user can be issued a cryptographic wallet. When a property is sold, its digital token is transferred from the seller's wallet to the buyer's wallet. These transactions can be tracked and recorded in a blockchain.

Similarly, vehicle registrations, sales, insurance, driving license, etc., can be recorded in a blockchain, for better management. The registration details of the vehicle – its make, model, Registration number, etc. – can be hashed to form a digital token; this digital token will be sent to the wallet of its owner. Whenever the vehicle is transferred to a new owner, this token will be sent to the wallet of the new owner; all such transfers, etc., regarding a vehicle can be recorded in a particular block; thus, the blockchain will ensure that the records cannot be hacked.

Almost every government department is built around a database; in many cases, these databases continue to grow; thus, blockchains can add to the integrity and security of the databases.

9.6.8 IoT and Blockchain

The **Internet of Things** is the upcoming concept wherein all the machines, appliances, devices, and systems are given unique identifiers, and receive and transmit data to and over the Internet without any human intervention, making them part of the Internet; such a system would cause a revolution about the way the Internet functions; more devices will use the Internet than humans. Real-Time Analytics will make it easier to predict and anticipate parts failure, for example, in an aircraft. IoT is a gamechanger in healthcare, transport, logistics, home automation, military affairs, and numerous other fields. IoT enables the assets and their crucial components to directly broadcast vital information to the owners and manufacturers. For example, at present, CCTV surveillance software can alert an owner if someone enters his house. With IoT, it can alert the neighboring devices automatically. Similarly, vital installations like powerplants, defense factories, etc., can be linked up to IoT to prevent sabotage. IoT can help maintain assets and to protect them from vandalism or theft.

However, not every asset is IT-enabled. This makes it difficult to extend IoT to most legacy assets like old houses, cars, etc. To obviate this, legacy assets can be added an extra layer of IoT-enabled parts. The simplest way is to add a smart lock to the asset. Then the asset becomes a part of the IoT. At present IoT has limited reach; however, the introduction of IPv 6 is going to increase the reach of IoT.

Blockchains can be used to record important communications in IoT network; for example, an aircraft company may record the information flow from crucial parts of a plane in a blockchain, so that that information cannot be ignored, deleted, or altered later on; in case of a serious failure, such information will be used in understanding the failure. Similarly, those data which are vital and must be protected at all costs, like the working conditions inside a nuclear reactor, or the surroundings of a chemical plant manufacturing hazardous material, can be monitored with the help of sensors, cameras, and other devices that record directly into a blockchain. Since these are vital information, the sending devices will encrypt it with the public key of the authority competent to study it; for example, the conditions around a hazardous chemical factory can be encrypted with the public key of the Pollution Control Board; only the said Board will be able to decrypt the recorded information with its private key. Thus, contentious monitoring processes can be automated and recorded in a trustless environment.

Since the devices on the IoT can directly communicate with databases, and they can be bought and sold online, their ownership changes can be recorded in a blockchain; the device will collect the public key of the buyer. If a smart car is sold, and the transaction is recorded in the blockchain of the RTO, the car itself will change its ownership by obtaining the public key of its new owner from the database and replacing the seller's public key. Then onwards, the car will respond only to the signals from its new owner's devices. Government agencies at all levels should consider and examine new uses for blockchain technology that could make the government more efficient in performing its functions (US Congress Joint Economic Committee, 2021).

9.6.9 Traceability and Supply Chain Management

Everledger (2021), a company that uses IBM blockchain, offers complete traceability for diamonds and other gemstones. The gemstones are analyzed at the producers' level, and the unique characteristics of a stone are encrypted to create a digital signature; this digital signature forms the core of a token that is recorded in a blockchain; subsequently when the stone is sold to agents and jewelers, and finally to customers, the details of these transactions are updated in the token and also recorded in the blockchain. This provides complete traceability and transparency to the gemstones, providing a clear pedigree. As the diamond trade is beset with unethical mining and trading, such a reliable database adds to the value of the products. Similar systems can be built for tracing the origins and supply routes for less valuable goods too.

9.6.10 Public Register of Antiques and Artefacts

Everledger (2021) proposes another product based on IBM blockchain: a ledger of antiques and artworks to be stored in an IBM blockchain. Here too, the unique characteristics of an antique or artwork are used to create a token that will be recorded in a blockchain; subsequent sales are relocations of that artwork are also tracked in the same blockchain. This will assure both provenance and traceability of antiques and artworks.

9.7 Conclusion

Blockchain is a paradigm shift in the way data is guarded and shared. Instead of protecting data behind layers of security, blockchain makes it immutable at every stage. This does not mean blockchain is tamper-proof; it only means tampering with a blockchain by trying to change an entry in the middle of a finished block, which is more difficult than hacking a database to change an entry. Blockchain replaces the Trusted Third Party with a trustless program. It can realign a lot of fields with an orientation towards more open and safer public and private spaces. Various aspects of cybersecurity will be vastly changed with the use of blockchain technology.

References

Bitcoin, 2021, www.bitcoin.org, [accessed 12 August 2021].
Blockchain, 2021, www.blockchain.com, [accessed 12 August 2021].
Coinbase, 2021, www.coinbase.com, [accessed 10 August 2021].
Ethereum, 2021, https://ethereum.org, [accessed 10 July 2021].
Everledger, 2021, www.everledger.io, [accessed 12 August 2021].
Fromknecht, C., 2014. CertCoin: A NameCoin Based Decentralized Authentication System, https://courses.csail.mit.edu/6.857/2014/files/19.fromknecht-velicann-yakoubov-certcoin.pdf

IBM, www.ibm.com, [accessed 7 July 2021].

Nakamoto, S., 2008. Bitcoin: A peer-to-peer electronic cash system, Government of Estonia, https://e-resident.gov.ee/bitcoin-whitepaper/

Remme capital Ltd., 2021, https://remme.io, [accessed 12 August 2021].

US Congress Joint Economic Committee, 2021, https://www.jec.senate.gov/public/_cache/files/aaac3a69.e9fb-45b6-be9f-b1fd96dd738b/chapter-9.building-a-secure-future-one-blockchain-at-a-time.pdf, [accessed 12 August 2021].

Whitepaper database, 2021, https://whitepaperdatabase.com/monero-xmr-whitepaper, [accessed 12 August 2021].

Wood, G., 2021. Ethereum: A secure decentralised generalised transaction ledger, Istanbul version, 80085f7, 11 July.

Chapter 10

Blockchain

V. Srividya

Professor, PSG Institute of Management, Coimbatore, India

Contents

DOI: 10.1201/9781003175872-10

Objectives

1. An Overview to Blockchain and its Origin
2. Describe the Structure and Working of Blockchains
3. Identify the Various Types of Blockchains and Their Evolution
4. Understand the Various Applications of Blockchain Technology and Its Benefits
5. Outlines the Infrastructure Needed to Implement Blockchain Technology

---

10.1 Introduction to Blockchain

The Internet of Things (IoT) refers to a network of interconnected objects that can sense and share data among those objects in the network with or without human intervention. IoT has been widely adopted in many sectors and industries across the world. The usage of IoT is advantageous, nevertheless due to the innate characteristic of interconnectedness it has brought in security. This security issue can be solved by the use of blockchain technology. Blockchain can be observed as a significant development in Industry 4.0, which secures all the transactions among the interconnected objects by providing a distributed ledger technology (Tinmaz, 2020). Blockchain can be used in all businesses involving an interaction among the various stakeholders on a networked business model. For example, it can be used to track the produce from the place of cultivation through the entire supply chain to the retail store through automation and integration. The procedure will be secure with the possibility of accurately detecting the pilferage or spoilage as each member in the supply chain will have access to the entire data like quantity, quality, and time, which they can validate. Data is encrypted, making data that is stored or transferred secure, thus eliminating tampering of data. Hence, blockchain technology will have profound applications to industries such as supply chain, logistics, or any other industry with processes or procedures involving transfer or sharing data. Blockchain is a secure technology that can help prevent frauds and identify unauthorized use of data (Wang et al., 2019).

10.1.1 What Is Blockchain?

Blockchain is a digital record of transactions. Each and every transaction recorded is called a block. Each block is linked with the other block, thus forming a chain. The name blockchain is derived from each record (Block) process being linked together in a single list (Chain). The information or data in every transaction on a blockchain is converted into a code through encryption and is secured through a digital signature thus ensuring its security. The blocks are open to anyone connected on the network and entries made to it can be viewed on real-time basis. The data stored on a single blockchain has a common history that is transparent to all network participants, thus limiting the misuse. The blocks can be stored anywhere in the world on multiple servers making the storage decentralized. Changes on any block are agreed among all the network participants and updated in all blocks simultaneously. The technology works based on a consensus or agreement of the participants, thus removing a third party or intermediary to validate the transaction and secured through the distributed ledger system maintained by all participants, making it difficult for unauthorized changes.

Blockchain technology can be used to track or exchange anything of value like cash, asset, and documents in a transparent way, avoiding the traditional institutions, intermediaries or parties by innovatively using peers to validate the transactions. It can handle the security issues and is also cost effective.

10.1.2 Origin of Blockchain

The origin of blockchain can be traced with the introduction of Bitcoin by Satoshi Nakamoto in a white paper published in 2008. Blockchain is mistakenly considered synonymous to Bitcoin. Bitcoin is a digital currency that was built with blockchain technology. Bitcoin is simply one among the many that uses blockchain technology. Bitcoin was conceptualized as an alternative to traditional payment methods to eliminate mediators, save time, reduce cost, and remove the risk. The Internet has altered the use of technology in various industries extending to the transfer of payments. Traditional modes of payment need a medium (Cash) and an intermediary (Financial Institution) to transfer the payments. Payments through online modes are routed through a third party for verification and validation. Online payments through the Internet or mobile are efficient, convenient and quick but have not completely eliminated the mediators and there is always the risk of compromising the information. Blockchain technology is built to remove these inefficiencies.

For Example, if you would like to transfer payments to your family at a different location through net banking, you need to log in to your bank's online portal and enter your account details. The payment is routed through a payment partner called aggregator. A one-time password is sent for verification to you. On approval, the amount is transferred to the designated account after authorization by your bank's core banking system. A transaction fee is charged for using the service. Blockchain technology can be used to transfer funds directly to the party eliminating an intermediary (bank or the aggregator). Here the transaction details are digitally configured into a block that is shown online and can be seen by all the parties in the network who validates the transaction to ensure accuracy. The validation is a permanent, undisputed and transparent record of the transaction and the block is added in the public ledger and forms part of the chain. The money is transferred immediately and no charges are deducted.

10.1.2.1 Demerits of the Current Transaction System

Cash – Cash as a physical asset has limited usage and can be used when in direct contact and in smaller amounts.

Access – A substantial part of the global population has no access to financial services lest the technology. The United Nations sustainable goals for 2030 and the national financial inclusion strategy launched by more than 50 countries in 2018 aims to improve financial inclusion (National Strategy for Financial Inclusion Report 2019-24 A report by RBI) substantiates the claim for exclusion.

Bank – Transactions through a financial institution like a bank is suitable for remote and larger transactions. The transaction is validated through a trusted central authority the bank; however, there exists a time gap between transaction and settlement due to the clearing process. Though it can be reduced using online methods, the transaction cost and service charge increase.

Trust – Transactions using online technology are routed through a third party to process the electronic payment and verify the authenticity and validity with the bank's core banking system. There is always a possibility of mistakes, fraud, or misrepresentation.

Reversibility – The transactions using physical currency or online can be reversed. The need for third parties to mediate in case of dispute or take corrective measures increases the transaction cost.

Risk – The risk of loss of information and confidential information exposure is high, especially in online transactions.

Satoshi Nakaomoto provides a solution to the traditional system's discrepancies in the seminal paper on 'Bitcoins' based on blockchain technology, where a payment system would work on cryptography and proof of work instead of the trust-based central authority was introduced. The technology would allow any number of parties willing to transact without the support of an intermediary, thus reducing the cost and intermediation problems. The transactions will be time-stamped and approved, making them impossible to change or modify, which also addresses overspending. A peer will replace the intermediary needed to validate the transactions to peer mechanism to validate transactions, thus substituting a central to collective control making the system robust and secure (Nakamoto, 2009). Blockchain technology serves to solve the security and trust issue. The technology, though initiated as an alternative to payment system, can be applied to any Industry like manufacturing, services, banking, healthcare, technology, and offers several opportunities to the Industry Revolution 4.0.

10.2 Blockchain Mechanism

A blockchain is a collection of blocks that are linked, similar to a chain hence the name blockchain. Each block contains information and is time stamped preventing tampering of information stored. Each block has three components the data, a hash, and a hash of the previous block as in Figure 10.1.

The data or information can be anything based on the type of blockchain. Note that example 1 pertains to transfer of cryptocurrency and example 2 has information of a contract to transfer drugs (Figure 10.2).

Hash is simply the encryption of data, it is the transformation of data or bit string into shorter fixed length values making it easier to store and index the data for retrieval. It has all the content of the data and is unique to the particular block. Any change in the data will also alter the hash (Figure 10.3).

The hash of the previous block is the link to the previous block, this technique of linking to the previous Block makes the transactions secure.

Notice that Figure 10.4 has three blocks linked in a chain. Each block has the data, a hash, and a hash of the previous block. Block 1 is unique as it does not have a hash to the previous block to which it is linked and is called the Genesis block. Thus, the first block created on a chain is called the Genesis block. The link to each of the blocks is the "hash to the previous block". When

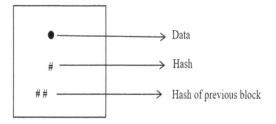

Figure 10.1   Components of a Block in a Blockchain.

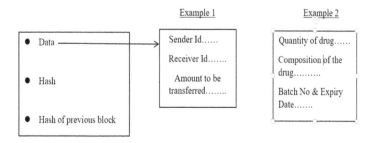

Figure 10.2   Examples for Data in Blocks of a Blockchain.

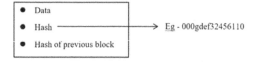

Figure 10.3   Example for a Hash in a Block of Blockchain.

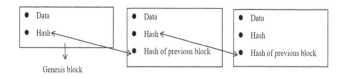

Figure 10.4   Examples for Linking Blocks Using *Hash of previous block* in Blockchain.

the hash in block 2 is tampered, only the block 2 hash is modified, the "Hash of previous block" in Block 3 will show the original value, the difference will reveal the tampering. So, the hashing link secures the chain. It is however possible to create and change multiple hashes within seconds and tamper the entire block. This is averted by using the proof-of-work mechanism. Proof-of-work refers to the creation and adding of blocks. Blocks can be created only through solving complex mathematical problems. In the case of Bitcoin, it is called as mining. The miners take minimum 10 minutes to create a block and add it to the chain; therefore, the time taken for creation and addition will make it impossible for tampering of all the blocks in a chain. Hashing and proof-of-work makes blockchain a secure transaction.

The other way blockchains secure themselves is by using the distributed ledger mechanism. Anyone interested can join the network and become part of a blockchain. Once joined, let's call them the nodes, each node has access to not only their block but the entire history of the blockchain. The history can be used to check and verify the authenticity of the transaction. Whenever a new block is created it is sent to all the nodes, each node verifies the authenticity and approves it by adding to the existing blockchain. It is by consensus that it is decided to either add or reject a block.

Hence, we can say that blockchain works on a peer-to-peer basis. Blockchains are secured for the very reason that if anyone wants to change any of the information on a block then they have to work on all the blocks connected in the chain, redo the proof of work for each block and also get the consensus of at least 51% of the participants in the network which would be a herculean process. Thus, preventing the tampering of information and ensuring security.

10.2.1 Components of a Blockchain

Origin – Participants have access to the history of the transactions and will be able to identify the source of the transaction and changes that has been made over time.

Irreversible – Transactions are protected with cryptography and cannot be altered once entered on the block.

Consensus – All the participants in the network needs to accept any changes and validate the transaction.

Distributed Ledger – The blocks are stored in various nodes and changes once validated is reflected simultaneously in all the blocks.

Shared Ledger– All the participants have access to the history and can see any modifications made to the ledger i.e., multiple copies of the same data is stored in various devices at different locations.

10.3 Types of Blockchain

There are four types of blockchain networks.

10.3.1 Public Blockchain

They are open to anyone and everyone hence is termed public. An interested person with an Internet connection can join the network. All the participants have access to all the information on a block and the history of the blockchain. Most of the public blockchain works on open-source platform and any participant can create, add, or verify a block. The acceptance of a new block is through consensus algorithm like proof-of-work that has the approval of majority of the participants. Every participant works for the betterment of the network as they are incentivized for doing the same, e.g., Bitcoin. Here there are no restrictions and works completely in a decentralized manner.

The advantage of a public blockchain is the anonymity of the participants. Since it works on a open distributed ledger technology there is no need to identify the participant. The greatest disadvantage is the complexity and low speed in creation of a block and the time taken to arrive at a consensus. The scalability of public blockchains are also limited due to bandwidth and high energy consumption.

10.3.2 Private Blockchain

They are closed networks that are owned by individuals or businesses. Access is not open to all and is only through invitation and hence can be called as permissioned blockchains. The network is controlled centrally and governed by guidelines. Participants are sanctioned specific rights and restrictions in the network. Hence the rights and limits to access information, create, add or verify a block is at the discretion of the network. The private blockchains are more controlled than the public blockchain, e.g., hyperledger.

The advantage of a private blockchain is the speed in processing the transaction which is possible due to fewer number of participants. Since fewer nodes manage the data, decision making is quicker, making private blockchain scalable. The blockchain technology was built on the components of distributed ledger but by having a centralized setup private blockchains have defied the core of blockchain. Fewer nodes verify and validate transactions, the authenticity depends on the credibility of the nodes. It is easier to compromise the security of lesser nodes as against all the nodes in public blockchains.

10.3.3 Consortium Blockchain

It can be considered as a subset of private blockchain as they are governed by a group of businesses or Individuals instead of a single entity. It follows the same principles of a private blockchain where the entry is restricted to the participants.

Few nodes have the control rights to access, create, add, or verify transactions on a block. The rights and controls will be customized based on the requirements of the group, e.g., Quarum.

They work on a collaborative model where they share some information example Bankchain. Usually banks, governments, etc. can form consortium blockchain where there are collective advantages due to synergy and individual benefits to each of the collaborating members.

10.3.4 Hybrid Blockchain

It uses a combination of both the features of a private and public blockchain. The nodes have the control as to, who can access which data in the chain. It allows businesses to keep part of their data secured and partly transparent. A hybrid blockchain uses the private blockchain to create the data blocks and encrypt them. These are then stored in a public blockchain without compromising the data privacy (Sharma, 2019), e.g., dragonchain.

This technology helps in businesses preserving their security and privacy and at the same time improves the scalability by being transparent.

10.4 Evolution of Blockchains

Blockchains have evolved from the time they were established during the construction of Bitcoins, where the focus was on money that was created virtually and circulated within the network with no presence of a central external monetary authority. The key to this technology is the creation of the block through the mining process supporting the traceability from the origin making it secure without intervention of external entity. During the construction of Bitcoin, the foundation and its principles were well defined that it could be used to support any type of transaction that can be thought of, as quoted by Nakamoto in *2010 "The design supports a variety of possible transaction types that were designed years ago. Escrow transactions, bonded contracts, third party arbitration, multi-party signature, etc."* (Satoshi Nakamoto Institute). The application of blockchains to a variety of other services and industries can be viewed as an evolution of blockchain to the next phase.

Blockchains can be used for various applications in finance and investments in areas such as lending, trading, mutual funds, crowdfunding, and in other areas such as law, healthcare, education, insurance etc., that needs records, transfer of properties, credentials, rights, etc. Blockchains per se may not be able to support all of the diverse activities, it needs special data codes and supports for each of the cases based on the demand of the transaction type. Thus the scope for blockchain applications is large. To generalize the application, for each type of transaction the parties involved specify the conditions cryptographically, on satisfying the conditions the transactions occur automatically. Hence the network only carries the function of evaluating the adherence to the conditions (Silva et al., 2020). Nick Szabo introduced a concept in 1994 proposing the use of any decentralized ledger as a self-executable contract. The contracts could thus be converted into codes and run on blockchain technology. These digital contracts that could execute itself on satisfying prerequisite conditions were later termed smart contracts. Smart contracts are the most powerful applications of blockchain technology (https://hackernoon.com/everything-you-need-to-know-about-smart-contracts-a-beginners-guide-c13cc138378a).

10.4.1 Smart Contract

Smart contracts are business rules that are converted into codes. The business rules converted to codes in the smart contract runs on top of an open blockchain ledger, therefore it can be applied to all business partners permitted on the blockchain. It is often confused with existing automation software or stored procedures of an organization; however, it is much more than automating processes and can be stretched across multiple organizations. Since smart contracts are codes of business rules they are only as good as the code it is programmed to perform. Data is fed into the blockchain and used for execution by the smart contract through an external source. These data feeds are called oracles. The oracles can be hardware or software connecting data and the contract. The smart contract once made cannot be altered therefore the accuracy of data fed is important, all though it uses the blockchain technology it does not necessitate validity of the data (Mearian, 2019).

A smart contract works on the following principles. The smart contract is a digital agreement that are a set of rules and regulations which are agreed upon by the parties to the transaction, they are digitally coded and published on a blockchain. Using the principles of decentralized ledger of the blockchain technology the code allows for automatic execution of the transactions on satisfying the rules and regulations. In a smart contract the codes cannot be reversed even by the parties to the agreement once they are published. The codes enforce the verification, sanction, validation, and hence the execution of the contract based on the decentralized consensus mechanism. These guidelines ensure the fool proof mechanism of the autonomous functioning of the smart contract (Ethereum, 2018).

Smart contracts can be used to transfer or exchange any asset or information without the need for an intermediary in a transparent and conflict free manner, thus has wider applications in trade, commerce, law, regulation, business, and management. They are far superior to digital contracts as they could eliminate the third parties thus reducing risk and cost. The growth in IoT connected devices will increase the use of smart contracts in future. Smart contracts will offer standardized method for accelerating data exchange and processes between IoT devices. Smart contracts are widely used in sectors such as financial services, utilities, transportation, and others that rely on process efficiency, logistics, and supply chain.

10.5 Business Applications of Blockchain

Blockchain had its inception in the finance sector and was perceived to be widely used in the financial services vertical. However the robust nature of its framework has far reaching potential and has benefited many industries, sectors, and verticals enabling innovative forms of organizations and processes. Blockchains have redefined the traditional organizational structures and catalyzed them to evolve into a self-organized one. Some of the applications of blockchain are discussed as follows.

10.5.1 Manufacturing

Blockchain technologies has the potential to transform the conventional work systems of manufacturing firms. Blockchains can be widely used for engineering design, protypes in foundries, production technologies, material provenance, supply chain monitoring, asset tracking, quality assurance, regulatory compliances, etc. Integrating IoT and blockchain offers an effortless way for exchange of data using smart contract in blockchain-enabled systems and can address every aspect from raw material sourcing to delivery of final products (https://www.bakertilly.com/insights/how-can-blockchain-technology-help-the-manufacturing/). Manufacturing firms with complex supply chains can benefit from the verification and transparency offered by blockchain. The technology can be used to improve business across the value chain. For example, the after-sales service department by using IoT and predictive analytics can offer preventive maintenance before a breakdown happens in an equipment. The movement and usage of the equipment can be captured by the blockchain and on time interventions can be made.

10.5.2 Healthcare

Healthcare providers like hospitals and doctors have to regularly share information to laboratories, pharmaceutical companies, pharmacists, patients, insurance companies, etc. and there is a need for all the stakeholders to work coordinately and share information. Issues related to provenance, traceability, immutability, and security of information is very high in this Industry. Mukherjee and Singh (2020) write that blockchain networks can be used to access, share, and transfer information across the chain safely and securely. Some of the usages of blockchain technology in the healthcare Industry are maintenance of clinical trial records, patient history for treatments, preservation of consent forms, and applications of insurance claim records.

10.5.3 Supply Chains

A supply chain is an optimized process that delivers goods and services from an organization to a customer, it integrates all the functions and processes within a company, the crucial part is the linkage with processes across companies to form a cohesive and efficient business model. In the real world, process chains links across companies that are related in multidimensional flow of information and products. The continuous uninterrupted flow of information is the vital element of supply chain, the challenge here is the collation of sufficient data that are dependable, accurate, traceable, and unalterable over time. Blockchain technology can solve these challenges and also effectively shrink the intermediaries thus improving the efficiency and reducing the costs (Silva et al., 2020).

10.5.3.1 Drug Supply in Healthcare

The supply chain in the pharmaceutical industry is the most complicated and dynamic. It integrates the supply chains of research laboratories that design the drugs, drug manufacturers, drug and medical device distributors, and healthcare service providers. It is a case where it is salient to have multidimensional flow of information and services among the parties that are also transparent enabling efficient and effective functioning individually and collectively (https://www.pwc.com/gx/en/industries/pharmaceuticals-life-sciences/publications/pharma-2020/pharma-2020-supplying-the-future.html).

Blockchains has severe implications for pharmaceutical supply chain management, its decentralized ledger offers transparency and security in the shipping process. As soon as an order to purchase a drug is received, the information can be encrypted into a smart contract. The smart contract then manages the execution of the contract throughout the supply chain from the manufacturer to pharmacist along with all the intermediaries. The smart contracts cannot be reversed and will work at every level based on satisfying the preconditioned factors like dates, composition, quantity, etc. This ensures trust and genuineness of the transactions (Mayank, 2018).

Blockpharma is a French start-up that traces drug sales online. Blockpharma uses an application interface that can plug into the pharmaceutical company's information system and capture the product information and QR codes when the companies releases the drug. The application then records and verifies all the points of shipment in the entire supply chain until it reaches the customer. The app allows the customers to know the origin and safety of the medicines and can prevent patients from consuming counterfeit medicine, the app also can alert the pharmaceutical company in case of any tampering.

10.5.3.2 Documentation and Verification

Digital documents are easily altered and modifiable. Organizations would want to create non-reversible histories of their business process, accounting or auditing procedures for later use. Blockchain technology provides a solution by time stamping the documents and making them secure.

Tierion a Connecticut-based firm provides a platform to users to verify documents using the Bitcoin blockchain technology. Tierion platforms may be used for variety of systems applicable to many industries that uses third parties to authenticate or validate credentials like insurance companies that uses medical records for claim settlement, educational credit transfers, credit analysis by financial institutions, licenses, or award authentication. For example, Tierion built a protocol called chainpoint to anchor data. Here, anyone connected to the network can anchor documents to the blockchain. Anchoring refers to the process of linking documents to the exact blocks in a blockchain. The credentials can be verified easily online using anchoring and is useful not only for employers but also for the individual users. Chainpoint can be used to anchor into multiple blockchains and has been widely adopted by many companies in the supply chain vertical. Since it is possible to anchor large volumes of data and easy to verify data on this platform without the need for any intermediaries (Hamilton, 2018).

10.5.3.3 Trade Financing in NBFCs

Factoring or receivables discounting is the process of pooling and selling receivables to an NBFC to fund the working capital requirements of suppliers/manufactures. This not only supports the short term needs of manufactures but all of the suppliers in the supply chain who are selling on credit. Supplier-to-manufacturer invoice discounting processes is complicated since each party involved is expected to maintain ledgers separately, update them, and also share them frequently. Human errors, delays, and risks are inherent to this system resulting in delay in payments and inability to meet the working capital gaps.

Mahindra Group, a large conglomerate in India with diverse businesses such as automobile, agri, mobility, retail, finance, etc., has partnered with IBM to use blockchain technology to disrupt the traditional method of receivables discounting. The cloud-based application has changed the trade finance transactions through a permissioned distributed ledger. The blockchain-based supply chain finance solution will help the parties involved in the transaction to have access to the shared ledger and participate in the updation limited to their sanctioned area. This ensures efficiency, consistency, trust, and transparency, while safeguarding sensitive information (Mahindra and IBM to Develop Blockchain Solution for Supply Chain Finance Cloud-based blockchain app to speed invoice discounting, 2016).

Mahindra is looking at extending this technology to their other verticals, with the success of blockchain technology in providing far superior supply chain solutions in receivables financing and expects tremendous growth in business through offering new products. IBM expects that this technology will change the way businesses communicate and work with each other and foresees application of this technology model to various other businesses.

10.5.3.4 Agriculture Financing

Blockchain technology can be used to support agriculture and agri-based small business too. Most of the farmers and unorganized small agri businesses do not have documentary support of their produce or the transactions which are mandatory to take loans. Financial Institutions and lenders need valid documentary support as collaterals for lending or advancing loans. There are a number of startups in this space that tries to bridge the gap using blockchain technology.

Companies like beermaker Anheuser-Busch InBev have partnered with BanQu to track farmers. Anheuse BInBev is interested to know the details of the produce supplied by the farmers that are used as raw material for the products manufactured by them. BanQu provides a blockchain platform to underprivileged farmers and producers in Zambia, Uganda, and India, that creates a digital trail of their transaction. BanQu service sends a message to the farmer with the details of their transaction after every sale they make, which can be used by farmers as proof to avail financial services like banking, borrowing, or lending. At the same time, it helps companies like Anheuser BInBev to identify the cultivator of the produce they use in manufacturing their products. BanQu was founded in 2015 by Gadnis, who designed an app that could be used on any mobile phone or on the Internet so as to make it accessible to anyone with just a basic model of the mobile phone with short messaging service feature. Farmers interested can sign up for the free services. The platform is run on a private blockchain, meaning only those who have the permission can access or be part of the chain. This ensures to maintain data immutability, privacy of the customers and also allows them to use the data for their advantage like proof or collateral to avail finances (Zhong, 2019).

10.5.4 Education and Academia

The educational sector has to be futuristic embracing changes in technology, before it transcends to other sectors. The educational system across the globe is evolving rapidly and has transformed itself to be flexible, student centric, skill-oriented, open access platforms leading to development of new business models. With an anywhere anytime method of learning and advancement in technologies, there are also perils of authentication related to course delivery, interactions on open access platforms, protection of rights, review, evaluation of students, transfer of credits, and stacking of credits. Blockchain technology has been widely used in various applications in the educational sector for the teaching learning platforms, student interaction, examinations, record maintenance and management, verification of credits, and has been able to bring in its features of security, control of access to data, transparency, verification, and authentication of data (Ali et al., 2019).

Sony Global Education has partnered with IBM to develop a platform using blockchain technology to share student records (https://www.cbinsights.com/research/industries-disrupted-blockchain/April 2,2020). Open access programs use the blockchain technology for teaching and management of the programs. Here, courses are offered by various faculty across universities and is open to any participant.

Learning machine a start-up in collaboration with MIT Media lab launched an open infrastructure using blockchain technology where students can share or verify their official records in digital format anywhere anytime. They joined Hyland software in 2020 that offers software solutions for wide applications in healthcare, education, government, manufacturing, and financial services (https://www.learningmachine.com/education).

10.5.5 Crowdfunding

The most popular application of blockchain technology is in the field of finance. Every financial asset like derivatives, collateralized borrowings, debt, or equity is based on a contract that is transparent and secured which has to be validated by a third party and/the regulator. Blockchains can be used to substitute the traditional modes to provide safer, faster services eliminating the intermediaries.

Crowdfunding is described as the process of raising funds by start-ups and companies from a pool of investors called as the crowd. The salient feature is that the demanders and suppliers of funds are connected through an online platform, the process is promoted through social media. The crowdfunding platform acts as an intermediary here and works on commissions (Heminway and Hoffman, 2010). Apart from the demanders, suppliers of funds (crowd), and the crowdfunding platform there is a passive member, the financial institution where the money is deposited. The funding options widely used are "All or Nothing (AON)" or "Keep it All (KIA)". As the name suggests in the AON model, the project is floated only if the goal of raising the required fund is achieved, else the project is stalled. In the KIA model the demander (fundraiser) keeps all the money irrespective of receiving the required funds or reaching the goal.

One of the use of blockchain technology in nonconventional finance is crowdfunding. It works on, mining the tokens/crypto currencies by the miners (suppliers of funds). The tokens/crypto currency are held by the miners to be invested in projects that interests them. The technology also works on a decentralized ledger format that works independently on the basis of peer to peer and consensus mechanism. The suppliers will only fund those projects that interests them ie. The one that matches their risk return objective. The advantage is the elimination of the intermediary.

Real Estate Asset Ledger (REAL), a firm based out of Singapore, offers crypto investors to purchase fractionalized non-ownership economic rights from varied property portfolio. They use the crowd funding platform on blockchain technology to create and maintain a transparent record of the investment made into purchase of residential and commercial properties and management of the portfolio invested (https://smarticoinvestor.com/real-real-estate-asset-ledger-ico-good-bad-ugly-real-estate-icos-pt-1/August 2017).

10.5.6 Banking

Banks are no longer defined by their basic function of lending and accepting deposits. Their roles have transformed during the last two decades and are involved in agency activities like portfolio management, transfer of funds, and utility activities like offering Demat accounts or social development activities. Banks currently are defined by the universal activities that they perform like selling mutual funds, insurance, or project consultancy they provide. The move to core banking facility has also redefined their functioning as it requires access to information across verticals within a bank and also across banks. Blockchain technology provides a safe and easy platform for these services.

BankChain is India's first consortium of 27 banks including State Bank of India (SBI), ICICI, AXIS Bank among other institutions that has adopted blockchain technology. The consortium has been formed to integrate and share information of customers to prevent money laundering and financing terrorism. The technology partner in the consortium is a pune based start-up named prime chain technologies. The first private blockchain of the consortium called the Clear Chain (c2) supports the sharing of the information on a permissioned basis so as the information is accessible and shared among authorized nodes within the consortium. The technology partner expects an exponential growth in the benefits of adopting blockchain technology when the number of collaborators increases and observes that the traditional competitors like banks and insurance companies forms consortium to explore new technologies to bring synergizing effects (https://economictimes.indiatimes.com/industry/banking/ finance/banking/sbi-to-use-blockchain-for-smart-contracts-and-kyc-by-next month/articleshow/61715860.cms?utm_source=contentofinterest&utm_ medium=text&utm_campaign=cppst). The blockchain technology has huge potential and its adoption can be extended to other areas of banking as well like securitization, advances, payment, international transfer, etc.

10.5.7 Cryptocurrency

Cryptocurrencies are digital currencies. They are virtual yet they provide the highest security and usability. They work with cryptographic principles on blockchain technology. The most popular cryptocurrency is the Bitcoin that relies on Bitcoin Block Technology followed by Ether which runs on a Ethereum Blockchain.

Bitcoin was the first cryptocurrrency that was introduced on blockchain technology in the world. Any individual having access to Internet and an account in the Bitcoin blockchain can transact in Bitcoins. To transact in Bitcoins all the participants (nodes) to the transaction should have an account. Creation of an account is called as a wallet which is similar for all cryptocurrencies and is done through a wallet service provider. To use the wallet, a key is required, it is a pair just like a locker key. It has a public key that is visible to all the participants in the network and also serves as the identity of the user. Every wallet also has a private key which is known only to the user, like the password. If the access to private key is lost the access to the account (wallet) and the money stored in it is lost. Any transaction can be carried out only through the wallets. To transfer funds, the details like the recipients account and the amount has to be entered in the wallet which is visible to all the participants on the network, the transactions will be verified for authenticity and legitimacy by miners and transacted ie. added to the block.

Bitcoins can be brought from the Bitcoin exchange just like any other commodity by exchange of any currency. Bitcoins can also be created through a process called mining. Mining is the process by which new transactions are validated and added to the 'blockchain'. The participants involved in mining are called miners. Mining requires dedicated hardwares and hence not all participants to a network are involved in mining. Any transaction created on the blockchain has to be verified and validated to complete it. On validation, the transaction is added to the block. Once they are added as a block, the details cannot be modified or tampered thus making the transactions secure. Other features of blockchain the peer-to-peer network, decentralized ledger, and encryption mechanism are applicable to cryptocurrency (www.blockchainexpert.ux).

10.6 Benefits of Blockchain Technology

The blockchain technology offers a variety of benefits due to its structure and the nature of its components. Some of the benefits are (https://blockgeeks.com/guides/what-is-blockchain-technology/):

1. It is decentralized and hence not owned or dependent on a central authority. In a centralized system data is stored at a central location which is exposed to many vulnerabilities In a decentralized system data is stored with all participants in the network so risk of loss of data/tampering is avoided.
2. The centralized entity acts as a trusted intermediary and every transaction goes through it for validity. Blockchain technology is based on direct interaction with the parties and effectively removes the intermediaries and reduces costs.
3. The speed of transaction will be slow or delayed in the case of a centralized system but in a decentralized system the transfers are faster as they are not dependent on a single storage point for verification and validation. In blockchain technology all the participants will validate the transaction, making it quicker and safer as it is impossible to alter data in all locations.
4. The transactions are transparent as in the case of public ledger any one who is connected on the Internet can see the details of what was transferred from whom to who along with the time. Though transactions are transparent the privacy of the parties are protected as they are not identified by their names or valid IDs but by cryptography.
5. The cryptographic hash makes the documents immutable and hence transactions are secure.
6. Multiple assets can be transferred in a single transaction between the parties in the network. The transfer of asset and payment can happen simultaneously thus reducing the delays in settlement process and avoids reconciliation.

7. Blockchain maximizes efficiency, security, and transparency and minimizes costs and frauds.
8. A blockchain provides the features of contract like offer and acceptance and hence can be used to assign title rights.
9. Blockchains provide secure, quicker, and convenient service thus improving the satisfaction of the users.
10. Blockchains greatly improve auditability and streamline paperwork.

These benefits of the blockchain technology make it popular for its usage in documentation, verification, governance, transfer of funds, or confidential data.

10.7 Infrastructure Needed to Implement Blockchain

The blockchain technology is versatile for many applications in businesses, government, legal, governance, or activities that deals with transfer of information, images, and documents. Blockchains use the good building blocks of computing together to create effective decentralized applications. An understanding of the components of computing will give an insight into the infrastructure needed to build a blockchain. The essentials of computing are storage, process, and communications. The components of storage are (i) token storage – tokens are stores of value e.g., assets, documents. Their main activity is to issue or transfer. (ii) Database – They store structured metadata that can be used to retrieve data quickly through queries. (iii) File systems – They are systems to store large files indexed in the hierarchy of directories and files. (iv) Data marketplace – These are systems that connect the data owners with the data users and can be considered as the core infrastructure as most of the applications would be based on these services. Processing in a blockchain technology is performed through a system of "smart contracts" in a decentralized manner. It may operate on a sequential business logic or combinational business logic or a HPC (high performance compute). HPC can be used for heavy lift like weather forecasting, simulation, machine learning, etc. The third essential element of computing, "communication", is about connecting networks and transfer of assets or information in the same state (McConaghy, 2017).

It should be noted that blockchain technology is not just about the software but there is a need for a substantial investment in hardware too. The energy required for solving complex cryptographic problems, necessary to create a hash and get it verified in each block is high, especially when it is a public blockchain and the chain is long. So, the blockchain infrastructure may require the use of uninterruptible power supplies (UPSs) in a way that other infrastructures do not. It will need investments into specialized CPUs, cooling, power supplies, and energy metering. Businesses need to plan for the hardware needed to support the computing, i.e., storage, process, and communication of assets or information needs to be taken care of and the additional network capacity and Interface with existing application of the organization like ERP. Internal governance mandates also make it important to maintain ongoing real-time and historic visibility into blockchain-related infrastructure activity. This visibility is necessary to mitigate the risk of inadvertent human error, to understand the real cost of blockchain participation, and to develop replicable best practices for continuously driving down cost and risk as the business engages in a growing number of different blockchains. A rigorous audit of the activities have to be undertaken for regulatory compliances (https://www.raritan.com/landing/blockchain-infrastructure-blockops-wp/).

10.8 Conclusion

Blockchain is not a technology by itself; it rather combines multiple technologies like encryption, distributed ledger, and authentication protocols for the technology called blockchains. Since its inception in 2009 to be used on crypto currencies the technology has evolved and it is perceived to be only in the infancy stage. Industry 4.0 and IoT has given Bitcoin technology various opportunities as it provides the much-needed security and trust to the stakeholders connected by different technologies and networks. Blockchain thus can be viewed as enablers in the process of industry revolution and has the potential to transform itself to suit varied needs of businesses.

References

Ali, A., et al., 2019. Blockchain-based applications in education: A systematic review, www.mdpi.com/journal/applsci, doi: 10.3390/app9122400.

da Silva, T.B. et al., 2020. Blockchain and industry 4.0: Overview, convergence, and analysis, In: Righi R.R., Alberti A.M., Singh, M. (Ed) *Block Chain Technology for Industry 4.0,* Springer, pp. 27–59. 10.1007/978-981-15-1137-0 [accessed 6 April, 2020].

Ethereum, 2018. What are smart contracts EthereumWiki? http://www.ethereumwiki.com/ethereum-wiki/smart-contracts/

Hamilton D., 2018. Tierion: Utilizing the bitcoin blockchain to verify documents, https://coincentral.com/tierion-guide/11

Heminway, J.M., Hoffman, S.R., 2010. Proceed at your peril: Crowdfunding and the securities act of 1933. *Tennessee Law Review* 78, 879.

https://www.bakertilly.com/insights/how-can-blockchain-technology-help-the-manufacturing/, Date accessed 20 Apr 2021

https://www.bankchaintech.com, Date accessed 5 May 2021

https://www.blockgeeks.com/guides/what-is-blockchain-technology/, Date accessed 20 Apr 2021 https://www.cbinsights.com/research/industries-disrupted-blockchain/April 2, 2020, Date accessed 5 May 2021

https://www.economictimes.indiatimes.com/industry/banking/finance/banking/sbi-to-use-blockchain-for-smart-contracts-and-kyc-by-nextmonth/articleshow/61715 860.cms?utm_source=contentofinterest&utm_medium=text&utm_campaign=cppst, Date accessed 10 May 2021

https://www.hackernoon.com/everything-you-need-to-know-about-smart-contracts-a-beginners-guide-c13cc138378a, Date accessed 8 May 2021

https://www.pwc.com/gx/en/industries/pharmaceuticals-life-sciences/publications/pharma-2 020/pharma-2020-supplying-the-future.html, Date accessed 20 Apr 2021

https://www.raritan.com/landing/blockchain-infrastructure-blockops-wp/, Date accessed 25 Apr 2021

https://www.smarticoinvestor.com/real-real-estate-asset-ledger-ico-good-bad-ugly-real-estate-icos-pt-1/August 2017, Date accessed 28 Apr 2021

Mahindra and IBM to Develop Blockchain Solution for Supply Chain Finance Cloud-based blockchain app to speed invoice discounting, 2016, https://www.mahindra.com/news-room/press-release, https://www.coindesk.com/ibm-blockchain-mahindra-supply-chain

Mayank, 2018, https://hackernoon.com.

McConaghy T., 2017. Blockchain infrastructure landscape: A first principles framing manifesting storage, computation, and communications, https://medium.com/@trentmc0/blockchain-infrastructure-landscape-a-first-principles-framing-92cc5549bafe.

Mearian, L., 2019, https://www.computerworld.com/article/3412140/whats-a-smart, [accessed 16 December, 2020].

Mukherjee P., Singh, D., 2020. Business applications of blockchain the opportunities of blockchain in health 4.0, In: Righi, R.R., Alberti, A.M., Singh, M. (Ed) Block Chain Technology for Industry 4.0, Springer, pp. 149–163. 10.1007/978-981-15-1137-0 [accessed 6 April, 2020].

Nakamoto S., 2009. White paper on bitcoin: A peer-to-peer electronic cash system, https://bitcoin.org/bitcoin.pdf

National Strategy for Financial Inclusion Report 2019-24 A report by RBI, https://rbidocs.rbi.org.in/rdocs/content/pdfs/NSFIREPORT100119.pdf

Satoshi Nakamoto Institute. Re: transactions and scripts: dup haBlockchain and Industrysh160, https://satoshi.nakamotoinstitute.org/posts/bitcointalk/126/#selection-69.0–117.41

Sharma T.K., 2019, https://www.blockchain-council.org

Tinmaz H., 2020. History of industrial revolutions: From *Homo sapiens* hunters to bitcoin hunters, In: Righi R.R., Alberti A.M., Singh, M. (Ed.) *Block Chain Technology for Industry 4.0*, Springer, pp. 1–27. 10.1007/978-981-15-1137-0, [accessed 6 April, 2020].

Wang, Y. et al., 2019. Understanding blockchain technology for future supply chains: A systematic literature review and research agenda. *Supply Chain Management: An International Journal* 24, (1), 62–84.

www.blockchainexpert.ux, Cybrosys Limited Edition, E-book on Blockchain.

Zhong, C., 2019, https://www.greenbiz.com/article/innovator-banqu-builds-blockchain-and-bridges-traceability-small-farmers-livelihoods.

Chapter 11

Cybersecurity

P. Sudhandradevi[1] and V. Bhuvaneswari[2]

[1]*Ph.D. Research Scholar, Department of Computer Applications, Bharathiar University, Coimbatore, India*
[2]*Associate Professor, Department of Computer Applications, Bharathiar University, Coimbatore, India*

Contents

DOI: 10.1201/9781003175872-11

Objectives

By reading this chapter, the learner will gain knowledge on

1. Basics of Cyber Crime
2. Cyber Security techniques
3. Preventive Measures
4. Cyber Crime Initiatives in India
5. Cyber Security Tools

11.1 Cybercrime: An Overview

Cyber crime is a crime where a computer is either the major resource or loophole for cyber violences. Crimes lurks are just shelter below the dark web. It can't be physically sensed at the same time it will spread through the network and do all illegal deeds. There are two factors to spread cyber crimes. The first factor is the attackers can hide behind their terminals far from principles, liberty of using the latest software, and networking techniques and by snooping others activity. The second factor is breaking all the securities to access everyone on the Earth just to steal the information. Dark web refers that all parts of the Internet is not accessible in the search engine such as Google or Bing. Cyber crimes are generally separated into two categories: a crime which targets either network or computer and another user device to participate in criminal activities.

The first cyber crime in history is recorded that two thieves were able to infiltrate the French Telegraph system and commit data theft. The advancement of web technologies is the next evaluation of the cyber crime timeline which was happened in the 1990s. In this decade through the Internet connections, viruses were spread to reach the technologies. The first malicious attack was documented in the 1970s at the beginning of computerized phones as a target. Long-distance calls are found through techy-savvy people by tracing the series of codes. They were recognized as "Phreakers"; they learn to corrupt the sensational data by adapting hardware and software.

Figure 11.1, in history, the next wave affected was in the 2000s when the evaluation of social media came into humans' lifestyles. Each individual is pouring their information into a profile database to create a data deluge of personal information and the rise of vulnerability. The latest wave of this evolution is the global criminal industry by targeting anything and everyone with the presence on the web. In this decade, dealing with cyber crime is a major problem because of a loophole in the laws and the hackers are highly skilled in both webspace and dark web (Herjavec, 2019).

11.1.1 Growth of Internet

The rapid and vast adoption of technologies is changing the world in all illegal activities. Around the globe, cyber crime damages are estimated as a massive hit of $6 trillion Internet users by 2021. Surfers who spend an enormous time on the Internet are vulnerable to cyber issues. Cyber crime is happening without the knowledge of users, attacks are categorized such as computer attacks, hacking, online scams, malware, and denial of service attacks. Data breach is

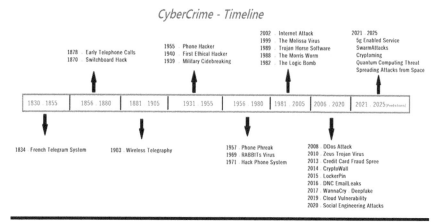

Figure 11.1   Timeline of Cyber Crime.

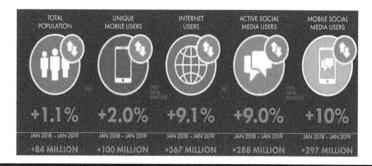

Figure 11.2   Growth of the Internet.

evolved as important cyber crime that produces harm to individuals in the trusted or untrustworthy environment.

Figure 11.2, in history, the next wave is affected in the 2000s when the evaluation of social media came into humans' lifestyles. Individuals are pouring all their information into a profile database. Data deluge of these profile information will increase the risks of the cyber vulnerable. The latest wave of this evolution is the global criminal industry by targeting anything and everyone with a presence on the web (Kemp, 2019).

11.1.2 Evaluation of Data

Figure 11.3, the data growth is mind-boggling but at the same it's completely understandable in structure. The most important thing is data exists in an

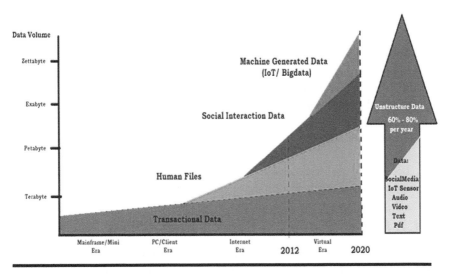

Figure 11.3 Evaluation of Data.

organization, e-commerce, ERP, and mail, while those are still important because of the evaluation of technology as well as the smart gazettes. While treating the data as assert, it becomes the lifeblood of an organization, social media, and digital marketing. As per statistics in 2025, 80% of the data is unstructured, which is generated by social media, video, audio, IoT, streaming, and geo-data and there will be 4.8 billion of techy (Ucros, 2017).

11.1.3 Causes of Cybercrime

Cyber crooks can cause the damages through the data breaches just for popularity in society, change the living cost, and to ruin the reputation of either organizations or individuals (Pande, 2017). The reasons behind cybercrime are listed below:

Revenue

People are interested in earning money and to have an expensive lifestyle. It also motivated them to be a public figure.

Revenge

This revenge happens because of political targets, personal complaints, and disgruntled employees so that hackers can use cybercrime as a weapon and while raising their voices. In an organization, the disgruntled employee will attack the website if they have reason to be annoyed or leak the sensational data.

Recognition

Hackers such as individuals or group members target big-branded websites, knowing that they will cause hits to publicity if they can get away with it. The main focus of cyber criminals are banking sectors, smuggling, retailers, and defense and government bodies.

Cyber Espionage

Because of political, economic, and social motivations, the government agency will act as a snoop on other people/networks.

11.1.4 Classifications of Cyber Vulnerabilities

Cyber vulnerabilities are classified into four major groups such as individuals, organizations, society, and government. They are categorized based on digital crime (Siege, 2019).

11.1.4.1 Individuals

The cybercrime involves spreading malicious viruses or by causing illegal activities online. This includes phishing, cyberstalking, email spoofing, and child pornography.

Phishing

In this type of cybercrime, which sends spam, junk emails, and text messages, in such a way including personal data such as password and debit card number. Spam is electronic junk of unwanted messages sent through email, text messages, or instant messages without the recipient's permission.

Cyber Stalking

An online harassment where the user is exposed to an excess of online messages and emails. They will threaten the users by knowing their witness and make the person feel concerned about their safety. Social media, websites, and third-party apps and browsers are the major resources of cyberstalkers.

Email Spoofing

It refers to email that appears too originated from one source when it was sent to another source and may cause monetary damage.

Child Pornography

Around the globe, the Internet is a major tool used to abuse children sexually. Criminals will interact via chat rooms or inboxes. The government has spent a lot of time and money to monitor the chat rooms frequently to reduce and prevent children from abuse.

11.1.4.2 Organization

With the online presence, the hackers will be able to hack the websites illegally, then it became a serious consequence for the company to deal with. The most common types of cybercrime will happen in private sectors or organizations for various reasons and it also affects the employees, associate stockholders, and business partners.

Data Breaches

Security incidents in which information is accessed without authorization. It collapses the business and consumers in a variety of ways. It can occur due to explosion system susceptibilities, weak PINs, drive-by downloads, and targeted malware attacks.

Cyber Extortion

The act of cyber crooks is monitoring malicious activity against a victim; they threaten the victims by demanding payments or any other requirements, e.g., denial of service attack.

Warez Distribution

Computer ware is a pirated version of the software or other online materials distributed via the Internet. It violates the original copyright law and illegally produce the unauthorized documents to the administrations. Warez files spread through fake torrents, Internet IP addresses, and steal the digital copies of copyrighted documents and distributed worldwide.

11.1.4.3 Society

Cyber criminals are targeting the society with techniques such as digital gazettes and social networks for their benefits. They are listed below.

Online Gambling

In this case hawala transactions, money laundering, is reported. It provides all the same types of games known as poker, casinos, slot machines, and blackjack.

Online Fraud/Forgery

The growth of Internet services and the mobility takes the opportunities for the criminals to perform frauds and online scams. The online scams are categorized into prize scams, money scams, dating or romance scams, and investment scams.

11.1.4.4 Government

The most serious offense against the government bodies is terrorism. These types of crimes will hack the government websites and defense websites and usually, they are terrorists or the enemies of other governments.

Cyber Terrorism

It is kind of terrorism where the medium is resources to threaten the government in its cyberspace. It has the different actions such as the spread of online propaganda, destruction of information, or any segment of administrative or social objectives via computer networks.

Software Piracy

Software piracy is an attack and accesses the personal or financial details illegally; these types of computer offences come under the Criminal Code Act 1995. It is sophisticated criminals who exploit vulnerabilities using computers and other devices. These attacks include the following:

i. **Unauthorized Access or Hacking:** Iit gains permission to access the computer devices without seeking permission.
ii. **Malware:** Iit is software that monitors the activity of Internet users and damages the computer. Malware is also used to steal usernames, passwords, or other sensitive information. A type of malware includes viruses, worms, spyware, Trojans, or bots.

iii. **Denial of Service Attacks:** Computers are flooded with website data. This type of attack more frequently targets business data, rather than individual data. In this attack, the computer can be resolved by performing a scan of the computer using up-to-date anti-virus software.

Computer Hacking

Hacking a system may cause technical ability to steal, modify, or destroy the data for social-economic or government motives. The hackers are catalysts as follows:

i. **White Hat:** Ethical hackers refer to the person who protects the system from outside hackers.
ii. **Black Hat:** They have extensive knowledge to break the computer networks and security protocols. They are popularly known as crackers. The main motivation of crackers are political issues, economic growth, and personal gain. The system keeps the information with them and exploit the system for personal or organization profits.
iii. **Grey Hat:** Grey hackers are blended black and white hackers to find out the security vulnerabilities without the owner's knowledge and report to the administrators to fix the security bugs with a consultancy fee.
iv. **Blue Hat:** They are beginners in hacking. Blue hackers are security professionals and they find the gaps and bugs in computer software before deploying the event.

11.1.5 Classifications of Malware Attacks

Malware stands for "malicious software" and it will install the malware into the system without the knowledge of the user. If a third party benefitted by doing unwanted tasks on the computer, the malware is written to distract/annoy the user, capture data from the host, and transmit it to the remote host. The various categories of malware represented on the Internet are (Love, 2018):

Adware

Adware is a type of attack that affects the advertisements. They are redirected to some other marketing page or pop-up page for promoting products or events. These advertisements are financially sponsored by related product organizations.

Spyware

The Spyware software is installed without the permission of the end user or host to hack the sensitive information from the target device. It tracks the cookies and it can act as a key logger to sniff the passwords and other information. Mostly it affects the people who spend their time surfing.

Browser Hijacking Software

Hijacking software copied along with the software over the Internet. They are installed in the host computer without the prior acknowledgment of the authorized user. The software is customized and redirect the links to other unwanted pages.

Virus

A piece of malicious code is programmed to damage the computer by customizing certain modifications in the file, occupy memory space, and replications of code to decrease the performance of the computer. Without human intervention, it can't be activated until or unless the executable file (.exe) is executed.

Worms

Worms can blow out through the web by finding the ambiguities in the operating system via electronic message. The network resources are like memory and bandwidth and force the network will be affected by replication and spread of worms.

Trojan Horse

Malicious codes or zombies are designed to install in the host machine by pretending to be useful software. It will damage the computer by manipulating the data and creates a backdoor, so it can be controlled in remote access. Trojans contaminate the other computer network or replicate the malicious code.

DoS/DDoS

These attacks used to make unavailable online services and down the network traffic from various resources. The infected devices are known as botnets on users' computers. Those computers are controlled by remote hackers. The remote hackers send spam or other malicious activity through this botnet. During the network downtime, the system will be hacked.

11.2 Cybersecurity Techniques

The goal of cybersecurity is to protect the computer networks from the unauthorized attempts or threats of blackmailers to publish their private data. There are some techniques to tackle cyber-attacks and they are listed below (Pande, 2017).

11.2.1 Authentication

This is one of the fundamental security techniques that aim to assure the users credentials on the system. The most important secure mode in authentication is password technology. In mobile phones, a SIM card will be inserted, so SIM cards are equipped with a unique one-time password, for secure communication. Authentic message should be prevented from either unauthorized people or spy. When the PIN or password is transferred over the insecure medium, it is possible to seize the credentials by untrustworthy people. This problem is encountered by encryption technique. The different types of authentication methods are (Rouse, 2018):

Single-Factor Authentication

Single-factor authentication is a simple and common authentication method. It requires authentications like PIN, keyword, OTP, and passwords that permit them access to service. It is known as primary authentication. It provides high usability and familiarity and low in easy guesses or stolen via data breaches.

Two-Factor Authentication

Two-factor authentication (2FA) asks for two-factor verification for the user identity. It includes then generated by records, one-time passwords, or PINs. The major function of the 2FA method is to improvise user security. By using 2FA method, 80% of data breaches can be prevented.

Multi-Factor Authentication

A multi-factor authentication method leverages two or more independent factors to grant the permission to access the system. The MFA security involves password, PINs, mobile phone, security token, fingerprint, face ID, and location information.

11.2.2 Encryption

Figure 11.4, encryption ensures that without the proper key application will be locked. This encryption method is solved through mathematical problems such as factoring large primes and it is complex for dealing with time and resources. The distribution of the key will be accompanied by potential security risks. While encoding the message, the same key is used for decoding the message. The security level is similar to the particular key either it will public key or private key. Asymmetric encryption utilizes the key to encrypt the text and private key to decrypt the same text (Bradford, 2014).

11.2.2.1 Encryption Algorithm

The encryption algorithm is responsible for strengthening the security issues. The algorithms are DES, Triple DES, RSA, AES, and TwoFish; they are listed below (Bradford, 2014):

Data Encryption Standard (DES)

The data encryption standard is unbreakable; it increases computing power and decrease the hardware price. DESs have rendered a 56-bit encryption method exclusively for complex data.

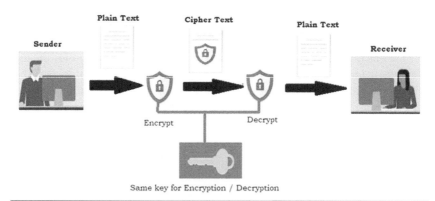

Figure 11.4 Encryption Methods.

TripleDES

TripleDES is more secure than DES. When DES was cracked, they introduced TripleDES method. It is three times better than the DES method. In the TripleDES method a message will be encrypted by using the same key message and will decrypt and again encrypt by giving an effective 168-bit key length. This is robust and effective for sensational information or data.

RSA

The RSA technique is used to encrypt and decrypt the message by using cryptographic algorithms. The asymmetric encryption functions have two different keys, such as private and public. In many aspects, Internet uses the RSA algorithm and some protocols include SSH, SSL/TLS, OpenPGP, and S/MIME to establish secure communications among the browsers with the same key length. In public-key cryptography the key can be accessible for the public and in private key cryptography is restricted for public access.

Advanced Encryption Standard (AES)

AES is a symmetric-key algorithm and uses asymmetric block ciphertext. It has three key sizes, such as 128 bits, 192 bits, and 256 bits for each key size and there are different rounds of encryption technique is available. It requires a level of computing power, data storage, and is impossible in the present scenario.

Twofish

The twofish algorithm works with a complex key structure and is difficult to crack the network. Twofish key has various sizes such as 128 bits, 196 bits, and 256 bits. This is one of the fastest encryption algorithms for both hardware and software. It appears in free encryption software; they are VeraCrypt for drive encryption method, PeaZip for file archives, and KeePass for open-source password manager tool.

11.2.3 Digital Signatures

The digital signature is used for identification when a person sends data through the device to make sure of his/her authenticity for security and safety measures. It is aware of who created the documents and not to interrupt the transmission of the data. Based on algorithms, digital signatures have been created. The

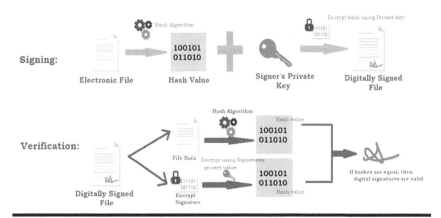

Figure 11.5   Functions of Digital Signature.

function of the Digital Signature Algorithm (DSA) is similar to the public-key encryption algorithm that generates an electronic signature.

11.2.3.1 Digital Signature Algorithm (DSA)

A digital signature is created by using mathematical algorithms that are associated with asymmetric encryption. A pair of numbers is created by digital signatures for data transmission. It allows the receiver to authenticate the origin of the message. DSA algorithm will generate the digital signature at the starting point of the data transmission. It ensures security with the signature and adds some messages privately. By getting the same decryption algorithm with the same public key, the user will verify their credentials.

Figure 11.5, key generation algorithm will generate the keys; those created keys are used to sign a document. Digital algorithms use a performed hash function to make the message digest. DSA with message gives the digital signature and then is transferred to the original data that has been sent. For verification, the same hash function is used as a verification algorithm.

11.2.4 Antivirus

The treats of computer viruses are written as short programs that generate unwanted commands without the explicit permission of users and assumed to perform in immoral aspects. The two functions of anti-virus software are:

1. The installation of anti-virus prevents the system from malware.
2. If already installed, it scans the system whether it is affected by viruses or not.

Figure 11.6 Types of Antiviruses.

The windows operating system is mostly affected by the target groups. The various types of antiviruses are given in Figure 11.6.

11.2.5 Firewall

Figure 11.7, firewalls are designed to avoid unauthorized access to a computer. While a firewall is connected to the Internet, hackers directly attack the network. Most of the operating systems are connected with firewalls and turned on by default. The entry and exit of the intranet are passing through the firewalls, if it meets the security rules it accepts otherwise it will be blocked by a firewall.

11.2.5.1 Functions of Firewalls

The firewall has several functions to protect computer networks that can be described in the following points (Hatori, 2019):

a. As a network security post, all traffic that enters and exits the network must go through the firewall. Firewalls will try to filter the traffic following the security breaches that have been determined when traffic occurs.

b. Prevent valuable information from being leaked without knowledge. Firewalls are installed with File Transfer Protocol (FTP) so that data traffic is controlled by the firewall.

Figure 11.7 Firewall.

c. Record user activity. While accessing data, network users will go through a firewall that records the log files to develop security systems. Log files are accessed while firewalls provide statistics on network usage.

d. Prevent the modification of third-party data so that they remain safe.

11.2.6 Steganography

Figure 11.8, steganography is one of the encryption techniques used along with cryptography as an extra-secure method of protecting data. The technique is applied to images, a video, or an audio file. The characters are written with hash functions; it protects from pirated copyright materials and helps to avoid unauthorized access. This technique includes secret messages without ringing alarms. An image file is covered with medium. An image represents in 3 bytes are having high-resolution, for hidden data, and the result of the image is embedded with the data. Here, every pixel is used to hide 3 bits of information (Shulmin and Krylova, 2017).

Steganography Key's Function

a. In secret key steganography, the parties who have the secret key can read the secret message.

b. In pure steganography, it assumes that no other party is aware of the communication.

c. In public key steganography, both private and public keys are used for secure communication.

Examples of steganography software are QuickStego, Xiao, and OpenStego.

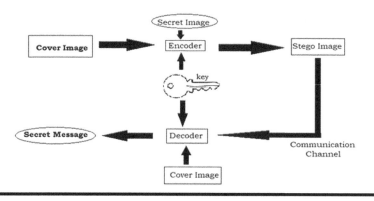

Figure 11.8   The Functionality of Image Steganography.

11.3 Preventive Measures

A preventive approach is important for organizations of different sizes that have different threats, risks, and vulnerabilities. The idea of using preventive measures includes hardening defences as much as possible so that the potential payoff is worth it. Some of the preventive approaches are described below (Pande, 2017):

11.3.1 Generating Secure Passwords

Many people find it hard to choose the right password and remembering the passwords becomes a difficult problem for everyone. Requirements are needed for strong passwords.

Passwords Affecting Factors

i. **Steal it:** Don't enter the password when somebody is monitoring or avoid keeping a familiar name as a password.
ii. **Guess it:** As per human thought, men will use four-letter vulgarities as passwords and women will use the name of their boyfriend, husband, or children.
iii. **A brute force attack:** Passwords are easy to guess when it has the combination of alphabets, numbers, and special characters, e.g., "kavi1993".
iv. **A dictionary attack:** Dictionaries have hundreds and thousands of word lists or both, until your password is found, e.g., "qwerty", "abcdef".

Do's:

i. Use at least 8–15 characters, not more than 15 characters because it is hard to remember.
ii. Best practice is to use random characters. Passwords consist of one uppercase and lowercase; numbers, and special characters are considered as strong passwords.
iii. Not use the same password for so many times.
iv. Don't use dictionary words.

Don'ts:

i. Don't add single-digit or special characters in starting or ending of a term, e.g., "smile1", "Smile@".
ii. Avoid keyboard sequences that will be familiar for everyone, e.g., "qwerty", "99999", "12345".

iii. Don't double the term, e.g., "smilesmile".

iv. Simply don't reverse the word, e.g., "elims".

v. Don't remove the vowels, e.g., "sml".

Protecting Ways of Passwords

i. Always choose private passwords; don't use somebody's password.

ii. Use password manager software.

iii. Choose two short words to concatenate together with special characters. e.g., " smile%93".

iv. Choose biometric instead of passwords.

v. Use multifactor authentication.

11.3.2 Two-Factor Authentications

Two verification was launched by Google to prevent Google sign-in from unauthorized access or unknown devices. To ensure the user, Google has to provide an OTP in addition to the password. Each time when a user signs in to a Google account, it will ask the user mail-id and password for verification as the first step of verification. In addition, Google adds an extra layer for security once the user logs in; the unique verification code will be sent to the user's phone. It won't allow the bad guys access to the Google account. In three-step verification, it additionally asks for recovery mail-id. The sample screenshots of two-factor and three-factor authentication are shown Figure 11.9.

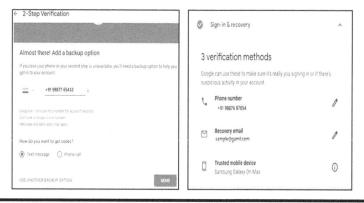

Figure 11.9 Two-Factor Authentication and Three-Factor Authentication.

11.3.3 Using Password Manager

When the password is negotiated, there are many possible ways to trace the account. Sometimes passwords are hard to remember, so they designed password managers. Password managers can store the passwords, are help for recovery, and manage the credentials. It encrypts the different types of passwords and is saved along with a master password; only particular users can recall it.

11.3.3.1 Functions of Password Managers

By using encryption algorithms, the company can generate different kinds of passwords. For better security purposes, password managers use 256-bit encryption protocols.

    i. Password manager stores the password in the cloud or local drive.
    ii. In the cloud, passwords will be stored and can be accessed anywhere and anytime.
    iii. In the local drive, passwords stored have the smaller amount of access.

11.3.3.2 The Functionality of KeePassX Password Manager

KeePassX is an open-source software, published under the GNU General Public License, and a cross-platform application and lightweight password manager. KeePassX password manager generates a random password for better security and a graphical user interface is designed with the help of Qt libraries.

Step 1: Credentials of KeePassX Password Manager

Figure 11.10, the first step it asked the user to give details such as user names and passwords. It creates a key file and is stored in the database. To add more credentials, it requires a URL, attachments, and remarks in a single database. Then it allows the user to customize the groups for making it more friendly by giving icons and titles for each entry. This database is encrypted by using either AES or Twofish along with a 256-bit key. Further, the entries are sorted in groups, which are customized and integrated functions that allow users to search either in the record or database (Reichi, 2020).

11.3.3.3 Features of Password Managers

    i. **Simple user interface**: Designed as per user comfortable.

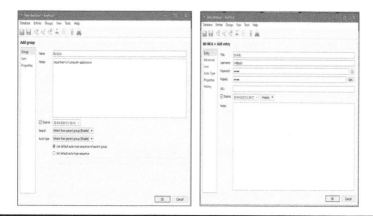

Figure 11.10 Credentials of KeePassX Password Manager.

  ii. **Portable media access**: Without installing the software, it can run on a compatible computer.

 iii. **Autofill**: Instead of entering the password and other information, it will be done through the autofill option and one-click option.

 iv. **Password generator**: Iit accepts strong passwords, give suggestions for weak passwords, and sometimes it generates alternate passwords.

  v. **Two-factor authentication**: Iit ensures the authentic users by providing passwords, PINs, and OTP if it meets the security criteria it enables the user otherwise it unlocks the database.

 vi. **Security**: Uses the AES encryption or Twofish algorithm to encrypt the database.

vii. **No installation**: It doesn't require any installation steps.

Examples of password managers: LastPass, 1Password, DashLane, Sticky Password, KeePassX, and Dashlne.

11.4 Cybercrime Initiatives in India

The growth of technology and the dependence on computers is increasing exponentially. Therefore, as a government, they need to monitor/upgrade information security infrastructure and restructure the cyber policies for effective security measure. The government of India has taken some initiatives to counter cybersecurity attacks and are given below (Pande, 2017):

11.4.1 Ministry of Home Affairs (MHA)

The Ministry of the Home Affairs is responsible for miscellaneous activities to maintain internal security as well as domestic policies (Ministry of Home Affairs, 2020). The ministry is responsible for internal security, border management, center-state relations, administrator of Union Territories, and disaster management. The department of Ministry of Home Affairs contributes:

i. Internal Security – Dealing with Indian police service, central police service, internal security and law and order, the grant of visas and other migration.
ii. Protection of Human Rights.

11.4.2 National Crime Records Bureau (NCRB)

NCRB is a repository of information on cybercrime and cyber attacks; it coordinates with Indian police, Information Technology department, and cyber specialists to enforce the law and improve public security and safety measures. NCRB is responsible for monitoring cyber attacks, cybercrime analysis, developing IT capability, and network tracking.

11.4.3 Computer Emergency Response Team – (CERT-In)

Cert-In has been designated under the IT Amendment Act 2008 to serve as a national nodal agency for the department of Information Technology. The purpose of CERT-In agency is to respond to computer security incidents, forecast and alert of cybercrime activities, guidelines to overcome form vulnerabilities, and to promote IT security practices.

11.4.4 National Counter Terrorism Center (NCTC)

The Indian government analyzed the importance of counterterrorism initiatives and proposed the National Counter Terrorism Center for providing intelligence inputs to decision makers to plan accordingly for counterterrorist activities. The NCTC is supposed to coordinate between various state and central government agencies and serve effective ideas of monitoring and organizing all the aspects of terrorism measures.

11.4.5 Indian Penal Code (IPC)

Table 11.1, cybercrime involves illegal activities that are traditional such as theft, forgery, defamation, and mischief, all of which are subject to the Indian

Table 11.1 Cybercrime Law in India: [IPC Acts – IT Acts]

S. No	Cybercrimes	Descriptions	IT/ IPC Sections
1	Harassment via Social Networks	A fake profile is created on social media and sends word, gesture, or act planned to insult. Sexually explicit act.	Section: 509 IPC, 66 A IT Act, 67 A IT Act, 67B IT Act
2	Cyber Terrorism	Terrorists are using virtual and physical storage media for hiding information and record their illicit business.	Section: 69 IT Act
3	Email Account Hacking	An email account is hacked and explicit emails are sent to people in the victims' address book.	Sections: 43 IT Act, 66 IT Act, 66 A IT Act, 66 C IT Act, 67 IT Act, 67 A IT Act and 67B IT Act
4	Software Piracy	Malicious programs like viruses, worms, backdoors, Trojans, and bugs are destroying or gain access to some electronic information.	Sections: 43 IT Act, 66 IT Act, 66 A IT Act and 426 IPC.
5	Child Pornography	Pornography is the largest business on the Internet. Child pornography is illegal in many countries.	Sections: 67 IT Act, 67 A IT Act, 67B IT Act
6	Phishing and Email scams	By sending defamatory messages or threatening messages via email. Phishing involves fraudulently acquiring sensitive information by hiding as a trusted entity.	Sections: 66 A IT Act, 66 IT Act, 66D IT Act, 420 IPC

Penal Code (IPC). The exploitation of computers gave a new identity to cybercrimes that are addressed by the Information Technology Act (IT Act), 2000. The cybercrime acts and penalties are described below (Sudhandradevi, 2018):

11.4.6 National Critical Information Infrastructure Protection Center (NCIIPC) of India

NCIIPC is known as a government organization to protect a critical information infrastructure in India. Critical information measure includes research and development, national security, economic growth, and public healthcare for the entire nation. The NCIIPC will perform:

   i. Purpose of critical sectors and sub-sectors
   ii. Study on information infrastructure to find critical issues
   iii. Day wise or month-wise of cyber alert/advisories reports
   iv. Malware exploration
   v. Tracking zombies and malware distribution
   vi. Aware of cyber forensics events
   vii. Awareness and training of Annual CISO Conference for Critical Sectors
   viii. 24×7 operations and helpdesk

11.5 Cybersecurity Tools

Cybersecurity is one of the top priorities for many companies. The result of the attacks is divesting consequences to the target, together with a status and economical loss. So, every organization is required to implement to monitor the activities and to achieve the finest security. Cybersecurity tools needs prevent the networks from unauthorized access, outbreaks, and protecting the system from the attacks. Some of the cybersecurity tools are described based on the categories (George Mutune, 2020).

11.5.1 IBM QRadar Advisor and Watson

Watson uses artificial intelligence as the best security tool by organizations. AI is a self-learning and self-evolving system. IBM QRadar tracks the threat detection section and eliminates the section. It gathers information and links both online and offline within the system. It formulates a strategy to encompass it and when an incident raises it will kill the threat.

11.5.2 Kali Linux

One of the penetration testing tools in cybersecurity is Kali Linux. For security auditing, more than 300 different tools are included in an operating system. Kali Linux is used to scan the networks and IT systems to avoid any susceptibilities. The major advantage of this tool will provide various security levels to the users. It does not have any advanced cybersecurity expert. It is only capable of monitoring the host and manages the networks via a single click.

11.5.3 Netstumbler

Netstumbler is a free cybersecurity tools for network defense and designed for the Windows operating system. Open ports of the network will be identified through the security experts. The purposes of tools are developed for the Windows system; therefore there is no provision of source code. WAP-seeking approach will search for open ports, the most popular tool for defense. It is capable of identifying vulnerabilities over the network among the other security tools.

11.5.4 Splunk

To monitor network security, Splunk is a useful and robust tool. It is used to find either historical searches of threatened data or network analysis simultaneously. Splunk is easy to access, strong in process, and contains an integrated user interface. Splunk will capture the index or collate data in searchable repositories and generate reports, alerts, graphs, visualizations, and dashboards in real time.

11.5.5 Nmap

Nmap stands for network mapper tool. It is an open-source software that is used to scan the vulnerabilities in the web and IT systems to find the present vulnerabilities. Nmap maps the potential attacks on the network by regular monitoring service. The mapper feature includes hosts connected in the networks, firewalls types, packet filters, secured network, and status of the operating system.

Keys to Remember

- **Admin privilege**: To control the system.
- **Adware**: When a user is offline, the software automatically downloads or displays the material.
- **Backdoor**: Another way to access software or hardware, rooted by intelligence agencies.
- **Bot**: Program automatically execute tasks or program as per guidelines by the creator.
- **Brute force attack**: Eventually guessed the passwords correctly, when an attacker tries so many times.
- **Bug**: An error or failure in the program code that may cause unintended interactions.
- **Catfishing**: Generate a fake identity on social media and target a specific victim for trick.
- **Crypojacking**: The victim mistakenly installs the program in their device and secretly mines the cryptocurrency.
- **Cryptography**: Protecting information by converting it into a secret message before sending it to the public or particular receipt.
- **Data breach**: Sensitive or confidential information are intentionally released to an unknown environment or untrusted person.
- **DDoS**: Distributed Denial of Service. Attack that occurs when numerous systems penetrate a targeted network.
- **DoS**: Denial of Service. Attack that interrupts the service to makes waste of time, effort, and money.
- **Dumpster diving**: Observing through junk for accessing the code or other sensitive information.
- **Firewall**: To stop unauthorized oncoming and outcoming traffic on the Internet.
- **Hacker**: To steal data and information, cyber attackers use the software and social engineering methods.
- **Hijacking**: Process of taking over a live connection between two users so that the attacker can cover up as one of the users.
- **IP address**: Internet Protocol Address. It identifies the address of each computer by using a string of numbers with the help of Internet.
- **IP spoofing**: By using a false IP network address without the user's knowledge.
- **Malware**: Malicious software. A kind of software program intended to harm or permit unauthorized access to systems.

- **Password**: A secret term or axiom that is used to access a computer.
- **Phreaker**: A person hacks the telephone system, to make free phone calls.
- **Pretexting**: Hackers create a false sense of trust by impersonating a remote co-worker.
- **Ransomware**: Unless the ransom is paid, victims are threatened to block, publish, or corrupt their data.
- **Smishing**: That exploits text message or SMS which redirects to some web pages, email, or phone numbers.
- **Spam:** Unwanted advertising or other information sent via mail or other messaging services.
- **Spoofing**: To gain a conviction on someone the attack disguises themselves as another. The attack is maybe a person or program.
- **Trojan:** A malicious software program that disguises itself as a harmless computer program and ability to execute attacks that steal information, interrupt functionality or damage the data.
- **Two-factor authentication:** For heightened security, it attaches the phone number or email address of the user to access the account.
- **Virus**: A piece of code that harms the computer functionality and service. Typically attached with the files, applications or downloads that appear to be non-threatening essentials.
- **Vishing:** Never respond to hoax calls which claim to be from banks/organization. Beware of VoIP attacks as it allows caller identity to be spoofed.
- **VPN**: Virtual Private Network. Permits user to create a safe connection between another network by using the Internet.
- **Warez**: Slang for pirated software.
- **Wiretapping**: The interception of electronic communications to access information.
- **Worm:** Worms lead viruses and have infected system. Since mainframes were the only computers in survival.
- **Zero-day exploit:** An unknown bug or flaw happens when a flaw is oppressed and attackers release the malware before the flaw is repaired.

Self-Test

1. To protect a computer from viruses ____should be installed on the computer.
2. To protect the computer against unauthorized access _____should turn on.
3. ____describes a program that can run independently and travels from one system to another to interrupt computer communication.
4. _____ are challenged by people to gain personal information, perverting from their individuality.
5. ____is the way of finding out the right credentials by repetitively trying all the permutations of possible credentials.
6. _____is the altering of data, not suitable unless changes are incomplete.
7. _____ is an intentional or unintentional transmission of data from the organization to an external unauthorized organization.
8. _____ is the process of finding vulnerabilities on the target.
9. A number of the device is connected to the Internet where each device has a greater number of bots that can run is known as _____.
10. _____ are the common methods of authentication for network security.

Use Cases

1. Generate some tips to set a secure password in email. Create a two-step and three-step verification for your Google account.
2. Find some popular password managers and evaluate them based on the performance.
3. Is the free antivirus safe to use on your computer? Justify your answer.
4. List the popular websites that you access frequently and state those that are secure or not.
5. What is the pre-causation to protect your computer or PC from harmful software?

References

Bradford, C., 2014. 5 common encryption algorithms and the unbreakable of the future. https://blog.storagecraft.com/5-common-encryption-algorithms, [accessed 23 March, 2020].

Hatori, N., 2019. Understanding firewall and functions and how firewall works on computer networks. https://medium.com/@hninja049/understanding-firewall-and-functions-how-firewall-workson-computer-networks, [accessed 24 March, 2020].

Herjavec, R., 2019 in Blog. Cybersecurity CEO: The history of cyber crime, from 1834 to present. https://www.herjavecgroup.com/history-of-cyber crime, [accessed 18 March, 2020].

Kemp, S., 2019 in Blog. Digital 2019: Global Internet use accelerates. https://wearesocial.co/sg/blog/2019/01/digital-2019-global-Internet-use-accelerates. [accessed 18 March, 2020].

Love, J., 2018. Malware types and classifications. https://www.lastline.com/blog/malware-types-and-classifications/, [accessed 22 March, 2020].

Ministry of Home Affairs, https://mha.gov.in, [accessed 26 March, 2020].

Mutune, G., 2020. 27 Top cybersecurity tools for 2020. https://cyberexperts.com/cybersecurity-tools/, [accessed 27 March, 2020].

Pande, J., 2017. Introduction to Cyber Security, Uttarkhand Open University, Haldwani, 152. pp, ISBN: 978-93-84813-96-3, [accessed 21 March, 2020].

Reichi, D., 2020. "Keepass Password Safe", Stable release 2.44, GNU General Public License, https://www/keepassx.org, [Accessed March 30, 2020].

Rouse, M., 2018. Authentication in cybersecurity. https://www.searchsecurity.techtarget.com/definition/authentication, [accessed 23 March, 2020].

Shulmin, A., Krylova, E., 2017. Steganography in contemporary cyberattacks. https://securelist.com/steganograpghy-in-contemporary-cyberattacks, [accessed 25 March, 2020].

Siege, 2019. Types of cyber crime. https://www.pandasecurity.com/mediacenter/panda–security/types-of-cyber crime/, [accessed 22 March, 2020].

Sudhandradevi, P., 2018. Design and development of multi-layered framework for categorization of cyber vulnerabilities and cyber laws. M.Phil. Dissertation , Bharathiar University, Coimbatore, 52 pp. [accessed 28 March, 2020].

Ucros, M., 2017 in Blog. Ladyboss, here's why you should study big data. https://medium.com/@melodyucros/ladyboss-heres-why-you-should-study-big-data, [accessed 19 March, 2020].

Chapter 12

PLC and SCADA as Smart Services in Industry 4.0 for Industrial Automation Techniques

J. Vijayakumar[1] and R. Maheswaran[2]

[1]*Associate Professor and Head, Department of Electronics and Instrumentation, Bharathiar University, Coimbatore, India*
[2]*Computer Operator, Department of Electronics and Instrumentation, Bharathiar University, Coimbatore, India*

Contents

DOI: 10.1201/9781003175872-12

Objectives

By reading this chapter, learner will gain knowledge on

1. Automation Systems
2. Automation System in Industries
3. PLC and SCADA
4. Industry 4.0
5. How to apply PLC and SCADA in Industries

12.1 Introduction

There are many instruments in industrial automation wired to form a network. Programmable Logic Controllers (PLC) are used to make them work. Programmable Logic Controllers are computers based on the industry used to track inputs and control the output based on the input logic state. The device is often installed in remote areas and to monitor the functions of these systems. This system is called the Supervisory Control and Data Acquisition System, abbreviated as SCADA. SCADA system enables devices and components to monitor, control, and coordinate in real time from a remote area, with data acquisition from one server location for planning and analysis. The term "Industry" is generally defined as an organized, cost-effective activity associated with production/service/trade. The term automation is defined as the functioning of machines without notable human intervention by implementing various technologies. Automation achieves better performance than the manual mode of operation. The need for automation increases significantly; a control system needs to be, without difficulty, programmable, flexible, reliable, stable, and value-effective. The modern automated industries depend on distinct manufacturing processes and their maintenance through PLC. These subjects, seemingly unique, are positively related due to the fact PLC programming, in most instances, is based totally on those models. Another topic is the use of web panels and the SCADA system as a part of the tracking process. As Industry 4.0 is approaching, employing SCADA with the developing IoT (Internet of Things) technology appears very suitable. SCADA concentrates on controlling and supervising the process, where the IoT focuses on analyzing the machine's data to increase productivity. SCADA will provide the data to the IoT. IoT also includes interoperability, scalability, and security to the data obtained using the IoT platform. Besides, the IoT offers cloud computing and bit data processing.

12.2 Classifications of Automation Systems

The automation systems can be classified based on integration, flexibility, and the industrial operations process. The classifications of the automation system are as follows.

12.2.1 Fixed Automation

Fixed automation has specialized equipment in mass manufacturing, which has a permanent set of operations and has been configured to be useful for this system. Such automation has been used by continuous flow and discrete mass production systems. Distillation, conveyors, paint stores, switches, lines, etc., are a few examples of this type. This method is mainly used for mechanical types of machinery to execute fixed types of operation and regularly operate the same processes to generate many homogeneous parts.

12.2.2 Programmable Automation

It has been used to configure the machines and variable sequence of operation using electronic controllers. For reprogramming, the machine or sequence of the method adopted nontrivial programming efforts also needed. The production method is not modified often so the investment required for implementing the programmable instrumentation is less. This kind of automation technology is used to utilize mass production where the job selection is less, merchandise volume is moderate to heavy, and generally of conjoint output. These have been ascertained in mills like steel rolling, paper, etc.

12.2.3 Flexible Automation

This type of automation is usually computer-controlled, which has used in Flexible Manufacturing Systems (FMS). The human operators are sent the codes by the software. They identify the devices and their position in the process, and the primary level adjustments are processed automatically. The computer sends instructions/settings to all the machines involved in the process. The necessary tools can be loaded or unloaded automatically, and their processing commands are carried out. The products have automatically transferred to the next machine after processing. These have usually used batch processes and job shops with high product types and medium to small jobs. Multipurpose Automated Guided Vehicles (AGV), CNC machines, etc., usually use these devices.

Fixed automation can be used in the following circumstances:

1. Minimal changes in the product type, including its mass, form, number of equipment used, and material
2. Predictable and steady demand minimum period of 2 years, so that the production capacity requirement is also constant
3. Mass manufacturing is needed at a time
4. Costs are essential due to competing market conditions. Therefore, the automation systems have to be improved to optimize the specific product.

Flexible automation, on the other hand, can be adopted in the following situations:

1. Innovative products are needed. The production system should be in such a way that alterations such as different parts can be added to produce the product.
2. Product life spans are short. Conventional and revolutionary development changes the requirements of production.
3. The volume of output is medium, and demands aren't as foreseeable.

12.2.4 Integrated Automation

It depicts the complete automation of a production plant, coordinated by the digital process of all functions and data working under computer management. It includes technology like software and producing, planning the technique using computer aids, computerized numeric controller tools, machine-controlled storage and recovery systems, standard machining setup, machine-controlled material handling systems like robots, conveyors, automatic cranes, digital programming, and manufacturing management. It can be used for incorporating a commercial framework into standard data. It symbolizes the complete integration of method and management processes using ICT. The Computer Integrated Manufacturing (CIM) and Advanced Process Automation Systems provide typical examples of these technologies. It can be seen from above; the variety and sophistication of the automation systems are growing from fixed automation to CIM. Automation's level for a different production establishment lies in production and assembly characteristics, working environment and competitive pressure, labor wages, and job necessities. It must be noted that the consequent increase in productivity must explain the expenditure on automation. To offer an example, it compares and contrasts the correct contexts for fixed and flexible automation.

12.3 Industrial Automation Systems

It uses computer-aided systems and technologies to perform several industrial functions in a well-managed way. The industrial automation systems are generally classified into two types:

- Manufacturing automation systems
- Process plant automation systems

12.3.1 Manufacturing Automation System

The production industries manufacture the finished products using machines/ robotics from raw materials. Food and beverage, paper mills, ceramic and glass, clothing, and textile are few examples of manufacturing industries. Nowadays, it has become a trend that most of the manufacturing units are completely automatic in all stages, like handling the material, machining, assembling, inspection, and packaging. Manufacturing automation has become very useful and versatile by employing industrial robotic systems and computer-aided control.

12.3.2 Process Plant Automation System

In process industries, such as cement, paper, pharmaceutical, petrochemical, etc., the output result is many chemical procedures based on unprocessed resources. Thus, the process plant is optimized to achieve more efficient high-quality control of the process's physical variables.

12.3.3 The Functional Elements of Industrial Automation

The automation system used in industries is a combination of many elements used to perform various functions for controlling, supervising, instrumentation, and managing operations as required in the industrial process. In some systems, these elements are made to communicate among themselves for sharing information needed for coordination among them and for operation optimization in a plant or factory or process. Below, we have classified the elements present in the industrial automation systems and discussed the technology's nature employed to perform the specific function.

12.3.3.1 Sensing and Actuating Elements

These components interface directly and physically connected to the equipment and machines involved in a specific process. The sensing devices or components used to translate the physical signal such as displacement, stress, or temperature to pneumatic or voltage or current form are convenient for analysis, decision-making, and controlling the input. These inputs are handled through the computer, which is in pneumatic and electrical forms. These input values convert into corresponding physical data like force, flow rate, or heat before acquiring the desired change in the outputs. These biological control inputs have been obtained using actuation elements.

12.3.4 Industrial Sensors and Instrument Systems

Scientific instrument systems and engineering sensors have a spectacular variety of mass, price, complexity, and these types of machinery have been used in the recently developed industries. However, all elements are connected in a specific form to provide a particular kind of signal. There are various tasks involved in the automation systems. The figure below shows the configuration of a typical sensor system. In Figure 12.1 the sensor system shown above decomposed into three of its major functional components, along with the medium in which the measurement takes place. These are described below.

12.3.4.1 Physical Medium

The physical medium indicates the object in which the physical process is taking place and the associated physical variables related to this process are being monitored or measured. For an instant, consider hot gas in a furnace for measuring the temperature. Here, the hot gas in the furnace is regarded as the physical medium or the pipe section containing fluid in the liquids flow rate measurement.

12.3.4.2 Sensing Element

The sensing element will be affected either by physical or direct contact by the physical medium phenomenon. In some cases, it gets affected due to indirect contact with the process in the physical medium. In some temperature monitoring systems, the thermocouple probe has been used as a sensing element. This probe often comes in direct contact with the flue gas from the boiler-furnace,

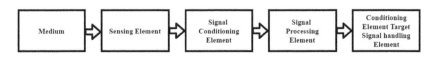

Figure 12.1 Functional Configuration of a Typical Sensor System.

or one can use an optical pyrometer to compare the brightness of the hot object with a lamp from a distance via the window. Here the optical pyrometer comes in indirect contact with the process happening. In most cases, the sensing element comes in direct contact with the medium, resulting in some property changes chemically or physically in the sensor corresponding to the variable measured. These changes are the necessary variable that has to be measured. An example of this is the change in resistivity due to the heat change in a resistant thermometer wire. In some cases, the sensing element will directly generate the signal with the change in input, for example, thermocouple. A thermocouple generates a voltage correspondingly to the temperature change between its ends.

12.3.4.3 Signal-Conditioning Elements

The signal-conditioning elements are used to alter the signal's nature produced using a sensor (sensing element). The conversion of the signal from the sensor to another form, often electrical depends on the sensor; independent signal conditioning sections are the features of a set of sensors. For example, the output of an RTD (Resistance Temperature Detector) changes resistance, which depends on the change in temperature in its environment. The RTD is employed in one arm of the Wheatstone's bridge to convert the resistance change to voltage. So this bridge construction acts as a signal conditioning element. These conditional signal modules have been used with specific sensors but not for variable conversion like ambient referencing of the thermocouple. Signal conditioning usually involves analog circuits that produce an electrical signal, either current or voltage, in a specific range.

12.3.4.4 Signal Processing Elements

The signal processing elements have been included in the setup to process the first stage's signal generated to perform various functions such as filtering (removal of unwanted signal), linearization, diagnostics (assessing the sensor's health), etc. Because of this, these are usually more general-purpose in nature.

12.3.4.5 Target Signal-Handling

The target signal-handling element functioning depends on the targeted application and performs various functions on it. Therefore, it may contain display modules of data/signal, recording or/storing modules, or direct feedback to a process control system. Examples are a chart recorder for temperature followed by a computer-based process control interface, an Analog to Digital Converter (ADC), or a digital display instrumentation tape recorder. The previous description does not fit in all cases; few variations have been observed in some cases. The subsystems mentioned previously are separated based on their function and their physical property for measuring the variable. Nowadays, the sensors manufactured have been built with digital communication capabilities using network, parallel, or serial communication protocols. These sensors have commonly termed "smart" and digital electronic processing systems embedded into them.

12.3.5 Industrial Actuator Systems

The actuation system is used for converting the signal generated by the computing system to a form that can be applied to the process. So, that desired variation in the physical variables has been produced. These are similar to sensors, but they convert the controller's output to electrical voltage or pneumatic pressure. The conversion has been carried out in two steps. The actuator converts the signal into some other physical variable like heat, torque, or flow in the first stage. The actuators and sensors are variable converters; the sensors are low-power devices, while the actuators are high-power devices. In most cases, the actuator first produces displacement from the electrical signal, converted to other forms. Following the above variables and energy conversion requirements, the actuation systems have been constructed as shown in Figure 12.2; an actuator system has been categorized based on major functional components.

12.3.5.1 Electronic Signal-Processing Elements

This kind of element accepts the control system's electrical command. This command undergoes processing in various ways. For instance, these command signals have to filter to avoid a particular frequency signal in input to eliminate resonance. For the precision operation of the actuators, these have inbuilt closed controlled feedback units in most cases. Therefore, in most cases, electronic signal-processing units contain control systems for actuators themselves.

Figure 12.2 Functional Configuration of a Typical Actuator System.

12.3.5.2 Electronic Power Amplification Elements

The electronic power amplification elements sometimes consist of power amplification stages of the linear type, termed servo-amplifiers. In the rest of the cases, it may contain power electronic drive circuits such as motor-driven actuators.

12.3.5.3 Variable Conversion Elements

The variable conversion elements have been used for changing the signal's nature generated by electronic power amplifiers. The variable conversion element alters the electrical signal to non-electrical form, generally in motion form. Servo/stepper motor, electro-hydro servo valves, current to pneumatic pressure converters, etc., are examples of these elements.

12.3.5.4 Non-Electrical Power Conversion Element

The non-electrical power conversion element has been used to amplify the power further if required, usually using pneumatic or hydraulic mechanisms.

12.3.5.5 Non-Electrical Variable Conversion Element

The non-electrical variable conversion element has been used further to transform the actuated variable to the desired form. These are carried out in several stages. Conversions in flow valves, motion-to-flow rate, mechanisms used for the rotary to linear motion conversion, and conversion of heat from flow rate using other hot fluids or steam, etc., are examples of these elements. Other miscellaneous components are auxiliaries for lubrication/cooling/filtering, reservoirs, prime movers, etc., sensors for feedback, features for show, remote operations, and safety mechanisms, the ability handling level is considerably high.

12.4 Programmable Logic Controller (PLC)

The PLC stands for Programmable Logic Controller, and is a modern controlling device and produces the output. It is widely used in robotics, transmission lines, controls the process, and automatic systems for sequence control. In general, a PLC is an industrial computing system based on microprocessors that perform the functions mentioned below in industrial operations in real time:

- Monitoring input and the sensor
- Control or diagnostics are performed by executing the logic sequence, timing, and counting.
- Actuators or indicators can be driven.
- It can be used for communicating with all computers.

The PLC's modular design, standardized hardware technology, capabilities for communication, and development in the program development environment are the reason that contributes to its advantage. The advantages of PLCs are mentioned below:

- Simple assembly model and easy to connect
- Modular extension scope of the memory input and output
- Programming atmospheres are simple, and the debugging aids and standardized task libraries can be easily used.
- Capability to communicate with other programmable computers and controllers

12.4.1 PLC's Evolution

Earlier to the development of microprocessors, sequence control and manufacturing logic have been implemented for operating control panels, including contactors and switches, relays, timers, and counters based on electronics or mechanical indicator lights. Moreover, microcontrollers' or microprocessors' growth in the early 1980s immediately directed the construction of Programmable Logic Controllers, with main advantages over microcontrollers or microprocessors.

- PLC programming is more straightforward than physical cabling components, and only the cables are required to connect the input/output terminals.
- The PLC can be reprogrammed as the programming tools are user-friendly.
- PLCs need considerably less space.
- PLCs can be easily installed and maintained, and they can rely much upon today's technology-based on solid state.
- It can be easily connected to the devices, monitored, and supervised by an automated distributed plant system.
- The system based on PLC favorably compares process complexity and control panel beyond a specific size.
- Plant sensors and actuators' wiring has reduced drastically due to the PLC's capability to admit the digital data in parallel, serial, and network

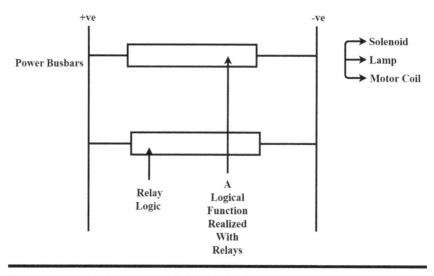

Figure 12.3 The Structure of Relay Logic Circuits.

modes since a single cable run to remote input/ output units. Due to this, local wiring can be done.

■ Fast maintenance services, diagnosing the problems, and troubleshooting without interrupting operations in the plant.

Since it evolved from the relay control panel, the PLC inherited the concept applied to such panels. The control panel has organized systematically to form a rung containing each control, facilitating the physically wired control logic easy for modification and maintenance. The PLCs retained their ladder logic even after development; here, the control circuitry is defined as rungs on the ladder. Each rung starts with one or more than one inputs and generally ends containing the single output. The structure of relay logic circuits and an example of ladder logic is shown in Figure 12.3 and Figure 12.4.

12.4.2 Application Areas

PLC is suitable for various automated tasks. It is used to provide a simple and economical solution to many tasks in automatic industries such as

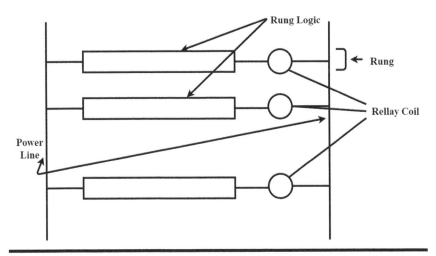

Figure 12.4   PLC Relay Ladder Logic Program.

- Control sequence or logic flow
- Proportional Integral Derivative (PID) structure control and computing
- Coordination and communication among the function
- Operator control and observing
- Start-up and shut-down of the manufacturing unit

All industrial technology requiring the regulation of routine, discrete signal operations are a possible contender for Programmable Logic Controllers' usage, e.g., machine tools, molding and extrusion equipment, programmed assembly equipment, programmed testing equipment, and textile machinery. PLC is used to handle significant Input/output and operations like communication, bit-level computation, and regular decimal point arithmetic. In other words, it is primarily a microprocessor and a real-time computing device. A standard set of components of a PLC system is shown in Figure 12.5.

12.4.3 Central Processing Units

Generally, a micro-programmed processor can rarely handle many data of width 8, 16, or 24 bits. Besides sometimes extra circuitries, like providing bit processing, often it has to operate on digital inputs and auxiliary quantities based on logical operators. Battery backup along memory is given for the following:

- Flags, counters, and timers
- Perform actions on the image for the signal states of binary I/O
- Operating system data

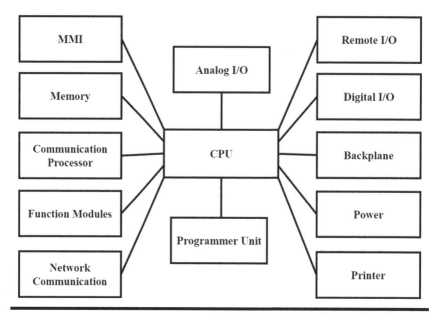

Figure 12.5 Conventional PLC Architecture.

The processor reads the program stored in the memory and executes the operation correspondingly during every scan. The binary operations are executed if the bit processor is present. The failure in industrial operation has been avoided by many central controllers in standby modes so that even if one fails, others can pick up the task.

12.4.4 Communications Processors

These processors can freely communicate information with the following:

- Supervisory Computer Systems
- Typical peripherals like keyboards, printers, and Cathode Ray Tubes (CRTs)
- Other controllers which can be programmed

EPROM or ROM has used to store the required information for every communication processor. These memories have been used so that that the processor memory needs not to be loaded. These processors are used to configure the LAN. These connections enable various configurations that can be used to interconnect the PLCs over a long distance. Mostly the protocols of the network are patented and cannot be used by everyone. But in the previous decade, the PLCs have been manufactured to support practical network protocol.

12.4.5 Program and Data Memory

The code and the information required for the execution have been stored in EPROM or ROM. These memories have often termed memory sub-modules. These have embedded within the processors. If needed, additional RAM also is plugged in.

Expansion Units

Input and output signal modules have connected with the Expansion Unit (EU). Interface modules are used to connect the EU and central controller in two patterns, as mentioned below.

Centralized Configuration

In this type of configuration, the EU can place in the slot where the central controller has placed or closed space to it. The cable's length has been restricted by the speed of the data transfer to the distant EU.

Distributed Configuration

In this type of configuration, the central controller and EU can be connected at a distance of even 1000 m. Another advantage of this configuration is a single central processor can connect with a maximum of 16 EU. Besides, the extra 4 EU have connected in centralized configuration with individual distributed EU and the central controller.

Input/Output Units

The PLC bus has connected with a host of I/O devices to exchange the data with the processor unit. These have been classified into special-purpose modules digital input and output modules and analog input and output modules.

Modules of Digital Input

It has converted the process's binary signals from peripherals to the internal digital signal level of controllers that can be programmed.

Modules of Digital Output

It has been used to transform the programmable logic controller signal levels into the binary signal essential superficially by the process.

Modules of Analog Input

It has converted the process's analog signals into a digital signal, which the controller then processes.

Modules of Analog Output

This has used for converting the programmable logic controller's digital values into the analog signals required by the process.

Special-Purpose Modules

This includes individual units for:

- Extraordinary accuracy positioning
- High rapidity counting
- Multi-axis synchronization and interpolation
- Online self-optimizing control

These are mainly used to protect the central processing unit from high computational loads involved in the method.

12.4.6 Programmers

The programs have downloaded into the CPU's program memory using external programming units. To support the graphical form of the program, external field programmers are used. These have provided several software features to help the graphic form and have also contributed with readily available kits for debugging and executing the program. For documentation purposes, the printers have also connected with the programmers. Rarely desktop computers have also been used as programming units by implementing special packages for programming. There are two ways of programming the programmers:

- The program can be directly entered into the plugged-in RAM with the central controller. To achieve this, one has to connect the programmer with the program interface's processor or modules.
- Programmer's EPROM sub-modules have programmed without the desktop (off-line) being connected. These have then combined into the central controller.

12.5 Supervisory Control and Data Acquisition (SCADA)

The software package used for online supervision of the process and functioning of the industry's equipment is SCADA. It has been installed in the control room. In the control room, it has categorized into three types based on the workstation.

The first type is the operating station; the user can only monitor the process in real-time. Next is the engineering station; here, the user can monitor and modify the process. The modification can be done only by the authorized person. This modification includes control logics, equipment and instruments parameter, etc. The last type is a server station; monitoring and improvement cannot be made, but the SCADA software's backup data can be stored and installed when the program is corrupted. In SCADA, it is generally termed a PLC (Programmable Logic Controller) or DCS (Distributed Control System) using Ethernet cable via Ethernet switch. All of these stations are connected through the centralized control system. All devices used in the field are connected to the SCADA from the area through screened pair cable. Again the output of the SCADA is fed to the PLC input panel via screened pair cable. In plants, the PLC has both digital and analog I/O signals. So I/O cards are installed in the PLC panel. Communications with the cards have been done via CPU. Based on the number of signals obtained from the plant, the quantity of cards used varies. Through PLC, we can monitor these signals and process parameters at different workstations. Today the SCADA has provided unlimited tags so that we can supervise many signals in this system. SCADA used to run on Disk Operating System, Virtual Machine System, UNIX, and recently in NT. SCADA may run on LINUX, too. SCADA is considered the best system for process monitoring and control function in integrated steel plants; a few of its features are as mentioned below, making SCADA most suitable in the industry:

- SCADA is ultimately a computer-aided software package that controls records and stores bulky amounts of process data.
- This system allows the industrial engineer to communicate with the actual process from all equipment and field sensors.
- The machinist assists SCADA in supervising the process's data with recommended action to maintain the system security.
- The remote terminal unit is considered a significant source of process data, which creates the system's online image.

Confidentiality
This system does not have any of those characteristics that provide communication confidentiality. If the lower-level protocols have provided no confidentiality, then that intercepted communication can be read easily.

Authentication
SCADA system has features for security, such as restricting the non-authorized persons by protecting with a password.

12.5.1 Implementation of PLC and SCADA in Industrial Application

12.5.1.1 Automated Effective Boiler System for Thermal Power Plant Using PLC and SCADA

In all power plants, the critical equipment is the boiler, which must be monitored at regular intervals. There is a possibility of an error to occur if it is measured manually. To avoid this, robust PLC and SCADA monitoring systems have been employed to prevent catastrophic failures. The working of the automated boiler system was developed based on PLC, SCADA, and sensors. Using a communication cable, the PLC and SCADA have interfaced. This industrial application's initial phase concentrates on transferring the inputs to the boiler at a specific temperature to keep a constant temperature in the boiler. The SCADA monitors the pressure, temperature, and water level of the boiler using various sensing elements. The output of the SCADA signal is fed to the Programmable Logic Controller, and it controls the thermal heat, water, and pressure range of this boiler. If the heating system or boiler's thermal and pressure level exceeds the pre-defined level, then the overall plant will be shut down. The automatic boiler ladder diagram is created using WPL soft, and InTouch Wonderware does SCADA design.

12.5.1.2 Necessity for Automated Boiler

The boiler is one of the essential elements in every power plant and the boiler automation is shown in Figure 12.6. That requires constant inspection and monitoring at regular intervals. It has a variety of segment boiling at power plants. This portion of boiling produces the steam's high-temperature vapor. In thermal power plants, the boiler vapor temperature is complex and challenging to regulate, leading to a poor understanding of the functioning principles.

Boilers suffer many serious injuries as well as property damage. It is critical that the boiler and steam turbine safely work. The boiler pipes get overheated and will damage if its too low a level. Too high a level interferes with steam separation and transfers moisture into the efficient turbine, decreasing boiler efficiency. The different control mechanisms can regulate the boiler set up to make it work properly, and several regulatory techniques have been implemented. To automate a power plant and reduce human interference, a Boiler Automation system needs to be developed. It is achieved by using the PLC and SCADA systems, which help mitigate human-induced faults and avoid tragic failures.

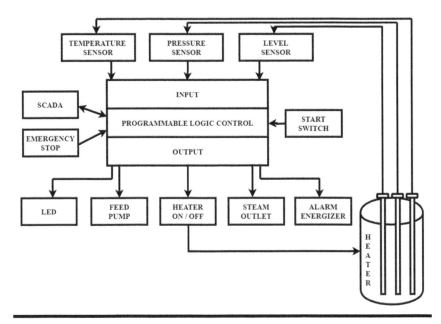

Figure 12.6 Block Diagram of Boiler Automation.

12.5.1.3 *Boiler Automation Using PLC and SCADA*

To automate the power plant and minimize the manual intervention, the PLC and SCADA systems have been used. By implementing and developing, these human-made errors can be reduced. PLC and SCADA have combined with communication wires. SCADA has implemented for monitoring the boiler thermal level and water as well as pressure using different sensors. The SCADA outputs are fed to the PLC to control the boiler temperature, water, and pressure level. The block of boiler automation is shown in Figure 12.7. This block diagram consists of sensors interfaced with PLC and SCADA to supervise and regulate the boiler, water, and pressure level plants' thermal level. Here the RTD Pt 100 is used for temperature measurement. The boiler pressure is calculated using an RT switch, and the amount of water fed into the boiler is calculated using float switches.

Operation of the Boiler

Water plays a substantial part in generating the mist. Pushbutton is initially turned ON, then the PLC, SCADA, and various sensors are turned ON. Using the water pump switch, the supply water pump is swapped ON – the coal in the coal compartment headed for the water pipe to the boiler. And the water from the tank can pass over two parallel pipes into the boiler, and its thermal level is

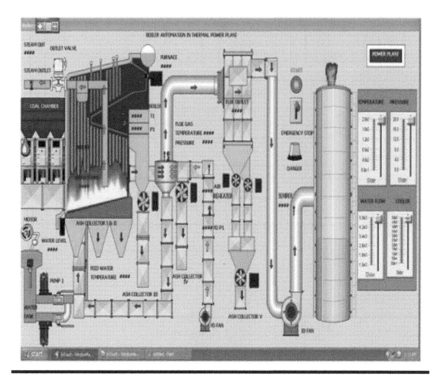

Figure 12.7   The Design of the Boiler Automation SCADA.

measured. One pipe records 130% of the flow rate, and the other records 75%. Suppose one pipe fails; it does not affect the process. The heater is turned ON with PLC. The forced draft ventilator is implemented to compel air into the boiler to enhance combustion productivity, and sensors have been performed to measure its corresponding temperature and pressure. The water is conveyed through an economizer, thus recovering the hotness in the departing gases, by removing their heat by water. After this, the heated water flows through a drum of steam and water. In this, the water level should be maintained at a minimum of 50%. Float switches are used for water level sensing. Float switches sense the change in level when the level is below or above 50% and sends the suitable control signal to the PLC. So, despite any changes in the disturbance variable, the water level can be conserved by proper PID controller tuning at 50%. Water in the drum of water is maintained at more than 75%. The motor will be switched ON when the water is less than 2000 liters. If the boiler's thermal heat and pressure surpass, then the whole system will be shut down. The corresponding automatic check valves are opened to prevent a terrible failure.

12.5.2 *Control Parameters*

- Control the steam drum's temperature, force draft, flue gas, induced draft, and feed water
- Control the force draft pressure, turbine inlet steam, induced draft, flue gas, and steam drum
- Level control in steam drum and water

12.5.3 *SCADA Design*

The SCADA automated boiler design is developed and implemented using the InTouch Wonderware software, and the increase in thermal heat, pressure, and the water level is supervised. The result is provided to the PLC to handle the full automation in a thermal power plant. Wonderware is a well-known Intouch HMI (Human Machine Interface) graphical and industrialized process control software that easily configures graphics. Powerful wizards allow users fast development and deploy customizable applications that connect to and delivers essential information. The design of the Boiler Automation SCADA is shown in Figure 12.7. Suppose the thermal heat and pressure become higher, the overall setup will be shut down, and the programmed control valves will be opened to release the high pressure and thermal heat inside the boiler to avoid boiler damage, and the outstanding flue gas will be cleared through the chimney.

Boiler automation has been designed and implemented in this application using PLC and SCADA. Various sensors have been appropriately used to measure thermal heat, pressure, and water levels. SCADA has popularly implemented monitoring the factors, and the PLC has implemented to handle the continuous function. If there is a slight increase in the thermal heat and considerable pressure change, the entire setup will be shut down. Later, the programmed control valves will be unfastened to release the steam and pressure. In the event of an emergency alarm, programmed control valves have unlocked to prevent a terrible failure.

12.5.4 *Internet of Things (IoT)*

The accessibility of data (the change in thermal heat, pressure, and water level) by the SCADA has limited within the sub-station or plant. To monitor and access the machine's data outside the plant any time IoT is employed with SCADA and PLC. Generally, the IoT is used for communicating between devices. It also ensures that the information is shared with the human as well as the machine. It has been used to integrate the real world into a computer-aided system. This helps in improving the efficiency and accuracy of the process. Besides, it is considered cost-effective.

12.6 Conclusion

PLC and SCADA systems are used for standalone units that can monitor and automate a specific machine function. PLCs can be networked; this type of network can manipulate a whole manufacturing line. PLCs may be tailored to monitor and control many sensors and actuators; they process electrical indicators and use them to perform preprogrammed commands for almost any application. SCADA systems manipulate and display industrial processes. SCADA is crucial for monitoring and permits effective decision making for optimization in industrial processes. IoT is used to analyze the stored data to make the plant function effectively. PLC, SCADA, and IoT are used in industrial automation to boom reliability, system balance, and performance, minimizing the need for human operators and the probabilities of human error.

References

http://www.ijsrcseit.com/paper/CSEIT184521.pdf, Date accessed 14 Mar 2021

http://www.ijsrp.org/research-paper-0615/ijsrp-p4264.pdf, Date accessed 12 Mar 2021

https://www.ispatguru.com/automation-in-steel-industry/, Date accessed 12 Mar 2021

https://www.jalpanshah.blogspot.com/2013/05/basic-of-plc-and-scada.html, Date accessed 12 Mar 2021

https://www.plcscadaacademy.blogspot.com/2018/01/, Date accessed 13 Mar 2021

https://www.reddit.com/user/Uvask/comments/fs8bkk/industrial_automation/, 12 Mar 2021

Index

Note: *Italicized* page numbers refer to figures, **bold** page numbers refer to tables